Getting in
Touch

THE GUIDE TO NEW
BODY-CENTERED THERAPIES

Getting in Touch

THE GUIDE TO NEW BODY-CENTERED THERAPIES

edited by

CHRISTINE CALDWELL, PH.D.

A publication supported by
THE KERN FOUNDATION

Quest Books
Theosophical Publishing House

Wheaton, Illinois ◆ Chennai (Madras), India

The Theosophical Publishing House
P.O. Box 270
Wheaton, IL 60189-0270

A publication of the Theosophical Publishing House,
a department of the Theosophical Society in America

Library of Congress Cataloging-in-Publication Data

Getting in touch: the guide to new body-centered therapies / edited by
    Christine Caldwell. — 1st Quest ed.
        p.   cm.
    "A publication supported by the Kern Foundation."
    Includes bibliographical references.
    ISBN 0-8356-0761-5
    1. Mind and body therapies.   I. Caldwell, Christine, 1952-   .
    II. Kern Foundation.
RC489.M53G47   1997
615.8'51—dc21   97-17060
                                                                          CIP

    6 5 4 3 2 1   * 97 98 99 00 01 02
        Printed in the United States of America

This book is dedicated to my son

Jesse

and

to all my students.

You have all taught me so much.

ACKNOWLEDGMENTS

STEVEN YOUNG, a family therapist who lives near me in Boulder, Colorado, once stated in a weekend workshop that unexpressed gratitude is a toxin. This idea hit me squarely between the eyes and contemplating it opened me up to the realization that I had been gratitude-deficient up to that point in my life. Since that day about five years ago, I have been working to reverse this deficiency with daily supplements of gratefulness. The Buddhist monk Thich Nhat Hanh once told me that what you pay attention to will grow, and sure enough, I have found that as I focused on acknowledging my friends, family, and co-workers, I have grown an abundance of love, kindness, joy, and integrity around me. Seeing gratitude in this light, I wish to express my appreciation to:

DON CAMPBELL, friend, gourmand extraordinaire, and teaching buddy, for steering me towards Quest and the path of increased creative productivity. Don, your open heart and extended hand have been a great blessing in my life.

THE NAROPA INSTITUTE, for being willing, in 1982, to take a chance on a mouthy young movement therapist and give her free rein to create a Dance Therapy Department and then a Somatic Psychology Department. All these years the Institute has given me a tremendous amount of academic freedom and support, and it was here, among a bevy of fascinating and creative people, that I germinated the Moving Cycle work.

The coauthors of this book, KATIE, RON, ARNY, MARJORIE, RICHARD, AL, PAT, ILANA, AND CAROLYN. What a vibrant, rowdy group you are! I especially appreciate your hanging in there through all my comings and goings with the structure and voice of this book. I marvel at the deep well of giftedness and creative energy you all represent, and count myself a happy woman that I know you and work alongside you.

I would also like to thank Quest editor Brenda Rosen and Mary Holden for their invaluable support and assistance.

CONTENTS

Introduction

THIS BODY OPENS

Christine Caldwell, Ph.D., LPC, ADTR
Founder, Naropa Institute Somatic Psychology Program

A few years ago a new client walked into my office. She came into counseling because she was in the middle of a divorce and wanted to deal with the issues and feelings that were arising. As we began to talk about what was going on in her life, I noticed that she would frequently rub her forehead when she encountered difficult feelings. When I asked her about this, she reported feeling headachy and tense as she was talking. As it turned out, she was a chronic migraine and tension headache sufferer. I asked her to describe the headaches in as much detail as she could. She used the words "pressure," "pushing," "gripping," and "clamping." She fisted her hands and gestured on either side of her head as she talked. I asked her to be aware of the physical position she was in. She reported that it felt like a position of struggle, of not being able to find a way out of something. I asked her what position she felt she was in with her estranged husband, and she began to cry, saying "The same; the same position."

Soma simply means body. *Psyche* typically refers to the mind. Somatic psychology, then, is the study of the body/mind interface, the relationship between our physical matter and our energy, the interaction of our body structures with our thoughts and actions. It draws upon philosophy, medicine, physics, existing psychologies, and countless thousands of hours of human observation and clinical experience to unify human beings into an organic and inseparable whole for the purpose of healing, growth, and transformation. As a somatic discipline, it values the physical body as a structural blueprint for our consciousness and our essential aliveness. It seeks to rectify a historical overemphasis on cognitive processes as central to human experi-

1

ence. It looks at physical states and symptoms as expressive of the central themes of our existence as illustrated in the case of the client above.

The splitting apart of the body and the mind, in which the body is the domain of physicians and the mind and emotions that of psychotherapists, has been so pronounced in Western thought in the last few centuries that the current idea of unity of the body and the mind felt like a somewhat odd and suspicious hypothesis when it was first introduced. Of course, in most traditional cultures, this splitting up of the human into parts is seen as laughable and as a symptom of Western craziness. It has only been in the last twenty-five years that the concept of the correspondence between physiological and psychological processes has been popularized and that many different forms of somatically-based psychotherapies have flourished. These forms seek to resensitize us to our birthright of healthy and optimal functioning by using the direct physical experience of the body as a healing tool. These systems also advocate our continued growth and transformation as humans through reclaiming our integrative being.

The above-mentioned client above did not think there was any relationship between her headaches and her divorce, except for bad timing. Many of us now would be more than willing to see these two events as related, and we owe this to the dissemination of somatic psychology principles in our culture. My client went on to explore her history with her headaches and realized that this pressure she put into her head corresponded to her core belief that she had to sacrifice, subjugate, and dismiss herself in relationships in order to receive love. This deal with the devil exacted a high price, and her headaches and divorce were the payment.

In a sense we could say that somatic psychology seeks a unified field theory of human nature. The field has no single founding mother or father, and it arose in many independent ways, as any good idea will keep cropping up. This makes for a field that holds a tremendous amount of creative diversity, and no clearly articulated central core. In this anthology, I intend to help to find our core, name and expand the principles of somatic psychology, and clarify its role in the evolution of the healing arts and transformational disciplines. I seek not to reduce our differences as authors, but to illuminate them as we acknowledge and foster our common ground.

This book draws together for the first time many of the current leaders in the field of somatic psychology. They have written about how they developed their systems and discussed some of their unique contributions to our understanding of the body/mind. All the authors have international reputations as clinicians and trainers. These chapters aim to give you the reader an overall sense of this exquisite field of healing. From this position of familiarity, you will be able to make choices as to how somatic psychology might serve you as a therapeutic form, a vocational training, or an adjunctive skill in your work. I hope also, for the readers who are already involved in this field, that this book gives you a sense of our head and heart and guts—what makes us a body—so that we may all move in harmony.

As you progress through this book, you may notice that many of these systems are similar to or compliment each other. As the editor, I was impressed with how much of the field has common roots, branches, and flowers. Because of this, it may be useful to look at four basic areas in which each author may exhibit unique contributions:

1. Theory

What are the author's theories about human nature? Most importantly, what are the author's views on health and illness? Some theories hold that we are inherently flawed or in conflict with society and that our health depends on how we manage this reality. Others state that we are inherently good and whole and that illness occurs when we are forced to go against our true nature. These kind of beliefs form the basis of any therapeutic modality and color everything about it.

Does the author emphasize early childhood experience? Current direct experience? Some therapeutic systems delve deeply into early experience, regarding it as vital for understanding how we currently operate. Other systems acknowledge early childhood influence, but state that healthy change does not occur through understanding what happened in childhood, but through locating oneself in the present moment. Figuring out who did what to whom is an act of leaving the present moment.

Does the theory require an analysis/diagnosis of the client by a therapist? Whether or not analysis and diagnosis occur, and how they occur, influences the power relationship between the therapist and client and locates the system along a continuum of orientation towards either understanding or experiencing.

What are the author's theories about how people change? Do we change through increased awareness or understanding? Do we change by releasing old energy patterns? Do we change through behavioral movement processes? These and other questions about theory can help the reader locate the author within the field as a whole.

2. Orientation

The author's orientation to the work arises out of his or her theoretical assumptions about the world. Does the author have specific ideas about how healthy functioning is restored? Or does the author believe that the act of following the flow of direct experience is sufficient to bring about change? This is basically a statement about whether the author advocates a goal orientation or process orientation. Some systems are much more interventionistic, while others view therapists more as witnesses. Another way to look at orientation is to examine the therapeutic relationship. Is it important or unimportant to the flow of the work? Is the therapist more a technician, a coach, or a remediating parent?

3. Forms/Techniques

Here we examine how the author's work actually works. Is the technique directive or non-directive? Does it involve touch, specific exercises, or experiments? Does it use regressive emotional states, or is it more a tracking of current experience? Does it use imagery? Is it done primarily in groups, with couples, or with individuals? Is it done in an ongoing series of sessions or in an intensive format? Is it short or long-term? Technique can be crucial in determining a good fit of individual to therapeutic system. We all learn and process our experiences in unique ways, and finding a system that fits our bodies and our learning style is essential.

4. Applications

Different authors apply their work in the world in different ways. Some go into corporations, some focus on couples relationships. Some are interested in individual healing as the basis for societal sanity. Others take their work into conflict resolution, peace work, and other community projects. Still others emphasize creative expression. Some systems focus more narrowly on healing, while others are interested in applying their work to growth, transformation, and societal evolution. By looking at these four areas, we can begin to discern how the various authors live and work. Though there are many commonalities, each system shines out in one or more areas as a unique contribution.

THE SPIRITUAL IMPLICATIONS OF SOMATIC THERAPY

Perhaps one of the most far-reaching contributions of all these authors and practitioners is in the realm of our understanding of spirit and spirituality. Western society tends to think of spirit as something disembodied, a part of ourselves free from the fetters of the flesh. In this field, nothing could be further from the truth. As theoreticians and clinicians, we have come full circle to the original meaning and intent of the word *spirit*, which shares a root with *inspiration*, both the creative kind and the inhaling kind. Spirit comes from the Greek word for "breath."

It is by breathing and being in our bodies that we locate ourselves and can transcend old, restricting forms of consciousness. When we align ourselves through our bodies, we can balance out the flights of fancy our thoughts are inclined to take, flights that can cause untold suffering when they become blaming and critical of ourselves or others. In somatic psychology we see the body as a temple, a sacred place. We counteract the toxic assumption that our bodies are what get us into trouble, that they are our weakness, our tainted and sinfully inclined, lower animal selves. How many of us have heard in church that we must leave behind the pleasures of the flesh, for they will lead us into sin? This pathologizing of the body has caused immense suffering, and somatic practitioners seek to dissolve this ancient and still-festering wound by recovering the body as the part of us that holds, contains, and takes care of all our other energies. It is our earth principle, our mother figure. If we care for it and live within it and in accordance with its needs, we heal both ourselves and the world.

We are interested in nothing short of a complete bodymind reunion, and it is through this reunion that we can make unity consciousness more possible. From where else does unity come from than from *all* the elements of creation? Only through a complete, contemplative return to our essence, our total body, can we locate that essence within the framework of all that exists.

In the summer of 1994, Jack Rosenberg, one of the founders of Integrated Body Psychotherapy (IBP), suggested that in twenty years it will be considered unethical to do therapy without a somatic perspective. This book attempts to keep us on that twenty-year track by creating an umbrella under which we all can stand, as practitioners, clients, seekers, philosophers, and lovers.

Chapter One

THE SOMATIC UMBRELLA

Christine Caldwell, Ph.D.

*I*n broad brush strokes, the field of somatic psychology operates on a few basic premises. One is that any event that occurs impacts our whole being—physical, emotional, cognitive, and spiritual. Indeed, any event must come through the sensory systems, permeating our flesh in order to register in the rest of our organism, including our mind. The only way that the mind becomes manifest is through the actions of the body in which it is embedded. Any event affects our physical structure as well as our emotions and our thoughts. If we think a pleasant thought, our muscles and organs are actually helping to create that thought with their squeezings and quiverings. Thoughts, in this system, are not just events of the mind, but are also physical events that take place throughout our organism. Somatic psychology sees this body/mind as a feedback loop or continuum rather than two separate though cooperative systems. Healthy functioning is a physical as well as emotional, cognitive, and behavioral experience, and dysfunction in any part of the organismic continuum will effect the whole system. Any therapy worth its salt must acknowledge this basic correspondence and operate from it.

ENERGY

The next premise is that humans are unique energy systems. Energy is the form and expression of aliveness. Most of us think of our energy in terms of how much we have or don't have on any given day, but we can define it in both practical and poetic ways. Literally, it is the force or power of our organism. We could also say that it is the fuel by which we can progress through life, that it is the divine spark by which we know ourselves to be human. We feel our energy as pulsating, much like a sine wave or an ocean wave. Our energy comes and goes, our emotions swell and ebb, our intense responses to life come in quiverings and shakings.

Energy, matter, and space seem to be the three ingredients of the universe; anything existing in the universe is comprised of one or more of these three elements. Somatic psychology pays exquisite and detailed attention to human energy. It is the form and process of our energy exchange with the outside world that determines much of our sense of who we are and how we act. Do I shrink when under stress, or do I blow up? What events sap my energy; which others flare it up? It is through these familiar energy patterns that we begin to know that "This is who I am." In this field, we examine how people absorb energy from the environment, how they process it, and how they express it back out, similar to a biologist studying how a plant absorbs sunlight, engages in photosynthesis, and excretes oxygen.

Events are seen as stimulating our energy flow. This energy flow is understood and labeled through how it impacts on the shape and density of our physical structure, which then determines our next energetic actions. When someone compliments me, blood rushes to my cheeks and makes them hot. My stomach feels fluttery, and I label this energetic event embarrassment. If I have been criticized, I will shrink in my chest area. Or, if I shrink in my chest area, I am likely to interpret someone's words as criticism. This energy is then discharged into the environment in the form of behavior, such as emotions, speaking, gesturing, and movement. Any of these energetic discharges can be spontaneous and healthy responses to the moment, or they can be reactive and conditioned reenactments of our historical relationship to energy. Whether we use our energy in responsive or reactive ways is seen as one of the core themes of somatic work. Energy is often seen as being overbound or underbound in the body, as a result of our using either tension or collapse as a defense strategy.

One of the important value statements made in somatic psychology is that our energy is so basic a life function that no part of it can be bad. Most pathologies are seen as a result of being punished for having or expressing our energy. How many stories have we heard or told about how someone was wrong for being too excited, too loud, too sexual, too much? Wilhelm Reich (1986) believed that modern society is a major repressive force that squelches and withers our energies, and that this repression was the basis for all illness. This view contrasts with Sigmund Freud's (1955) concept of the libido, which he saw as a form of primitive, unsocialized energy that must be controlled for society to operate. Body-centered psychologists believe that judging any of our energies as out of control and potentially dangerous is a self-fulfilling prophecy. Whatever energy we hate or fear will become distorted and wounded and will not be felt or expressed normally.

Somatic psychology is also interested in the energy loop of feeling and expressing. Feeling is generally equated with sensation and with the pulsatory flow of energy inside the body. It is an occurrence within the boundaries of the self that is the raw data of our experience and our sense of who we are. Our ability to stay receptive to inner sensation and energy in an unconditional manner is seen as a prime component of healthy self-identity. Many practitioners work to help clients reclaim sensation and energy pulsation by having them enter into a tracking and validating of sensory awareness (Gendlin 1978; Hanna 1987). It is Freudian free association on a body level.

Expression is also a prime component of healthy functioning. Though early practitioners tended to emphasize explosive, intense expressiveness (such as kicking, yelling, and pounding) as a strategy to counteract society's repression of expression, the field now employs gentler modes of expression as well for releasing old injunctions to restrict or diminish our movement, speech, and other expressions. Many clinicians now focus on expressions that most accurately communicate inner experience. Sometimes we have learned to exaggerate our expressions and need to find ways to disclose them more calmly.

Many clinicians will focus on a stage in the energy event where the excitement that is building is formed (Keleman 1975) or contained (Rosenberg, Rand, and Asay 1985). Albert Pesso (1973) believes that it is a basic human need to have limits, and containing our energy, even momentarily, is seen as important for our ability to make meaning out of our experience. For all somatic practitioners, however, therapy and general health involves physically expressing oneself through vocal sound and movement. Often this expressiveness is seen as a way to reestablish the healthy pulsation and vibration that is the natural shape of energy flow in the body. Habitually holding our energy inside tends to increase tense rigidity in our body structure, to depress our future energy, and to create rigid notions of who we are. Expressing our energy too quickly or chaotically, on the other hand, tends to diminish our sense of self and our effectiveness in the world.

Most theoreticians have developed theoretical models for this basic energy process. Stanley Keleman (1975) calls it the charge, formation, and discharge process. Events create charge in the body, which builds and is given meaning and personal identity. The charge is then discharged as expression and ends in relaxation. Pesso (1973) uses an energy-action-interaction-symbol formula. Integrative Body Psychotherapy (Rosenberg, Rand, and Asay 1985) calls it excitation-charge-release-resolution. Most of these models are derived from Wilhelm Reich's early pioneering work .

Most body-centered models believe that the body can be divided into energetic segments or zones, and that different segments, due to their form and function, store different memories, emotions, issues, and traumas. Often this analysis of body segments can be traced back to Reich, and to Eastern beliefs about chakras, or energy centers, in the body. Energy blockages in the different segments can distort affect, posture, and movement in characteristic ways and can result in specific physical and emotional illnesses. Generally, these areas are as follows, from top to bottom:

1. THE OCULAR SEGMENT (AROUND THE EYES)—contains issues around what we were allowed to see

2. THE ORAL SEGMENT (MOUTH, JAW, THROAT)—issues of communication, being heard, and the taking in of nourishment and rejection of toxicity

3. THE THORACIC SEGMENT (CHEST AND DIAPHRAGM)—anger and sadness, rejection and longing

4. THE ABDOMINAL SEGMENT (THE BELLY)—fear, issues of digestion

5. THE PELVIC SEGMENT (REPRODUCTIVE AND ELIMINATIVE ORGANS)—sexuality, vitality, survival, and support

Some practitioners also focus on the legs as the part of the body concerned with grounding (Hendricks and Hendricks 1991; Rosenberg, Rand, and Asay 1985; Smith 1985).

The Somatic Umbrella

Movement

Movement enjoys a central theme in somatic psychology. Movement is the way we define life—heart beating, lungs pulsing, brain waving; its absence is death. In this field, any movement is generally viewed as a type of vibration or pulsation that can be seen as a continuum from gross (locomotions such as walking) to mid-range (fluids pumping in the body, body gestures, and emotional quiverings) to fine (ion exchange, cellular metabolism, and electrical impulses). The pulsatory process is seen as the primal life movement—expansion and contraction—like breathing in and out, the squeezing and relaxing alternations of digestion, and the heart swelling with blood then fisting it out. In its simplest form, somatic diagnosis is an assessment of where the person is moving in his or her body and in life, and where he or she is not. Therapy is about restoring systemic motility and pulsation.

Body As Metaphor

Lastly, in somatic psychology the body is regarded as a template, blueprint, or metaphor for all experience. This is illustrated in how we use language. Saying that a person is a pain in the neck is a somatic statement. Getting an ulcer means something about one's abdominal energy flow. Dreaming about having no legs is a statement about standing and grounding. Somatic therapists listen to our words, images, and dreams about the body to assess how we view and organize our experience (Dychtwald 1977; Hanna 1987; Johnson 1983; Kurtz and Prestera 1976).

When we are influenced by another person, our whole being is affected. Our posture, stance, and gestures subtly shift to conform to our significant others. We teach our emotions to flow in ways that are attuned to the emotional climate of our family of origin. In this sense, we physically carry all the characters, stories, and archetypes of our childhood, and we carry them into adulthood as our sense of how the world works. Our families tend to act out unconsciously classic comedies and tragedies. If my mother played a Joan of Arc martyr/heroine to my father's alcoholic Attila the Hun, I will organismically take on a role that accommodates and mediates between these two. I will then strut and fret my hour upon the stage with gestures, positions, speech patterns, health issues, and other manifestations that relate not to the present moment, but to my historical habits of relating that I have been practicing since conception.

Somatic psychology seeks to dissolve these organismically-absorbed characters through direct experiences of our authentic energy and movement. In this way, we can live free of any ways that we may have needed to misshape ourselves in order to get through our formative years.

HUMAN DEVELOPMENT FROM A SOMATIC PERSPECTIVE

Somatic psychology holds unique ideas about human development. While the field acknowledges and extensively uses the ideas of the classicists Winnicot, Mahler, Piaget, and others, it also offers some distinct perspectives on childhood development. In particular, it looks at how developmental needs and tasks are routed through the body, and how physical interactions in the family impact psychological maturation. It recognizes that from conception until some time after birth we are out of gravity and in the horizontal world, being held first by the womb and then by our caregivers. When our body begins to move outside the womb, we experiment with gravity and make increasingly successful attempts to become vertical. This transition from horizontal to vertical, from out-of-gravity to in-gravity, is the blueprint for all developmental tasks and often echoes how we progressed up the evolutionary scale and developed in the intrauterine environment.

The work of Bonnie Bainbridge Cohen (1993) has made an important contribution to body-centered developmental theory. Cohen began her career as an occupational therapist, and from her specialization working with small children she subsequently developed Body-Mind Centering. She began by observing the developmental movement sequences of normal human babies—beginning with the newborn's ability to turn and raise its head, and as it grows, progressing down the spine to the ability to raise up on the arms, then to push onto hands and knees, then to crawl and so forth. She noted that when something interferes with these basic tasks, not only did the children's growing bodies become more susceptible to postural and orthopedic problems, but that these movement deficiencies also retarded perceptual richness, emotional maturity, and cognitive acuity. Cohen then began working with adults, taking them back through original movement sequences that had been skipped or inadequately experienced. Her Body-Mind Centering techniques have formed a bridge from early childhood movement experiences to later adult functioning—physically, emotionally, and mentally.

Marion North (1972) believed that personality could be assessed through observation of movement, and her work as a movement analyst led her to look at the movement patterns and sequences of children, studying the origins of personality in the early body expressions of newborns. She found that basic movement tendencies such as a tendency to be more energetic and fidgety, or withdrawn and hesitant were present at birth and persisted into adulthood. She also correlated these basic movement energies to character structure and felt that a child's movements were simply outer energetic expressions of inner temperament.

Irmgaard Bartenieff (Levy 1988) is also well known for her work with children. She began her work as a physical therapist and dancer and developed specialized movement games for children that emphasized the building of movement sequences that integrated physical needs with emotional and motivational ones. All three of these clinicians and researchers saw the early developmental movement tasks of children as essential to their later adult health and functioning, both physically and psychologically.

From the moment of conception, we need physical care, such as food, warmth, and protection. If we do not receive these, we die. As these are met, we need bonding, a sense of attachment first to mother's body, then to other people. Around birth we actually "imprint" on significant others, a biologically-driven form of learning that ensures our survival (Lorenz 1963). This bonding process is body-focused and body-oriented. It is accomplished through movement and sensory processes—touch, vocal sound, smell, vision, and movement synchrony. Is the baby held in a way that is stiff and braced, or is its body shaped to its mother's in a relaxed and comforting way? The ways in which we interact with the bodies of our infants form their first experiences of love and belonging. Love blooms first and foremost as a physical interaction.

Next, we need to be reflected. Jack Rosenberg and Marjorie Rand (1985) call this mirroring. This manifests in the physical interactions between the infant and his or her significant caregivers. This stage has to do with helping the child develop a sense of being both distinct from and related to others and is accomplished through physical cues that give the child's emerging motility plenty of approval and safety.

CHRISTINE CALDWELL

As a child becomes upright and begins walking in the vertical world, he or she has the increasing capacity to leave mother and go off on his or her own. This stage reinforces the sense of a separate self, often called healthy narcissism. The child establishes groundedness in gravity, his or her first feet-on-the-ground, this-is-me identity. This occurs in the context of being able to rebond at any time. The young child's ability to move towards and away from, choosing when to separate and when to rebond, allows the child to feel that both being separate and being together are safe, good, and under the child's own choice. This is often called rapprochement. This body dance of the need for both intimacy and separateness, both relatedness and distinctness, continues for the rest of our lives. We need relatedness in order to exchange essential nutrients such as love and affection and to avoid such toxins as self-centeredness or delusion. We need distinctness in order to separate from poisons such as disapproval or codependency and to receive such nutrients as solitude and self-reflection.

Space, Time, and Effort in Development

Because of the deeply physical nature of early development, somatic psychology has a lot to contribute to our understanding of it. We can look at our development in terms of space, time, and effort. First, development occurs through our relationship to space. Space has to do with how much of it we take up, how much room there is for us in the world, and how we face different directions within it. It is illustrated in how expanded or contracted our body is, how much space we use to move in, and where we draw our boundaries in terms of who gets close and who doesn't. It heavily impacts our ability to form healthy relationships. Our first physical imprints about space occur in the womb, during birth, and during postnatal bonding. We have needs for space to be enclosing and enveloping, and we have needs for space to be open and unlimited. Our developmental history with regard to space is written in our physical structure, expressive movement, attitudes, and beliefs.

Time is the next developmental orientation. It has to do with speed and pacing. Like space it is imprinted before, during, and after birth, and continues to be shaped by interactions within our family system. Having our rhythms respected while negotiating how to synchronize them with others is the task here. Does a child have permission to put her shoes on at the pace she wants, while still cooperating in the mother's task of getting everyone out the door and to school before the bell rings? Timing issues often manifest in energy and emotions. Are we quick to anger, slow to boil? Do we hurry through things, or hold everybody up? The body stores our timing issues as well, along with our expressive movement (such as going through our day like a hummingbird or a sloth), and in our attitudes and beliefs about being on time or missing the boat.

Energy is the third developmental issue. It has to do with power, which in physics is simply defined as the ability to do work. As embryos, infants, and children, we all received messages about how much energy is OK to have. "Sit still! Calm down! Shake a leg!" are all injunctions to change one's energy. The essential questions regarding energy are: Do I have enough energy to perform any action to its completion? Is it OK to have as much or as little energy as I feel? Our sense of personal power and accomplishment ride on these questions. Do we pop out of bed in the morning? Do we drag through the late afternoon? Do we feel we have power over what happens in our lives?

Somatic psychology has made two other interesting contributions to developmental theory. One is the emphasis it places on pre- and perinatal (before and around birth) experiences. It is likely that in verbally-based therapies the pre- and perinatal periods are not emphasized because we do not have cognitive access to them, most theoreticians believing that we don't truly cognize until we are one or two years old. But just because we cannot usually remember and talk about our experiences before age two does not mean that they did not have a deep impact on our formation. Because somatic psychology believes that the body literally holds all of its history, most practitioners believe that we store and can reaccess any event that happened to our body while we were in our body, all the way back to conception. This perspective was in fact mentioned by Freud (1955), but was taken up more thoroughly by his student, Otto Rank. Its influence today is seen in the work of Gay and Kathlyn Hendricks, D. Boadella, D. Chamberlain, and A. Janov, and also in the disciplines of Integrated Body Psychotherapy, Rebirthing, the Primalists, and Stan Grof's Holotropic Breathwork.

Another interesting contribution comes from Stanley Keleman (1985) and others who have carefully explicated the "anatomy as self-identity" theory. In this theory development is viewed as the formational interplay between movement and structure, from the cells all the way up to the adult body, from conception through death. Movement forms structure, much as the flow of water shapes a river bed, and structure shapes the flow of movement, just as a river bed will channel the flow of water. Since life is measured by energetic movement, and all energy vibrates in some way, all life pulsates. The nature of this pulsation, as it interacts with the formative process of cells multiplying to become tissues, tissues forming into organs, and organs into systems, determines who we are. The history of how this formative process took place—whether or not this process sustained insults to its integrity—determines our vitality and functionality.

Somatic psychology provides a rich addition to theories of human development. By paying more attention to the very real and physical issues inherent in the developmental process, we can understand and treat our children and each other with increased finesse and care.

PATHOLOGY IN SOMATIC PSYCHOLOGY

Any coherent body of psychological knowledge has beliefs as to the nature, origin, and process of illness. In somatic psychology a correspondence is seen between physical and (so-called) mental dysfunction. Any traumatic or wounding event will negatively impact the functioning of a person's body, emotions, thoughts, and behaviors. Many physical illnesses, such as ulcers, migraines, or skin rashes, are seen as potentially an expression of emotional and/or cognitive upsets. Physical illness is viewed as a metaphor for underlying issues. Backaches may reflect issues of support, uprightness, or burden. A sore throat may be the holding back of speech or sound. In this way a somatic therapist regards physical illness as a potential symptom of trouble in the somatic unconscious. This does not mean that we should ignore physical symptoms as medical issues but that we should look at illness as a continuum from the physical to the spiritual.

Because somatic psychology is so movement-oriented, pathology tends to be seen as a state of stillness or blocked movement in the body. If we need to either tighten or collapse to restrict our energy and movement, and if this strategy is used frequently, it becomes chronic and fixated in the body—what Reich called character armor. Many practitioners see this armoring as a persona or false self that reacts automatically and dysfunctionally in the world (Kurtz 1990; Keleman 1985). Defense mechanisms are literally physical states of posturing or positioning the body. These postures and positions can be classic in their nature, so that many clinicians will characterize body stances as schizoid, oral, rigid, and similar terms. Many somatic psychologists will "read" the body as a form of diagnosis, noting where the body is held, what shape results, and what emotions, beliefs, and behavioral strategies ensue (Brown 1990; Kurtz and Prestera 1976; North 1972; Pierrakos 1987). Some emerging work (Levine 1976; Caldwell 1996) looks at defense strategies as reflective of our animal history. Some of us, in the face of extreme stress or repeated danger, learn to use our bodies like a rabbit in the grass, freezing in order to escape detection. Others develop the badger strategy, using aggression and all-out attack as a way to defend against predation. These defenses are programmed into our physical behavior at an early age and most likely reflect strategies perfected back in our more primitive past.

Where do these blockages or stillnesses come from? Most somatic psychologists will agree with standard theory about the origins of psychopathology—abuse, abandonment, disapproval, reality not being validated, and other problems. All these states lead to a fragmentation of the essential self, with disowned parts being isolated, loathed, and projected, while compensatory false identities are practiced out of survival need. Somatic psychology develops these ideas further by physicalizing them. We look at abuse as an insult to the *form* of a person, altering his or her size, shape, and energy. Abandonment is experienced as a state of ache and emptiness in the body that only physical strategies can mitigate. Disapproval ultimately means disapproval of our bodies and how they operate, resulting in a physically-based shame that curls us in on ourselves (Lowen 1970; Smith 1985). When our reality is not properly validated, we learn to mistrust our senses and the body in which they are embedded in order to be cognitively in tune with the environment. Being crazy is a tangible, material state of twisted posture, tense musculature, and graceless movement.

TREATMENT FROM A SOMATIC PERSPECTIVE

It is in treatment that one sees the highly distinctive and creative body of somatic psychology. This uniqueness extends to both our orientation towards and techniques of clinical work. Body-centered psychotherapy enjoys two unique clinical perspectives—process orientation and use of direct experience. Somatic psychology tends to focus less on examining the client's story and more on the *process* of how the client operates within his or her story. The somatic clinician pays more attention to the client in the room than the client's past or what the client thinks about the past. Small gestures and changes in breathing are at times more significant than the family tree. The fact that her jaw tightens when the client speaks of her father is pursued as deeply as an explanation of feelings towards her father. Though several somatic disciplines do analyze bodies and movement, most do not see analysis as a treatment form (Grof 1985; Hendricks and Hendricks 1993; Keleman 1985; Mindell 1982; Rosenberg, Rand, and Asay 1985).

Treatment itself consists of the client having direct experiences that promote healing. In other words, it is only in here-and-now sensory and behavioral experience that change can occur. Gendlin (1978) calls this approach "felt-level experiencing." Talking about an issue until one understands it is not seen as transformative. Body-centered psychotherapists seek to reestablish the loop of feeling and expressing as their healing modality. Somatic therapists either design exercises that invite felt-level material, or simply urge the client to track and stay with sensation and feeling and allow them to completely reveal themselves.

Certain techniques are common to most somatic disciplines. Perhaps the most universal is the use of breath. Since breath is seen as one of our most life-affirming and promoting activities, breathwork is perhaps the primary intervention in body-centered therapy. Breathwork can be done by itself, often lying down and deepening respiration until it stirs up energy and feeling, or by asking clients to breathe more deeply as they feel and report memories, emotions, and beliefs. Breathwork is believed to clear blockages, resolve trauma, and promote healthy functioning (Christiansen1972; Grof 1985; Hendricks and Hendricks 1993; Keleman 1985; Lowen 1970).

A second common technique is expressive movement. Since a primary therapeutic goal is to reestablish movement, therapists encourage clients to allow their bodies to move with what they feel. Sometimes this shows up as expressive gestures such as hitting or kicking, and sometimes it involves dancing around the room with gleeful abandon. Movement enters into healing all the way from subtle shifts inside the body to wild locomotion. In this sense, sound is regarded as a form of movement—it is movement on a vocal vibrational level. Clients may be asked to make various vibration-inducing sounds, or they may be encouraged to vocalize their experience as a way to reestablish movement processes that have been blocked (Brown 1990; Grof 1985; Lowen 1970; Smith 1985).

The use of imagery is also common (Gendlin 1978; Masters and Houston 1978; Mindell 1982). Images can be referenced through the body or processed by the body. Images can come through dreams, memories, metaphors, or symbols. All images are somaticized; that is, they are worked with by allowing sensation, energy, and movement to guide them. For example, a woman might work with a dream image of a horse. A somatic therapist might ask this woman to feel the qualities of "horse" in her body, which may translate to a feeling of raw energy or forward motion.

Many (but not all) somatic therapists use touch with their clients. Touch can vary all the way from supportive hugs to deep manipulation designed to loosen body blocks. Many somatic therapists have specific bodywork training that assists them in touching clients in professional and appropriate ways.

THE HISTORY AND DEVELOPMENT OF THE FIELD OF SOMATIC PSYCHOLOGY

Somatic theory and techniques have been practiced on this planet since humans began to identify themselves as healers. Seeing illness or health in terms of dividing body from mind is virtually unheard of in traditional cultures. In the context of the current field of somatic psychology, however, its origins point to Freud.

As Freud (1955) began to articulate his theories of psychodynamics, he also laid some groundwork for somatic psychology. He had trained first as a physician before he developed psychoanalysis, and he recognized the body and body processes as the foundation of psychological states when he asserted that the ego is first and foremost a body ego, derived from bodily sensations. He noted the importance of the physical blocking or discharge of energy as crucial in the formation of psychological disorders. He later became fascinated with verbal analysis. The only vestige we see of his somatic perspective is his technique of lying patients on a couch, which he felt physically lowered their defenses by relaxing tense musculature and regressing clients to earlier infantile states.

It remained for Freud's colleagues and students, however, to elaborate on these ideas. Perhaps the most pivotal of Freud's colleagues was Josef Breuer. Breuer was fascinated with the nervous system and felt that it was organized around currents of energy and channels of excitement (Boadella 1987). He saw neurotic symptoms as surpluses of excitation, which could be discharged through three types of activity: ideational (dreams, images, and fantasies), motor discharge (body movement), and vegetative affect (respiratory, digestive, or cardiac distress). Because of his emphasis on energy discharge, he was the first to introduce catharsis into psychoanalysis.

Georg Groddeck, a contemporary of Freud, was also one of the first psychotherapists to see the connection between physical illness and psychological states. He believed that our emotions and beliefs are directly expressed in our bodies. In his clinic in Baden-Baden he combined diet, deep massage, and psychoanalysis in his work with patients, thus pioneering multimodal techniques and psychosomatic medicine.

Another contemporary of Freud was Sandor Ferenczi. He was also a psychoanalyst, but he modified the analytical method and developed "activity techniques" for his patients that stemmed from his observations of their expressive movements and postures. He would ask a person not to fidget, self-touch, or pluck at his or her body during a session in order not to dissipate the somatic tension the client was building up and unconsciously trying to dispel. He also used muscular relaxation to deepen free association and stated that the expression of emotion in movement actions can evoke memories from the unconscious, as memories bring about emotional reaction or activity (Smith 1985).

It took Freud and Ferenczi's student, Wilhelm Reich, to greatly advance somatic psychology by developing a coherent theory and technique that was body-centered and body-focused (Boadella 1985). He contributed many of the ideas that form the basis of somatic psychology today, and if any of us had to name a founding father in this field, Reich would be the name most often mentioned. First, Reich saw neurosis and even psychosis as a repression of both physical and psychic energy. This repression causes a person to form defense mechanisms that are physical in nature. He called this phenomenon "character armoring" and saw it as a chronic muscular rigidifying and posturing in various parts of the body.

The Somatic Umbrella

Reich developed a form of therapy that differed from psychoanalysis. He would ask a client to breathe heavily. Observing the client, Reich noticed reactions to the increased energy in the body such as changes in skin temperature or color. These reactions indicated blocks in the natural energy flow. He also used physical contact and touch in order to diagnose or release the blocks. The physical manipulation often led to a release of feelings and to the recovery of memories, and he felt it served to speed up other therapeutic processes that accompanied bodywork.

Reich viewed orgasm as an important function because it discharges excess energy and leads to a breakdown of neurotic character structures. In his theory he showed that full orgasm is absent in neurosis and that only a free mind in a free body can experience and express a total body orgasm, not just a genital one. Reich concluded that tension and relaxation are united biophysical conditions; psychological tensions cannot exist without physical parallels, and psychological problems cannot be relieved without correcting the body as well. His techniques—which involved clients lying down and breathing deeply in order to stimulate their energy and melt defensive armoring through cathartic moving and sounding—were radical and got him in a lot of trouble with the conservative American culture of the early 1950s. Reich died in prison, bitter about society's repression of the body and of his work. Yet his emphasis on energy, on defenses as physical structures, and on breathwork have subsequently come into the mainstream and formed a major underpinning of somatic psychology today.

Other practitioners, such as Frederick Alexander, Ida Rolf, and Moshe Feldenkrais, followed the developments of somatic psychology but went on to pioneer another branch of the somatic family tree—bodywork. Bodywork emphasizes the alignment of one's physical structure, realizing that when the body holds muscular imbalances, the resulting torsions and compensations produced stress, chronic tension, and disease. Most bodywork pioneers acknowledged that the psyche and emotions both influenced and were influenced by body tension (Rolf felt that the body *was* the personality), but their work focused on using physical massage and movement techniques to restore physical balance. Bodywork was not meant to be a form of psychotherapy *per se*, though all felt that physical alignment could restore emotional and mental harmony. In addition, people who became bodywork practitioners did not receive any psychotherapy training in order to become bodyworkers. This separation continues today, though more and more bodyworkers engage in some study of psychology as an adjunct to their work.

After studying with Reich, Alexander Lowen and John Pierrakos separated from him and founded the Institute for Bioenergetic Analysis in 1952. Their work is based on Reichian concepts such as the universal life energy and the muscular armor but differs in the form of treatment. Later Pierrakos left the Institute and continued independently, developing Core Energetics (1987), while Lowen stayed with the Bioenergetics Institute. Like Reich, Pierrakos was interested in the free flow of energy in the body and looked at the constellation of energy blocks as one of his diagnostic tools. Pierrakos also used intensification techniques to charge the body with feeling that would break through energetic blockages.

Lowen defined Bioenergetics as the study of personality based on the body. The personality is the way a person is in the world. A person moves and holds the body in characteristic ways which can be used for diagnosis. Reich was the first to discuss character analysis, but Lowen continued this focus and organized the character types systematically, along with their relationships to each other. Lowen describes five different holding patterns: holding together, holding on, holding up, holding in, and holding back, which define the schizoid, oral, psychopathic, masochistic, and rigid character types respectively. These five patterns are distinct in each person. They can be seen directly from the physical structure of the body and its movement habits. Therefore, Bioenergetics reads the body as a form of assessment.

In the therapeutic process Lowen emphasized increasing the client's awareness of psychological processes, such as unconscious fears and conflicts, and their relationship to tensions and rigidities in the body. He then focused on releasing tension and freeing blocked emotions, and finally, on supporting the client in finding interpretations of the dreams, memories, and emotions which might emerge from the unconscious during the bodywork. To support this process Lowen developed a number of exercises that magnify the tensions held in the body and force the client to release them. Since the release requires more energy, the client is encouraged to increase breathing. The therapist might also use pressure on tense muscles, or massage, or suggest expressive exercises as interventions in order to induce a release in the client. Similar to Reich, Lowen saw the orgiastic potency as a criterion for cure, but he also included the ability to express all emotions fully.

Breaking from mainstream bioenergetic tradition is Stanley Keleman. More than any other pioneer in this field, Keleman has attempted to articulate how movement creates the body and the body creates movement. He examines the vibratory processes of the body down to the cellular level and postulates that it is the quality of this pulsation that shapes our physical form. Clinically, he works with breath, movement, and sound to reestablish the charge, formation and discharge process that develops both healthy tissues and healthy people.

Charles Kelley first described his work in the 1960s as "neo-Reichian" but later named his Institute the "Radix Institute." He defined "Radix" as the source, root, or primary cause from which the substratum of energy, feeling, and movement are created. In the healthy person this radix pulsates, charges, and discharges in emotional release. Radix work is less analytical, involves less interpretation of meaning, and uses less verbal exchange between the client and therapist than Reichian therapy or Bioenergetics. The focus is on how a person is blocking emotionally and not on the emotional content. Kelley used a different characterology from Reich and Lowen. His work is based mainly on discovering how people block fear, anger, or pain. Since Kelley's background was in the psychology of vision, he emphasized visual awareness, eye contact, seeing and being seen, and visualization techniques. Kelley focused on two aspects: on opening first the ability for deep spontaneous emotion; and second, the ability to choose appropriate goals and purposes and effectively pursue them, since purpose and self-direction give control and significance to people's lives. Kelley avoided the medical and therapeutic model in his work. For him there were no patients and therapists, only students who worked with each other and whose feelings were opened to expression through education and personal growth processes under a teacher's supervision. Most Radix work is done in groups, which can be different from Reichian therapy and Bioenergetics. It is often done in residential intensives rather than in weekly sessions. Assuming that the intensive environment is protective, there are fewer pressures from work or home situations, more support from other group participants, and fewer opportunities between sessions to reestablish defenses. Weekly follow-up sessions help to integrate the work into daily life.

Many of the Reichian offshoot therapies, such as Bioenergetics, would be what Edward Smith (1985) calls "hard techniques," because they are neither subtle nor gentle. They tend to blast the client through his or her process and employ intense emotions as a therapeutic technique.

If we continue along the somatic family tree, we find a branch devoted to movement specialists. Many movement specialists began their work with no formal training in psychotherapy. Many were dancers who became aware of the therapeutic effect of their work and took their movement skills into mental hospitals. This was the birth of dance/movement therapy. Some of the early pioneers were Mary Whitehouse, Marion Chace, Blanche Evan, Liljan Espenak, Trudi Schoop, and Alma Hawkins (Levy 1988).

We also see in the field pioneers who blended other disciplines with the body to form their work. Robert Hall, a student of Fritz Perls with a background in Eastern psychology and Rolfing, argued that body and mind are functionally identical and that unfinished, blocked energy must be released from muscles of the body and expressed through movement as well as be psychologically finished. He is a cofounder of the Lomi school, which mixes Gestalt therapy with various forms of bodywork such as Reichian breathwork, body education techniques, Eastern spiritual practices, Vipassana meditation, Hatha Yoga, Aikido and Tai Chi Chu'an.

Thomas Hanna was a practitioner who blended movement reeducation with psychotherapy. He worked with somatic exercises designed to resensitize and remobilize blocked body parts, believing that the ensuing freedom of movement promoted the health of the entire organism.

Stan Grof began his career as a somatically-oriented psychologist through his studies of altered states of consciousness. From this base he developed Holotropic Breathwork as a means to explore and heal personal, pre- and perinatal, transpersonal, and cosmic states of being. He asks his clients to lie down and breathe deeply while listening to evocative music. Clients are encouraged to keep breathing, moving, and making sounds while feeling and expressing their experiences. When the process is complete, they are frequently asked to draw mandala images of their experiences to integrate what occurred.

The field of somatic psychology profoundly contributes to our understanding of healing and transformation. It combines all aspects of human experience into a unified field of work, using the physical body as a template or blueprint for change. As a field it continues to grow and be valued in the therapeutic community, to the point where now almost every therapeutic practitioner acknowledges and uses some of its techniques.

Currently, we are enjoying a glorious blooming of body-centered psychotherapy models that will take more than this book to cover adequately. As this work grows and expands, softer techniques and less analytical methodology have been added. More awareness practices and meditative techniques are being used. There is not as much use of explosive catharsis, stressful postures, invasive touching, or breathing into extreme states. The therapist is also less likely to interpret physical behavior or analyze body posture. It is more likely that the job of finding meaning in posture, gesture, and movement will be left to the client. This trend is exemplified by Kurtz's (1990) Hakomi Therapy, Gay and Kathlyn Hendricks' (1991) Radiance Method, Amy and Arnold Mindells' (1982) Process Therapy, my own Moving Cycle (1996), and others.

Looking Ahead

Somatic psychology is a diverse and rich field that has only recently begun to be recognized by people other than the pioneers who developed it and their students and clients. In the beginning, one had to apprentice with one of these pioneers to learn this type of work. While this apprenticeship model is still popular, several accredited master's programs and other academic opportunities have evolved that teach the general system of the field and offer extensive clinical skill training. (See Appendix One for a list of somatic psychology departments.)

There is much diversity in the field of somatic psychology. It is working to articulate its own unified body, and this anthology attempts to further recognize and articulate this common ground. As an aside, other interesting trends can be observed in somatic psychology. Quite a few somatic psychologists work as husband/wife teams (such as the Hendricks, the Mindells, the Grofs, the Rosenbergs, the Pessos, and the Browns). This kind of energetic balance and cooperation bodes well for the field. There is also an almost universal love of physics among somatic psychologists, perhaps because the body organizes around the laws of mechanical physics (new evidence suggests the body also behaves consonantly with chaos and fractal theories in mathematics), and because the frontiers of physics seem to correspond to what we are discovering about the body's innate capabilities.

Most somatic psychologists see in the future such a deep reclaiming of and regard for our bodies that all healing and transformational work will eventually involve this emphasis on the body. We tend to immodestly feel that we are healing society's Cartesian and religious mistakes (Dychtwald 1977; Johnson 1983; Murphy 1992; Pierrakos 1987; Smith 1985), and hope that in the upcoming century our call for organismic wholeness will resonate and vibrate throughout the entire body of humanity.

REFERENCES

Boadella, D. *Wilhelm Reich: The Evolution of His Work.* Boston: Arkana, 1985.

——. *Lifestreams: An Introduction to Biosynthesis.* New York: Routledge & Keegan Paul, 1987.

Brown, M. *The Healing Touch: An Introduction to Organismic Psychotherapy.* Mendocino, Calif.: LifeRhythm,1990.

Caldwell, C. *Getting Our Bodies Back.* Boston: Shambhala Publications, 1996.

Chamberlain, D. *Babies Remember Birth.* Los Angeles: Jeremy Tarcher, 1988.

Christiansen, B. *Thus Speaks the Body.* New York: Arno Press, 1972.

Cohen, B. Bainbridge. *Sensing, Feeling, and Action: The Experiential Anatomy of Body-Mind Centering.* Northampton, Mass: Contact Editions, 1993.

Dychtwald, K. *Bodymind.* New York: Pantheon, 1977.

Freud, S. *The Interpretation of Dreams.* New York: Basic Books, 1955.

Gendlin, E. T. *Focusing.* New York: Everest House, 1978.

Grof, S. *Beyond the Brain: Birth, Death and Transcendence in Psychotherapy.* Albany, N.Y.: SUNY Press, 1985.

Hanna, T. *The Body of Life.* New York: Alfred A. Knopf, 1987.

Hendricks, G. and K. Hendricks. *Radiance: Breathwork, Movement and Body-*

Centered Psychotherapy. Berkeley: Wingbow, 1991.

———. *At the Speed of Life: A New Approach to Personal Change Through Body-Centered Therapy.* New York: Bantam, 1993.

Janov, A. *Imprints: The Lifelong Effects of the Birth Experience.* New York: Coward-McCann, Inc., 1983.

Johnson, D. *Body.* Boston: Beacon Press, 1983.

Keleman, S. *Your Body Speaks Its Mind.* New York: Simon & Schuster, 1975

———. *Emotional Anatomy: The Structure of Experience.* Berkeley: Center Press. 1985.

Kurtz, R. *Body-Centered Psychotherapy: The Hakomi Method.* Mendocino, Calif.: LifeRhythm, 1990.

Kurtz, R., and H. Prestera. *The Body Reveals.* New York: Harper & Row, 1976.

Levine, P. *Accumulated Stress, Reserve Capacity, and Disease.* Boulder, Colo.: Rolf Institute, 1976.

Levy, F. *Dance/Movement Therapy: A Healing Art.* Reston, Va.: The American Alliance for Health, Physical Education, Recreation, and Dance, 1988.

Lorenz, K. *On Aggression.* New York: Bantam Books, 1963.

Lowen, A. *Pleasure: A Creative Approach to Life.* New York: Penguin Books, 1970.

Masters, R., and J. Houston. *Listening to the Body.* New York: Delta Publishing, 1978.

Mindell, A. *Dreambody: The Body's Role in Revealing the Self.* Boston: Sigo Press, 1982.

Murphy, M. *The Future of the Body.* Los Angeles: Jeremy Tarcher, 1992.

North, M. *Personality Assessment Through Movement.* Boston: Plays, Inc., 1972.

Pesso, A. *Experience in Action: A Psychomotor Psychology.* Albany: SUNY Press, 1973.

———. *Movement in Psychotherapy.* New York: New York University Press, 1969.

Pierrakos, J. C. *Core Energetics.* Mendocino, Calif.: LifeRhythm, 1987.

Raknes, O. *Wilhelm Reich and Orgonomy.* Baltimore: Penguin Books, 1971.

Reich, W. *The Function of the Orgasm.* New York: Farrar, Straus and Giroux, 1986.

CHRISTINE CALDWELL

Rosenberg, J., M. Rand, and D. Asay. *Body, Self and Soul: Sustaining Integration.* Atlanta: Humanics, 1985.

Smith, E. *The Body in Psychotherapy.* Jefferson, N.C.: McFarland & Company, 1985.

Chapter Two

THE RELATIONSHIP DANCE

Kathlyn Hendricks, Ph.D., ADTR

EDITOR'S NOTE: *The Hendricks' method was pioneered by two people who, be-fore they met, had already committed themselves to high-level healing and trans-formation, unconditional integrity, being widely useful, and channeling their work through the body. Kathlyn began her career as a dance/movement therapist, and Gay started as a psychologist who had deeply studied Wilhelm Reich. When they met and committed themselves to each other and to putting their work out in the world in a practical and far-reaching way, the resulting marriage created a system that blends consciousness, breath, expressive movement, integrity work, and a commitment to creativity that is highly effective.*

Together, Gay and Kathlyn have developed three branches in their work. Their body-centered transformation principles are discussed in their books At the Speed of Life *and* Conscious Breathing. *They like to say that they are their own best customers in the relationship work they describe in* Conscious Loving. *Most recently, they have become interested in communicating their basic principles to the business community.* The Corporate Mystic *explores this new focus. The purpose of their work is to demonstrate the creative power of authenticity, bal-ance, and gratitude so that all people can celebrate the true essence of themselves and others.*

Gay and Kathlyn Hendricks are perhaps our most "integrated in the larger world" practitioners, bringing their work not only to the workshop circuit, but into corporate boardrooms, to "The Oprah Winfrey Show" (among many other television and radio programs), and to institutions all over the world. Their understanding of how to manifest one's essence in daily life is the most advanced I know. This chapter deals with one of their prime commitments: understanding

29

and cocreating highly conscious and satisfying relationships. I considered this work of such a high caliber that I took their Conscious Loving training both for my personal growth and for my couples therapy training, and feel profoundly transformed because of it. I also readily reveal that Katie is my best friend and long-time teaching buddy. To stand together and coteach in a fully empowered and consistently fun way with another woman has been a great source of joy and inspiration for me.

*A*ll relationship is a dance with two steps. We are either coming close to or moving further from our partners. We sometimes call the "unity step" the "urge to merge" and the "individuation step" the "call of the wild." Every relationship is shaped by the individual's cycles of union and separation, and we all need to feel both whole and powerful in our relating. Everything else that we construct or think about relationships can be deconstructed to these two elements. Over and over when working with couples I find that their issues and desires can be stripped down to their awareness and comfort with these two pulsations.

What does this dance look like? When people are getting close, the movement toward can be as flagrant as barroom preening or as subtle as a nod. Getting separate may look as different as a glance over your partner's shoulder out the window or taking a retreat for several weeks or months. One part of the body may be getting separate while another is getting close, and your partner's body may be doing the same thing. This dance can get pretty complicated with the individuation-merging pulsations changing and flowing all the time.

A secret that most people don't realize is that the relationship dance is not symmetrical. Your partner will probably not always want to be close when you want to snuggle, and will probably be unaware of your impulse to go off on adventures exploring the world unless you speak up. Our cultural mythology would have us deny the power of this dance and instead learn to waltz in the commercial whirl of happily-ever-after. Marriage magazines don't talk about the day after the wedding or the weeks after the honeymoon, when your mate wants to go play basketball with the guys or take in a concert with old friends on the very night you'd planned a surprise intimate evening.

Relationship increases energy. Two or more people in close relationship have more energy together than any one individual experiences singly. One plus one is greater than two in this case. How people decide to dance with this increased energy determines whether the relationship thrives or slides into conflict.

Gay's and my primary purpose is to reveal essence in ourselves and in the people with whom we work. "Essence" is our term for who we are at the deepest level, our direct connection to wholeness and unity within ourselves and in the world. In our own relationship of sixteen years and in working with the thousands of people in our trainings and workshops, we've found that close relationship is the short path to revealing and sustaining essence. In this chapter I want to explore the most important things we've learned from our relationship dance and the dances we've been privileged to witness performed by our clients, students, and colleagues.

Our relationship work is unique in that it is based in the integrity of the body. It emphasizes taking one-hundred-percent responsibility for one's own experience and the results one is getting in the relationship, and it assumes that what feels like conflict can actually be the relationship trying to deepen. In our work, the couple doesn't just sit there and talk. What enables creative change in a relationship is consciously moving, right there in the room, what was unconsciously driving the relationship, taking ownership of that old strategy, and finding how one's essence really wants to move and express itself. When people come into our office, they can expect to move and make visible their relational patterns and to use that increased visibility towards greater intimacy.

When essence is revealed in the first sparks of relating, new motions, adventures in spirals, and tumbling assumptions roll through the old familiar corridors of routine. That's why people in love are often labeled crazy. They're unpredictable; they go out in the middle of meetings and turn cartwheels in the hall, cut their hair shorter on one side, wear purple shoes. The traditional myth continues at this point by asserting, "Have your fun now, because after you're married, it's all over." In contrast, I've seen that people can continue to reveal essence to each other and continue rekindling the sparks while becoming more deeply transparent.

The central tools I use in the relationship arena are all somatically-based and draw on the organic wisdom of the body. Countless times I've seen the body signal something that the person's mind hasn't yet registered. I call these signals "flags" because they send out discernible messages to pay attention to the context and the content in that moment. Something has erupted from the unconscious that is saying, "Notice me."

Here's an example. In a recent workshop Gay and I were working with a couple. In this context, they sat facing each other while Gay and I sat facing them. We encourage this face-to-face orientation because it supports the contact and directness that is necessary for essence to emerge. For this same reason, we ask couples to talk to each other more than to us. Ron said that he couldn't stand it when Melissa got angry with him. He just froze up and stopped breathing. We noticed that he had on a T-shirt that had a spiral on the front, with the apex of the spiral right over his diaphragm. It looked very much as if his shirt was a target.

A question we frequently ask in sessions is, "How are you experiencing that issue in your body?" When we asked him where he felt the impact of Melissa's anger he pointed to that spiral. As he was talking about the sensations he was experiencing he looked over at Melissa sheepishly.

We asked Melissa if she had any unexpressed anger toward Ron. A split second passed before she said brightly, "Oh, no," as she reached down to scratch her right leg.

"Yes, that scratching," Gay and I both pounced on her unconscious flag. Since scratching often is an anger signal, we asked, "What are you mad about?"

To Melissa's credit, she didn't spend any time being defensive. She instead focused her attention on wondering. In just a moment or so she realized she was angry about holding back her full expression from Ron. She thought initially that she held back her full intensity to keep from frightening Ron.

But here's what was amazing, and not at all unusual. As Ron and Melissa exchanged statements about how they felt while moving closer to and further away from each other, they noticed a stopping place, a moment where each of them shut down. They both began to see that holding back intensity kept them from noticing that they were scared to get really close. They had stayed in a kind of polite limbo jitterbug that wasn't close and wasn't separate. So in their relationship they had made an unconscious agreement to create a barrier to getting closer. They described the barrier as a kind of alarm bell that would go off when they became more intimate than they knew how to handle. They each had learned to associate getting close with getting hurt. Having a conflict about intensity and engaging in a power struggle were preferable to opening to their deep fear of intimate connection.

They completed this session by standing, facing each other, and then moving closer to and farther away from each other in the room. While doing so, they told each other the truth of what they were experiencing, and thus broke through into their essence. This movement had the effect of increasing their intimacy.

I've learned a fundamental relationship law in working with thousands of couples: "You're never upset for the reason you think you are." People in close relationships are often entranced by the drama of the dance and don't see that the source of their upset has nothing to do with the current conflict. The thinking is often, "I'm upset; you're here; therefore, I must be upset because of you and what you did or didn't do." I teach people to notice what is familiar about the dance—a tone, a feeling, an image—and to trace that familiarity to the original dance step that they keep repeating. People find that they have been locked into repeating a dance pattern and choose partners who will cooperate in their dance. In fact, I have been amazed to find how brilliantly creative people are in selecting the one partner who will tango toe-to-toe with them in interlocking issues. The controller will choose the passive player; the logical one will hook up with the emotional fountain. A man (or woman) tries to get his (or her) partner to do *his* steps in *his* rhythm rather than appreciate the possibilities of creating a new dance together.

Hundreds of time I have witnessed couples, business partners, and friends in close relationship uncover the hidden source of the conflict. Close dancing creates heat, and in that heat old wounds and old potentials surface. This increased heat brings transformation or trouble, depending on each partner's willingness to participate fully in the dance.

After an initial discussion of their goals and issues, I often have partners and families move together doing the relationship dance to find out where they have feelings that they don't express, where they haven't occupied the whole range of free flow between getting completely close and fully individuated. It can begin with my noticing an unconscious movement gesture either partner is making while talking about what is bothering them, and asking them to magnify it and play with it consciously. A typical instruction is "Stay in motion and move either closer to each other or further apart. You can move as fast or slowly as you like. Do your best to notice *how* you know 'that's far enough away' or 'that's close enough.'" After five minutes of watching a videotape made of their dance, clients can see, hear, and feel their entire relationship pattern. Everything is present in that short time period, because people in close relationship keep repeating the same basic pattern. Once they become conscious of what they are doing, they can express the underlying feelings and consciously identify what they want.

Most people have said that initially they were not aware of the signals that might let them know they wanted to get separate or closer. Many people base their relationship dance on the perceived expectations of their partners or society. Here are some of the questions people frequently pose: "What am I supposed to do? What's expected here? Is it okay to want something different than what my partner wants? If my partner wants to be separate when I want to be close, does that mean something is wrong in our relationship? I've never tried to notice whether I want to be close or separate—can I learn to do that?"

People gradually learn to recognize and act on the authentic signals that let them know what choice they want to make. I invite them to begin at a fundamental level with body sensations and core feelings as they move closer to and further away from each other. One person may move close and notice, "My cheeks are getting hot, and I feel a pressure on my chest." As she moves away she notices and remarks, "When I get to this distance, I feel the pressure sliding off my chest. The hotness in my cheeks is cooling off now, and I realize I feel safer somehow at this distance." These simple communications open up deep authentic connections for individuals and their relationships.

Another focus of somatic relationship counseling involves expanding the dance steps, so that partners are not stuck or dragged into repetitive cycles based on old unconscious patterns. Anything repeated enough times becomes invisible. It fades into the background and creates an invisible web that is sticky, a web that catches spontaneity and gobbles it up whole. This somatic approach loosens the hold of old patterns and brings conscious choice to the moment-to-moment experience of relating. For example, a typical pattern is the chaser pursuing the withholder. In this pattern partners would explore where each person learned that style of relationship interaction, often by exaggerating what they're already doing. I invite them to identify body sensations and emotions as they're moving. Then, I might invite them to try out different steps to notice how expanding or interrupting the pattern affects their relationship. I often have them switch roles, giving each partner the chance to try on the opposite pattern. I also ask them to invent an entirely different step with each other. From these explorations partners can expand their creativity directly and can learn a great deal about how their life dance unfolds.

Here's an example from a seminar. I had structured a simple movement activity for people to explore getting close and getting separate. I asked them to just go through the motions first, moving in automatic or robotic ways. After a few moments I asked them to consciously choose each movement toward or away from other participants. During the discussion that followed, one woman jumped up and said, "I did my whole life in the last ten minutes! That's *just* how I am!"

Society, as well as traditional family structures, supports routine and stability. In one of my favorite films, "A Thousand Clowns," there are two brothers, one straight-laced, one not. The straight-laced brother vigorously defends his schedule, his predictability, and his suits. The other brother (played by Jason Robards) is extremely creative, funny, and adventurous, but he can't seem to commit as an "adult." The film explores the question: Is it possible both to keep the open-ended qualities of childhood alive *and* to be commited? Much of the drama in relationships swings between these polarities of nesting and adventuring, or, as we put it, getting close and getting separate.

In our books we've identified and explored the phenomenon we call the Upper Limits Problem. Each of us has a thermostat setting for how much love and positive energy we can handle. When that limit is exceeded, we each have favorite ways of returning to a more familiar level. In relationship the macro or obvious expression of the Upper Limits Problem often occurs as an argument or broken agreement.

For example, toward the end of one of our week-long trainings in relationship transformation, one of the couples slid into the Upper Limits Problem. Libby was feeling sexy and touching Terry, leaning in toward him and flirting with her eyes. Terry said, "Is that a screw-me move?"

Libby froze, held her breath, and rather than tuning into what was authentic for her, began focusing on Terry's feelings asking him sharply, "What's going on with you?" When we invited her to notice her experience, she murmured, "I'm sad." Very quickly Libby recognized that she had filtered Terry's playful response through a well-established pattern that he, like her father, limited her sexual feelings.

When people get caught in the Upper Limits problem, they move and breathe less. They can understand the nonverbal messages of their relating by noticing the quality of movement and the quality of breath. For example, a woman's movement may become hesitant as she starts to talk about her sexuality. A man's breath may skirt high up into his chest when his wife touches him. I spend much more time noticing how people communicate than just what they talk about. I've found it particularly useful to notice what occurs when breath or movement shifts during an interaction.

As people are moving in the relationship dance of getting closer and more separate, these fluctuations and contractions are especially obvious. Some people hold their breath when they reach a certain closeness to their partner. Others shrink as they move away. When changing from closer to further away, in that transition moment, many people get smaller and suspend breath. Breath and movement often flow and freeze together. By noticing and flagging these patterns we can give partners access to feelings and experiences that have been simmering under the surface. I've noticed that people in close relationship often freeze breath and motion when faced with change, conflict, or, to their surprise, when things are going well.

Two keys to balance are full, harmonious breathing and free movement through the whole range of getting close and getting separate. What can open the flow again when people are stuck? I teach people to first recognize that they have fallen into fear, even though they may think they're angry. Behind most angry outbursts lurks an unspoken fear. People can regain harmony and flow by telling a simple truth, taking a centered breath, moving with curiosity, and wondering about their role in the issue.

Most people give lip service to the importance of honesty in relationships, but we've found that in practice, especially in the heat of conflict, those ideals slide into the mud of projection and power struggle. Most couples need lots of practice to be able to say something that restores flow and harmony, something that no one, especially their partner, could argue with. In our workshops and trainings, we help people to identify things they can say that produce connection and vitality. Instead of saying "You made me angry," they learn to identify their body sensations and to say a simple truth like, "My jaw is tight and I noticed I was holding my breath." We have seen thousands of relationship miracles occur when people communicate from the most basic level.

Chest breathing or breath holding are common ways that people freeze their experience in relationships. Chest breathing produces anxiety all by itself, regardless of the person's thoughts or feelings. Both chest breathing and held breath signal the body to engage in fight-or-flight responses. What many people don't realize is that those signals reach the brain faster that rational problem-solving thoughts can. So whenever you or your partner stop breathing full and relaxed breaths, your brain and nervous system think there's big trouble. Most people can't stop those responses; they're deeply wired in to our physiology. But I've noticed that people can learn to return to centered breathing quickly with a little practice. Centered breathing is covered in detail in one of Gay's recent books, *Conscious Breathing*. In short, when breathing in a relaxed and conscious way, a person's belly fills first before the chest. The stomach muscles relax on the inbreath to allow full expansion of the diaphragm. This style of breathing is literally the opposite of what most people do. It creates bridges between the survival brain and the creative brain and opens the possibility of seeing your partner as an ally again rather than the worst mistake you ever made.

Many people freeze or contract their muscles when they're stuck. Some people get smaller; some inflate themselves. Most people repeat the movement sequence that helped them survive the first threats to their essence. They recreate the postures and gestures that worked when their authentic response didn't. The whole parade of personae—clown, intellectual, martyr, loner, and so on—is glued to movement patterns. By simply moving with wonder rather than righteousness, people can unlock those old patterns and discover their authentic feelings and thoughts. I'll often ask a person to notice the place where he or she feels tightest and allow that part to move the way it wants to move. These simple movements open flow again and restore connectedness to self and others.

People are so used to defending themselves against real and imagined attacks that they often don't consider the bigger picture. Gay and I want people to wonder about what they really want, rather than just excavating what's wrong. The larger purpose of our relationship work and body-centered transformation trainings is to free creativity so people can design their lives and relationships consciously rather than by default or in defiance of the past. Another reason that our approach is based on the organic processes of the body is to expand choice. We look at healing old patterns in the context of the question, "Then what?" We ask: "What would you be doing with your energy if you weren't using it in this conflict?" We have been amazed to learn how few people actually ask themselves what they really want. The response we usually hear is, "Well, I know I *don't* want. . ."

Wondering is a body event. True wondering involves willing play and presenting of the sensations, feelings, and images that your body offers. In our work we cultivate wondering as a central tool for both healing and creating. Wondering is a whole-body "hmmm" that vibrates possibility out from between the cracks of frozen responses. Here are some questions we frequently use to stimulate wondering:

◆ What would be the completely healed, positive outcome of this?

◆ If you could design it any way you wanted to, how would you design it?

◆ What is it about you that requires this interaction, event, or outcome?

◆ Has either of you ever experienced anything like this in your life before?

People tell us that as they open to the intention and practice of wondering, their lives become more magical. Answers to seemingly intractable questions appear as they're taking a walk or cooking dinner. Once people let go of the need to control situations or their partners, true creativity can emerge. Wondering allows partners to step into the unknown safely. Truly, if people knew how to solve their problems, most would do so. It's *not knowing* and feeling helpless and stuck that drive most people crazy. Instead of struggling more or trying to change their partners, we encourage people to wonder, using the questions like those given above to jump start their own creativity.

People have said that because the answer didn't come immediately, they slipped into a sense of discouragement. When coached to realize that creative rhythms don't always work on clock time, people relax more into the play of possibilities. Through wondering, warring partners have created shared work positions, schedules that allow both to care for their children, new houses, careers, and programs for their community. I have come to have tremendous respect for the power of wondering.

Most people have difficulty being authentic in the relationship dance. In *Conscious Loving* we outlined the five stages of relationship, focusing a lot of attention on what we call the Choicepoint. After Stage One, Romance and Recognition, in sweeps Stage Two, The Inevitable. In this stage the heat and increased energy of close relating flush up shadows and unowned potential. Here people confront the Choicepoint, Stage Three, where they can turn in one of two directions. In the Unconscious Loving choice, people withhold the truth, big or small. The energy that it takes to withhold creates distance and withdrawal, and out of withdrawing the partner starts to look different, creating projection. That sequence—withhold, withdraw, project—can sometimes take only a split second, and is a major source of distance and misery in relationships.

In contrast, if people take the Conscious Loving choice, they wonder about what an issue has to do with them and they tell the inarguable truth. This level of choice and communication creates intimacy and more harmony in the relationship dance. Several years ago I realized that there are only two states in my relationship with Gay: harmony or withholding. If I'm not feeling loving and creating, I'll look for the withhold. Buckminster Fuller said that any idea you don't take action on within ten minutes turns sour. We've found that any truth that isn't communicated within a few minutes turns into withholds and projections, creating the trickle of distance that gradually erodes relationships in the bedroom and the boardroom.

People often don't know they are withholding. I've found it useful to identify what withholds look and feel like at the somatic level, since they are so crucial in the relationship dance. Withholding is always accompanied by contraction, whether tiny or whole-body. Withholding takes measurable physical energy. Most people have storage areas, places where they habitually hold back. This often depends on the feeling they typically withhold. Most people identify three feelings that cause the most trouble when left to fester rather than being communicated simply and straightforwardly. These feelings are anger, fear, and sadness. As Reich and other somatic psychologists have identified, each feeling involves particular muscular-organ systems of the body and can be identified by focusing attention on body sensations.

Anger withholds are often stored in the lumps and cords that show up in the shoulders, arms, and along the spine. Sadness often constricts the chest and throat; some people notice sadness first in sensations around their eyes. Fear is commonly described as the "butterflies" and queasy sensations around the navel area. I have been amazed to find how many people are unaware that body sensations are connected to emotions.

In the relationship dance much of the work involves identifying sensations in the moment and matching them to the emotion. The question "What feeling is that connected to?" creates a bridge between body sensations and emotions. The flags mentioned earlier are the easiest way to discover the body's messages and signals of withholding. When a person contracts to withhold, the body takes over communicating. A flag goes up, whether it's a held breath, a glance away, drumming fingers, a tonal change in the voice, or postural shifts. With a little practice, both clients and therapists can utilize these signals to open up areas that are virtually inaccessible if the focus stays on content or verbal exchange. The body is marvelously clever and persistent. Flags will not only continue but often escalate until someone notices and starts to inquire.

Here's an example of this pattern from my own life. Three days before going away on a retreat to write the sequel to *Conscious Loving*, I evoked one of the behaviors that drives us both crazy. I was negotiating some financial agreements with one of our colleagues and got scared and angry when talking to Gay about the details. Instead of continuing to talk about my feelings until they cleared up, I tried to handle it. As soon as I made that decision, my nose started to get sniffly and sneezy (incidentally, one of my first performances in high school modern dance class was entitled "The Sneeze," so you can see how long I've been favoring this mode of expression). Over the next two days my symptoms escalated; meanwhile, I had repressed the original issue and began to look at the possibility that I was allergic to hotel rooms. We were teaching a seminar at a retreat center, and the students later reported that I seemed not quite as present as usual.

On Saturday, in the middle of the night, I woke suddenly coughing and choking, which startled Gay out of his sleep and kept him up for an hour or two. As I was stretching the next morning, a faucet opened in my sinuses and I honked through several tissues.

At this point Gay asked what I was withholding, this pattern of sneezing and dripping instead of expressing being quite familiar to both of us. By this time I had convinced myself that I was having a reaction to something in the bedspread or the high level of mold and grass in the air. I made a case for this with several examples of how I felt much better when I was away from that site the afternoon before, and how my symptoms had returned as soon as I came back into the room.

Gay, predictably, became very angry and pressed me to inquire about the original withhold. I eventually did uncover the moment when I had gathered up my resources to control my feelings rather than simply express them. The usual miracle occurred. The moment I expressed my feelings, the symptoms disappeared. But by then we had decided to cancel the mountain retreat.

It took several days of exploring and inner searching to unravel this particular Upper Limits event. I realized that I was excited and scared to take the next step of cocreating more fully, and I was scared to show Gay what I had written so far. I was more committed to running the old drama of withholding than having an actual current relationship with Gay. And I had cast him as the enemy rather than appreciated his bringing an unconscious pattern to my attention. I felt very sad to be running an old pattern once again. After all, I've written books about the value of being totally transparent, yet I clearly hadn't mastered it in my own life. Gay also looked at where his withdrawing reaction came from, and uncovered old pain about his mother's commitment to not see him or let him get close.

The event gave us the opportunity to share deeper levels of fear and deeper levels of what we want with each other. We used it, and it was costly— days of distancing and nights of tossing. It was time to repair the breakdown in trust. I recommitted to full expression in each moment and to celebrating a fully evolved, cocreative relationship.

A story came to mind as we were recovering. In rabbinical school, the rabbi was teaching and told the children that he would place the great teachings on their hearts. One little girl said, "Why are you placing the teaching on our hearts and not in them?"

He replied, "Only God can place the teachings in your heart. We put them on your heart so that when your heart breaks, they'll fall in."

Something I encourage partners to remember is that the Choicepoint occurs over and over in relationship, especially when things are going well. The moment one person tells the truth and starts being curious, flow and harmony return to the relationship. As people free themselves from the limited movement and breath patterns that have restricted their possibilities, they begin to recover their deeper selves and the potentials of their relationships. The biggest benefit that people report is the rekindling of romance and the enhancement of creativity within themselves and in their relating.

It has surprised us and the people we work with to find how frequently couples share the same underlying emotion and fundamental issue. On the surface it may look as if they have completely different issues because their styles of coping have evolved in different family settings and environments. Over and over, as we explore with them, they find they are dealing with the same feeling, the same basic wound.

I have been teaching the relationship work in Germany over the last few years. On a recent trip I was working with a couple in a Hamburg seminar.

Peter and Otteline looked very different and had opposite body postures and mannerisms. Peter was large and bulky, with a lethargic quality and slow gestures and speech patterns. In contrast, Otteline was small, wiry, and quick. She darted from place to place and also spoke in short, staccato bursts. His complaint was that she was too clingy. Hers was that he wouldn't commit. We worked with their flags and the question: What might they be creating if they weren't engaged in this power struggle? When we asked this question, Peter sighed and touched his chest. When I called his attention to that gesture and asked him to be with the sensations, his defensive tone began to dissolve. He noticed the pressure he felt in his chest and said how familiar that was. As he let his awareness rest on those sensations, he realized that he had always felt unwelcome. He couldn't remember ever feeling oherwise, and had grown a large body to buffer himself from the sadness and pain of not being wanted.

As he spoke Otteline began to cry and reached out to take his hand. She said she could see that, as the last child in a family of nine, she had learned to outrun the same feeling that he had buffered. This recognition of their similar wound allowed them to become allies in loving and appreciating each other and knowing that part of their choosing each other was to heal the same trauma.

Seeing these basic similarities has given us increased respect for the power of the unconscious to select the partner with whom seemingly insurmountable wounds can be healed. We have noticed there is a big "if" to this possibility. If both partners are willing to use the heat of close relationship and to listen and speak to each other with wonder, miracles occur. Partners can then focus on celebrating each other's essence and unfolding their creative expression.

HOW WE CAME TO THIS WORK

Gay developed a somatic approach to his work after completing traditional clinical and counseling psychology training at the University of New Hampshire and at Stanford University. He began using somatic techniques such as breathwork and movement in the early seventies to augment his then largely verbal practice. As his experience grew, he came to rely more heavily on somatic practices because body-centered techniques, unlike verbal techniques, produced lasting results much more rapidly. His research into somatic psychology has produced over twenty books, including *At the Speed of Life, Conscious Breathing, The Centering Book, Learning to Love Yourself,* and *Conscious Loving.*

I came into partnership with Gay with a background in movement therapy. I was Joan Chodorow's first student in the late sixties, apprenticing at the innovative Santa Barbara Psychiatric Medical Center. My first explorations included leading hospital groups, conducting day treatment, and participating in and observing individual movement therapy sessions. During the seventies I studied with Irmgaard Bartenieff, Barbara Govine, and Trudi Schoop, among other somatic educators. My friendship with Mary Whitehouse influenced my development of improvisationally-based movement activities that could lead even resistant nonmovers into exploring their inner world.

Kathlyn Hendricks

In 1978 I entered the Institute for Transpersonal Psychology, where I received my doctorate in 1982. My graduate studies led me to value the spiritual basis of all somatic experience and to place a high priority on developing processes to encourage following authentic impulses.

Together, Gay and I have developed three branches in our work. Our body-centered transformation principles are discussed in *At the Speed of Life* and *Conscious Breathing*. We like to say that we are our own best customers in the relationship work we describe in *Conscious Loving*. Most recently, we have become interested in communicating our basic principles to the business community. *The Corporate Mystic* explores this new focus. The purpose of our work is to demonstrate the creative power of authenticity, balance, and gratitude so that all people can celebrate the true essence of themselves and others.

Chapter Three

ESSENTIALS OF HAKOMI
BODY-CENTERED PSYCHOTHERAPY

Ron Kurtz with Kekuni Minton

EDITOR'S NOTE: *Ron Kurtz is one of our better-known body-centered therapists. As an ambassador of the bodymind, he has taught and toured tirelessly for more than twenty-five years. His blending of many Western therapy forms with Eastern values of nonviolence have made him a bridge builder of great importance in this field.*

The word "Hakomi" has an interesting origin. It came to one of the early trainers in a dream, and he handed the unknown word to Ron on a slip of paper. They found out it is a Hopi word meaning both "Who are you?" and "How do you stand in relation to these many realms?" The word also has derivations in Chinese and Hebrew, having to do with laughter and existence. Hakomi got its start with these intuitive and spiritual underpinnings, and the system reflects these origins.

Kekuni Minton is one of Hakomi's current trainers. One of our finest theoreticians, he has the unique distinction of having trained in other somatic therapy forms, most notably Integrated Body Psychotherapy. He and I cotaught a theoretical survey course in somatic psychology at Naropa Institute for several years, and I have come to value highly his broad perspective, insight, and sensitive classroom demeanor. In the following chapter, Ron's voice is in the foreground, while Kekuni brings in a clarity of organization and a rich and broad view of this material.

*H*akomi is a body-inclusive psychotherapy that interweaves Western therapeutic influences with Taoist/Buddhist principles such as *mindfulness, awareness,* and *nonviolence.* The word *Hakomi* is a question, a Hopi word meaning "How do I stand in relation to these many realms?" or, more succinctly, "Who am I?" It is an inquiry into one's basic nature. Inherent in this method is the belief that this question cannot be answered by effort, force, or the therapist's imposition of his or her own agenda.

What's new about the Hakomi method? I think this is one of the main things: Hakomi is the evocation of experience in mindfulness. Mindfulness is a state of awareness that is an inward turning of attention, a simple noticing of what *is*—not an attempt to justify or explain, but simply "being with" current experience. Hakomi uses mindfulness in a precise way.

Mindfulness is not just another technique. It is a state of consciousness. We evoke experiences while the client is in this particular state of consciousness. The evoked experiences tell us what kind of models the client is holding about herself and her world. More importantly, the models are often immediately clear to the client. By evoking experience in mindfulness, emotions are often released that would be very hard to release any other way. This happens because the client knows what's happening. There are no tricks or manipulations here. The state of mindfulness is a deliberate choice on the part of the client to be vulnerable and sensitive. Clients drop their defenses when they become mindful. They choose to take what comes. If they feel painful emotion in this process, it is because they believe it is worth it in order to understand themselves. So they are willing to bring this material into consciousness where it can be worked on. This is not violence. This is the courage to face what is. Amazingly, this approach works much more quickly than any I had used before.

Another aspect of Hakomi psychotherapy is that it is experiential. We focus on bodily experiences, such as sensations, emotions, tensions, and movements. This focus on experience, rather than abstract notions, leads to more grounded insight and understanding. We discover the roots of psychological organization and we find meaning by working with here-and-now experiences. The body is alive with meaning and memory. We focus on experience, not for its own sake, but to learn how we came to be who we are, and how we shall move on.

I started practicing psychotherapy in 1970. By 1979 I'd developed enough original techniques and ideas to justify calling the combination a new method. The Hakomi Institute was founded the same year. Eight years later, Swami Rama told me that I was a person with a mission: to create a new method of psychotherapy. When I think about Hakomi, I think about it in those terms, as a new method of psychotherapy. However, before I talk about that, I would like to give a little more history.

I began my studies with the experiential, body-centered therapies of the sixties, which became the Western psychological roots of Hakomi. There are two more tracks that influenced me. The first was Eastern philosophy and practice. I had been practicing yoga since 1959. In graduate school I became interested in Taoism and Buddhism; awareness practices became part of my life. The last track is my life-long interest in science. My passion is systems theory, the branch of science that studies living systems. These threads —Eastern philosophy, psychotherapeutic technique, and systems theory— are the foundations of Hakomi. They are diverse and extensive and offer much that nourishes and teaches.

The Western experiential therapies I started out with (Gestalt, Bioenergetics, and so on) seemed, in my view, too forceful, at times even violent. In keeping with the Eastern philosophies I'd studied, I wished to be nonviolent, to encourage change without force. I began to look for gentler ways to access emotional material. I slowly found ways to incorporate mindfulness and other gentle interventions in my work.

I began to use mindfulness in this way: I would have an idea about what the client couldn't believe or experience. Let's say the person had low self-worth; he couldn't believe he was a worthy person. I would ask him to become mindful. Sometimes I would teach him *how* to become mindful.

When he was in a mindful state, I would offer a statement that was just the opposite of his belief about his worth. For example, if the belief was "I have little worth," I would say something like: "You're a worthy person." We call these statements "probes." I would set these statements up as little experiments (my science background). I'd say, "Let's see what happens when I say. . . " Then I'd offer the statement. I was looking for reactions. A person in mindfulness has no trouble noticing his or her reactions.

I slowly started doing more and more of these little experiments in mindfulness and both the client and I would observe the reactions. Sometimes the reaction would be intensely emotional, although it was arrived at completely without force. The statements I offered were always positive. The reaction was the result of the person's inability to accept this potential nourishment. If I could identify what the core issues were, I could help bring them into the client's consciousness through this use of mindfulness.

The introduction of mindfulness was more than just a new technique. It laid a new foundation. It influenced all the techniques. It gave the method an added depth. Adding mindfulness gave the therapy greater power and shifted the way all other techniques were used, for all techniques became experiments in mindfulness. In addition, it made nonviolence essential and that in turn made the personal development of the therapist essential.

I eventually deemphasized the more forceful (Gestalt and Bioenergetics) techniques in my practice. I used mindfulness to evoke emotions, meaning, and memory. One of the connections of Hakomi to Taoism and Feldenkrais work and the Gestalt notion of figure and ground is the notion that awareness itself lowers the noise. When you turn your awareness toward something, you automatically lower the noise. When you start to pay attention to something, that is, when you make it the signal (or the figure), other things will automatically fade out—the noise will lower by itself. If you draw attention to movements in slow motion, as Feldenkrais does, you will start to notice things that you did not notice before. This is mindfulness. Bare attention gives time for signals to develop. The more time you take, the more information you get. In mindfulness, attention is concentrated. The pace is slower. One's usual concerns are set aside. The focus is on present experience, as it is in other consciousness disciplines.

I built Hakomi out of such components as mindfulness and nonviolence because I found that they worked. It happened mostly by trial and error, not shaped by any grand plan. Like any stubborn fool, I had to find out for myself. I read. Ideas came to me. But I never accepted them without trying them out. When I tried mindfulness and nonviolence, they worked. If I created safety, people could become mindful. When I did little experiments in mindfulness, something important would be evoked. It was easy. It worked. And I liked the fact that it was nonviolent, full of compassion. It felt good to me. I wasn't thinking about the long run. I was using what worked and I really didn't see what was coming.

When I built Hakomi on the principles of nonviolence and mindfulness, it gave the therapy a strong spiritual foundation. Working out of those principles, which require respect, sensitivity, presence, and compassion on the part of the therapist, leads naturally to loving experiences and finally

ESSENTIALS OF HAKOMI BODY-CENTERED PSYCHOTHERAPY

to spiritual experiences. The method is pointed in that direction. Hakomi has been called "applied Buddhism." This spiritual direction has been built into Hakomi from the beginning. This only became clear slowly, as I developed the method and added techniques.

I used to think of psychotherapy as intrapsychic, that the client did all the work internally. The therapist suggested things but was basically not really involved as a person. My image of the therapist was the samurai, who was a master swordsman, but who did what he did without emotions, passion, or personality. His goal was perfect precision. I thought of myself as a therapist in that same way, as a precise technician, trying to be a master. It was no doubt inspired by a character flaw of mine, but I liked that image: precise, technical, without feelings or personal involvement. I took a secret pride in that.

Eventually I saw that the difficulties that emerged in therapy were the result of my personal limitations, my incomplete personhood. They weren't technical problems at all and it wasn't about mastery. It was my ego, my puffed-up attitude, and my inability to understand people because I didn't understand certain things in myself. It was about my ability to relate. Again, the focus shifted to something deeper than just technique. I came to a place where I concentrated for a few years on what I called the "healing relationship." For a healing relationship to happen, more than just safety was needed; what was needed was the cooperation of the unconscious. It required a relationship at the level of the unconscious, a deep, person-to-person connection—and that's a two-way street. Not only did I learn that I needed the cooperation of the unconscious, I also learned that I had to be worthy of it. I needed to earn it.

Some years ago, I read Michael Mahoney's book, *Human Change Processes*. He cited a few twenty-year-long studies which showed that "the 'person' of the therapist is at least eight times more influential than his or her theoretical orientation and/or use of specific therapeutic techniques." I took that very seriously. I realized I couldn't just teach people technical methods. I had to define, recognize, and teach "personhood." I had to help students develop their personhood, which to me is mostly spiritual development. We all have to attend to our personal growth and do a certain amount of emotional work. But beyond that, and especially when you wish to become helpful to other people, spiritual development is the natural and necessary next step.

The healing relationship involves two basic things. First, the therapist has to demonstrate that he or she is trustworthy, nonjudgmental, and compassionate. Second, the therapist has to demonstrate that he or she is present, attentive, and really understands what's going on for the client. If the therapist can consistently demonstrate these things to the client, he or she will earn the cooperation of the client's unconscious.

The unconscious is waiting for somebody who can do that. If the client has painful secrets, shame, confusion, and emotional pain, the therapist will need extraordinary sensitivity, understanding, and caring to become an ally of the unconscious. The unconscious has been managing this pain for a long time. It won't allow just anyone to become part of that process. The healing relationship is about gaining the trust and cooperation of the unconscious through compassion and understanding. If you can do that, therapy really happens. Building such a relationship doesn't have to take three months or three years. It can take as little as fifteen minutes; but creating it requires more than just technical skills.

The creation of a healing relationship in therapy requires that the therapist be a certain kind of person, a person who is naturally compassionate, and who is able to be radically present to give full attention to another, to see deeply into people, and to understand what is seen. This requires a certain state of mind. We could call this state of mind nonegocentric. The therapist needs to be free of as many ego-centered habits as possible when working with the client.

This step in Hakomi's evolution involved the spiritual development of the therapist. It involved the development of personhood, an expansion of understanding and insight into levels of consciousness beyond the ordinary, rational, and objective. To sustain this higher level of consciousness, one needs a base, a source of inspiration. One needs to find, recognize, and cultivate a source of spiritual (or nonegocentric) nourishment. With a stable connection to that source, confidence, calmness, understanding, and compassion come naturally.

Outside of therapy, there are many, many sources of spiritual nourishment. But in the present moment of a therapy process, the source I use is the client. I search for and find nonegocentric nourishment in some aspect of the client. This is very close to the Buddhist practice of searching for the seed of Buddha in every person. Or as Swami Premananda says, "The purpose of life is to see God in everyone and everything." When asked how this was done, he replied, "In the silence." The idea is to drop the "noise of self" and see the other as spirit. With this as habit, with this as a base, therapy becomes a shared, deeply heartfelt journey.

Working this way, compassion emerges spontaneously. With the mind quiet and attentive, understanding comes easily. The two qualities most important to the healing relationship, compassion and understanding, are the natural outcome of searching for nonegocentric nourishment from the therapist-client relationship. The development of that practice is a spiritual discipline, and its fruition is personhood and full human beingness. It is this approach that makes psychotherapy a spiritual practice.

So I started to focus on the state of mind of the therapist. I developed methods to explore and support the spiritual development of the therapist. My trainings and workshops now include a lot of work and practice around that. This brings us up to date on the development of the Hakomi Method. The principles of mindfulness and nonviolence were the beginning of the uniqueness of Hakomi, and the last step was the focus on spiritual practice and the state of mind of the therapist.

Now I would like to convey a sense of how the practice of Hakomi therapy actually works. One of the techniques of Hakomi is called *taking over*.

When an emotional experience is evoked in someone, the habits that manage that experience are also evoked. These management reactions are usually called defenses. For example, sadness is often managed by covering the face, tightening the muscles of the diaphragm, chest, throat, and eyes, hanging one's head, and collapsing the posture. All these are automatic reactions. A person doesn't think about doing them. They are habitual ways to manage emotional experience. I do not oppose these management habits or in any way try to break them down. I do exactly the opposite. I support all management behavior. If a person tightens his shoulders or covers his face, I might use my hands to help him keep his shoulders together or to cover his face. (Of course I first ask permission.) That's taking over.

Taking over also can be done verbally. If I offer somebody a statement such as, "You're worthy," and she reacts by hearing a voice in her head saying, "No, I'm not!", I might take the voice over. I would ask the person to be mindful again and, perhaps with the help of another person, we would repeat this exchange a few times: me saying, "You're worthy" and the assistant saying , "No, I'm not." The "No, I'm not" is also a management behavior. For the client, in her model of life, there's something wrong with feeling worthy. Perhaps it's too dangerous, or it makes her a target for others. That's the model, the belief system. Perhaps the experience of feeling worthy elicits some painful memories around feeling unworthy. So, we take over the voices or thoughts that manage this pain.

The usual result of taking over is this: the person relaxes their managing. Sometimes they relax it a little bit, sometimes a lot. If you manage your sadness by tightening your shoulders and I begin to help you with that, the message is: you're not alone with your sadness. You have an ally. It may be the first time you've gotten that message about your sadness, and receiving that message may be the most important part of the session.

Another result of taking over is that you don't have to work as hard. You're being supported. You can let go a little. It's not that you have to; nobody is forcing you to let go. You simply have been offered the opportunity. Letting go is up to you. And you can do it at your own pace. You can allow the feelings you are managing to come forth and be expressed. This is another way that nonviolence is incorporated into Hakomi.

When you are not opposed or made to feel wrong, when you feel like somebody is on your side, you may be able to go a lot deeper into your experience, deeper into your feelings than you could if you were struggling against it all by yourself. Taking over sends messages like these: I can see that this is difficult for you; I'm willing to help you handle this experience; I'll follow your lead; I won't force anything; I'll support your need to control your own process. Taking over sends these messages through the actions themselves; not through words. As such it speaks directly to the unconscious. Of course, the therapist has to be extremely sensitive to the client's reactions, must "get the permission of the unconscious" through following the client's nonverbal expressions—through following the body.

Typically, supporting management behavior leads to feelings of safety, relaxation of the management, deeper feelings and expression, deeper insight, and movement of the emotional process to its emotionally logical conclusion. It's paradoxical. A part of the person is trying to manage her experience, to hold it back or minimize it. The therapist offers support for that, and the person goes deeper into her experience.

So these two general methods, using evoked experiences in mindfulness and the nonviolent taking over of the management of the experiences evoked, are basic elements unique to the Hakomi method.

From a systems point of view, we can think of mindfulness as lowering the noise. A sensitive system is a system that can detect or pick out a weak signal from a noisy environment. To increase that ability, you either raise the level of the external signal or lower the noise in the environment. Mindfulness is a way of lowering the noise. Eastern philosophy teaches us that when the mind has become silent (when you have lowered the noise of bodily tension, busy thoughts, and concerns of all kinds), then the signal (which is the beauty and reality of spirit) will simply emerge. That signal, like the stars which appear when the sun goes down, is always present, hidden by the noise we make.

In body-centered psychotherapies, where the signals being sought are insights into bodily experiences, unnecessary physical tension, struggle, effort, and even pain can be considered noise. The noise is especially great when the struggle is one part of yourself against another, when unresolved issues generate conflicting impulses and compete for attention and control.

Mindfulness, which involves a relaxation of effort and a quieting of the mind, lowers the noise. Being mindful means deliberately bringing yourself into a sensitive and vulnerable condition. That's how it works in psychotherapy. If you're busy lifting weights and listening to the radio, and I come in and say, "You're worthy," you're not going to react much to my words. But if you're mindful, sensitive, and quiet, if your mind is open and simply noticing, the same statement can evoke quite a deep experience.

Nonviolence is a necessary part of this because in order for the client to become vulnerable (mindful), he or she has to feel safe. So, the first task of a Hakomi therapist is to make the other person feel safe. There are many ways to do this, but the most basic is to have an active, deep respect and compassion for all beings. Then the other truly is safe. All you have to do is convey your respect and compassion to the other person. If you are going to use mindfulness in therapy, nonviolence and safety are absolutely essential. It doesn't work any other way.

When the noise is lowered, whatever signal is being masked will emerge. It appears, as out of a fog. When the client is in a state of mindfulness and experiences are evoked, there is no confusion about the source. The client is clear that whatever emerges, it's hers. She knows that the emotional response is her own and that it's based on her own beliefs and history. The therapist is not asking her to believe anything. They're not having a discussion about what might be going on. The two of them are doing little experiments in mindfulness together and they're discovering the results. The client becomes vulnerable, she lowers the noise and the signals emerge. Using this method, we avoid interpreting or explaining a person to herself. She discovers who she is and how she's organized for herself, at her own pace, within a safe setting and with a trusted guide. So two of the main advantages of this method are that it supports personal responsibility (by showing clearly how experiences are organized by inner models and beliefs) and that it avoids confusion (by studying and processing evoked experiences in the here-and-now, letting a person discover who she is rather than theorizing about it).

Now, I want to talk about the place of the body in psychotherapy. Besides its focus on mindfulness, Hakomi is definitely a body psychotherapy.

Several things come to my mind when I think of the body in psychotherapy. The first is the notion of Wilhelm Reich (the father of body-centered psychotherapy) that the body is an expression of the psychological history of the person. The body reveals psychological information. You don't need to ask about it; a person's psychological history is alive and present in everything the person does and the style in which he does it. It's there in how people use their bodies, how they move, where the tension is, what the posture and structure are like, and the structure itself. So, you can look at the body for psychological information. In Hakomi we teach people how to read the body for such information. We learn about the person's history and his or her core models and beliefs from posture, movement patterns, breathing patterns, gestures, body structure, facial expression, pace, tone of voice, and on and on. All of this gives us psychological information. For me, this understanding of the expressions of self through the body is one basic component of body psychotherapy.

If I do an experiment in mindfulness and evoke an emotional experience, any meanings we find are grounded in bodily experience. The person may respond with something like, "Yeah, my heart feels like it's in my throat. My stomach is tight. I'm a little nauseous and I feel afraid." We're not discussing what might be true or what might have happened thirty years ago.

We're discussing what is happening right now. And what is always happening right now is that beliefs have strong bodily and experiential outcomes. The mind is hooked up to physiology.

So, one of the ways Hakomi is body-centered is that it uses experience as doorways to insight. If you're in mindfulness and I say, "Dogs are friendly" and you react with fear and disbelief, there's no question about what model you're holding. As soon as you're in touch with those beliefs and those emotions, clear memories are likely to follow. And when memories are present, explanations aren't needed. Even more important, when beliefs are conscious, doubt becomes possible. Change becomes possible. The key thing is to discover the connection between the beliefs and the experiences.

If there is conflict about the expression of certain emotions, Hakomi therapists support the actions that manage that expression (but only if we have permission to do so). This usually results in a deeper, more complete, and more satisfying release. Often, when emotional expression goes beyond an habitual boundary, spontaneous insight and integration follow immediately. The missing experience emerges and the process evolves into savoring and integrating that experience.

Of course it's not all that linear. We often loop back to earlier steps, spending time building the relationship, trying new experiments, and evoking new experiences. But the general drift of each session and the therapy process as a whole tends to move in the direction I have described.

We work with people's core beliefs and models of who they are and what kind of world they're in. We get to these models through the methods I've already presented. We call the process of uncovering basic models "going for meaning." We want to help people change their models. Again, this is not an intellectual process. It's mental, but it's not abstract. For the person holding the model, it's not theory, it just is. The deepest models are those that are beyond doubt. They are not in consciousness, but they are in use. They are organizing all experiences, all the time. These are old habits.

It's as if you had been wearing colored glasses all your life. If they are orange-colored glasses, you have never really seen the color blue. You don't know what blue is, or even that blue exists. All blues look black to you. And if you don't even know you are wearing orange glasses, if it has become so unconscious and automatic, you may never question the blacks you see. The deepest models you are using determine your perceptions and other behaviors. Your model is your truth. It determines what you can think, what you do, and what you feel.

One very significant thing about Hakomi is that it brings these models to consciousness clearly and easily. It quickly gets to the beliefs and meanings that run your life. It gives you the chance to examine and change those meanings. The use of mindfulness allows people to study the direct effects of their models. They learn, through their immediate reactions to various significant statements (or any other little experiments the therapist can come up with), exactly how they habitually organize themselves and their worlds.

To help people become conscious of the models they are carrying, I might do something like the following. Say I'm working with twenty people in a workshop setting. Around a big issue like safety, there will be quite a range of models. Some will feel perfectly safe. Some will be nearly terrified. I help the whole group to become mindful and when they're ready, I offer a statement about safety: "You're completely safe here." Twenty people will have twenty different reactions. Some people will sigh with relief. Some will have feelings or thoughts. For some, nothing much will happen. Some people will tense up. Some people will start trembling with fear. Some will think, "Bullshit." There will be twenty different ways to organize experience, because all twenty people are carrying different models.

After we help bring people's fundamental, unconscious models into consciousness, we then want to provide an experience that balances out any imbalances in the model. Some models are extreme and rigidly maintained. For example, a person might hold at a core belief that no one can be trusted. A devastating experience of betrayal can make this belief seem a good one to have, since it protects against further betrayal. A person with this core belief will be cautious with everyone and won't really trust anyone. The person may withdraw from contact and prefer to be alone because it feels safer than interacting with others. Such a model is unbalanced. The truth is that some people are trustworthy and some people aren't. Some people will hurt you and some people won't. You just have to be able to discover who's safe. To do that, you'll need three things. First, you'll need to know what you believe. Second, you'll need to know that trust is a real possibility. Third, you'll need to know what you feel like when you're with someone whom you deeply trust. You'll need the experience of trusting, which is the missing experience.

We work to create an opportunity for you to have that missing experience.

You won't know that you don't trust anyone until something happens in consciousness to illuminate that fact. If you haven't discovered it already, it becomes clear when you work with that issue. You suddenly realize you've never felt safe anywhere. Now the model is in consciousness. You're experiencing an underlying fear you've had all your life or since that terrible accident or whatever. The therapist helps you work with that fear, go through it, survive it, and finish it. With that done, you now have the possibility of feeling safe. The therapist helps to create that possibility.

A major part of the theraputic method is how you create the missing experience. Someone who has never felt safe in his whole life is going to have a very powerful experience when he finally does feel safe. It is important is to spend enough time with this experience to stabilize it and create access routes to it. Taking time with this feels quite natural to the client. We wait patiently for each new insight and each new aspect of the experience. Hakomi therapists don't lead here. We follow.

As the process unfolds, we support each development. But we never use force against "resistance." Pushing against resistance just creates more resistance. Force automatically evokes counterforce. So, we back off when we see that the client doesn't want to go that fast or in that direction. We try to understand why and help the client to understand. There's no rush and no need to push. But neither are we passive.

Once we get to the missing experience, we want to give the client time to fully absorb it, ground in it, memorize it, savor it, learn about it, and try it on again and again to see if she can integrate it. She may have a whole series of spontaneous insights. The therapist may just watch the client have insights. The client may speak about these insights or she may not. Something changes when this missing experience is savored and stabilized. The old model is wrong now, or at least incomplete. It must be revised. The new model has enormous implications on all levels, from physiology to relationships. It takes a long time to integrate the new model. In a typical session, it might take thirty minutes to arrive at the missing experience and another twenty to thirty minutes to savor it, but it might take years to fully integrate it. The person has been using the old model his whole life. A lot of things will have to be changed.

In order for the new model to become truly stable, the person has to use it in all kinds of applicable situations. Changes like this are integrated one decision at a time. I have an example. I once did a therapy workshop for a group of Rolfers. One woman, in her process, touched terror. It was set off by the statement, "You're perfectly welcome here." Her terror and fear were based on her model that she was not welcome anywhere. In fact, at the deepest level, she felt that her life was in danger. People didn't want her to be alive. These were the messages she had taken in as a child. She screamed with the terror, while several of us held her very tightly (taking over the physical contractions that helped manage her experience of terror)—with her permission, of course. She reported that screaming felt good; it was a relief to let it out. After a while, the terror subsided and her body relaxed. She could finally take in that she was welcome. The people there were all her friends. One after another, possibly for twenty minutes or so, each one said very quietly, "You're perfectly welcome here." She kept taking it in. She relaxed in a very deep way. Finally, she became ecstatic. She had had a wonderful, thirty-minute experience of feeling welcome, held, cuddled, and loved.

I saw her two weeks later. She told me that, a few days after the session, she was walking down a street on her way to a friend's house and she started to feel uncomfortable, thinking, "I didn't call them. They don't know I'm coming over. They're not going to be happy about me just showing up." In the middle of that internal dialogue, she suddenly heard a voice saying, "You're perfectly welcome here." She lit up. In an easy, light-hearted way, she continued on to her friend's house.

Every time she does something like that, every time a choice like that comes into consciousness, every time she chooses an option from the new model rather than the old one, and every time that choice is confirmed, she changes. She grows step by conscious step into this new model. Eventually, the new model becomes habit and sinks into the unconscious. This is how people change. They have a new model, they use it, and if it works, it becomes habit.

That is how Hakomi works: the practice of loving presence helps the client feel safe and understood. That makes mindfulness possible. The therapist then finds ways (little experiments) to evoke experiences in mindfulness. The meaning of the bodily experiences evoked are understood as direct expressions of core beliefs—models of self and the world that organize all experience. When these core beliefs are made conscious and understood, change becomes possible. Core beliefs that are limiting, destructive, unbalanced, or painful can be challenged. New beliefs can be tried and new experiences evoked. I call these missing experiences. Safety, peace, freedom, and aliveness are a few.

Another important thing about Hakomi: the beginnings of a basic spiritual practice are built right into it. If you're a client in Hakomi long enough, you get a lot of practice using mindfulness. You get a lot of experience doing self-study from a compassionate, mindful place. That's spiritual practice. That's a way of changing in a very basic way. As you begin to distance yourself from your automatic behaviors and egocentric models about who you are, as you calm down and relax, you begin to find another part of yourself, a different level. As you distance yourself from egocentric habits, you become able to make spiritual choices about things like ownership and competition. You become more at home in yourself and in the world, more friendly, less stressed out; all just from practicing mindfulness and studying yourself. And as missing experiences become part of you, there's not so much inner noise from conflicted subselves.

All therapy helps people move on in their lives, helps them towards fuller maturity and capacity. Hakomi is a particularly good platform for moving people towards and along their spiritual path. One Hakomi trainer, Halko Weiss, says that when the client begins talking about religion, it's a sign that therapy is over.

The primatologist John Napier said, "When did man emerge from the primates? The question is really irrelevant. He was there from the beginning." That is, the potential for humankind was there in the primates all along. Its manifestation was just another small step. One could ask, when does Hakomi become spiritual practice? The answer is, it was there all along. It's there in the use of mindfulness and the principle of nonviolence. It's there in the focus on experience and self-study. It's there for the client and it's there for the therapist. Therapy as spiritual practice—it was there in Hakomi from the beginning.

Chapter Four
_____

DREAMS AND THE DREAMING BODY

Amy and Arny Mindell

Editor's Note: Amy and Arny Mindell bring a rich perspective to somatic psychology from their background in Jungian psychology, dance, and dreams. Their work applies not only to individuals and small groups, but to whole communities and peoples in deep conflict. It may be fair to say that these two are the high ambassadors of intuitive process, bringing forth the dreamlike nonlinear associations in the body that so often hold our healing. A folk wisdom in the field states that we cannot solve a problem in the state of consciousness in which it developed, thus leading the Mindells into the realm of altered states of consciousness. Amy and Arny have explored and articulated even extreme states of consciousness such as occur in comatose patients; their discoveries have made a great contribution to the field.

It has been a pleasure and an inspiration to see the Hendricks, the Mindells, and the Pessos work so seamlessly as husband/wife teams. They model what successful and loving relationships can do when the energy they create is turned towards service in the world. The Mindells are also globetrotters, jetting between the United States and Switzerland in their trainings. This chapter introduces their work and reveals the sensitivities and intricate dances of a session.

I In the early 1970s while Arny worked in Zurich as a training analyst at the Jung Institute, he began a development of Jungian Psychology called "Dreambodywork." This work was based upon the discovery that dreams mirror body feelings and experiences of body symptoms. Since then his work has expanded into what is now called "process work" in the United States or

61

"process-oriented psychology" in Switzerland and other parts of the world.[1] Our work today is based upon the dreaming body and can be applied to dreamwork, bodywork, and also to work with people in comatose or near-death states as well as in psychiatric and large group conflict situations. In this chapter, we discuss the dreaming basis of process work.

DEFINING DREAMS

There are at least two kinds of therapists. One kind develops a great deal of expertise in understanding and has explanations for everything. Another kind of therapist seems more shamanistic, follows the mysterious, and relies more upon imagination. All of us have both capacities within us: one which understands and one which follows the process of dreaming.

Dreams and the dreaming process play a central role in process work. If we use the terms of Taoism, dreams might be called "the Tao which can be said," while the dreaming process is "the Tao which cannot be said." The *Tao Te Ching* says in its first lesson that the Tao which can be said is not the eternal Tao. Jung also differentiated the archetypal images of dreams from the archetypes which cannot be seen.

We can choose to work with what is unknown and unsaid instead of what is being discussed or reported on. Dreams can be said, described, explained, enunciated, and reported. The mysterious, ongoing, energetic evolution which appears to us in the form of dreams is like the wave function in quantum physics or the Great Spirit as understood by Native Americans. The wave function gives rise through observation to reality, and the Great Spirit lies behind the motions of everything known.

That part of process which can be stated appears to us not only in terms of visual dreams, but also in psychosomatic ailments, relationship problems, and world issues. Dreaming is the dynamic experience which expresses itself through body feelings, movement, visualizations, relationships, and unpredictable events in the world.

Very few people focus upon body feelings or movement, unless they are ill or have a movement injury. So it is not without surprise, that what we call dreaming is often mainly connected with visual images, that is, with dream figures. Thus, myths, stories, and images are central to the study of dreaming.

However, dreaming also can easily express itself through our movements. Body feelings, movements, smell, taste, the subjective sense of relationship, and the world around us are all aspects of dreaming.

Wave Functions and Reality, Dreaming and Dream

In a way, we find the same differentiation between dreams and the dreaming process in physics. Physical reality consists mainly of spaces and times which can be measured and agreed upon by all. But in quantum physics, the wave function, much like the idea of dreaming, cannot be seen in consensual reality. It is based upon what the mathematician calls "imaginary numbers." When the wave function or what we suspect must be an "elementary particle" is observed, probabilities of measurements can be predicted. Yet no one sees the particle itself; some physicists even say it is fruitless to imagine it. Physicists get around this problem by saying if you can't measure it, you can't discuss it.

But for psychologists, the situation is different. We may not be able to discuss the Tao which cannot be said, yet we feel best if we learn to follow it. We can only describe the body in terms of consensual reality; its imaginary or wave function aspect can only be experienced and followed. Following requires "metaskills," as Amy calls them, attitudes which believe in the flow of the unconscious.

In process work, following the unconscious is a basic metaskill. Emphasis is placed upon noticing the dreaming process, that is, the Tao which cannot be said, and learning how to help unfold it. We also study the interpretation of events which can be stated in terms of dreams and body problems.

Following the Tao which cannot be said requires in part the belief that the events to come are important, even though at given moments we cannot understand them. This is the sort of mystery school orientation we often find among shamans.

An Example

We remember a client who came to see Arny for the first time. She looked like she was in a lot of pain and seemed very dissociated. She complained about feeling exhausted and having a stiff neck. She said defensively that she had heard from both bodyworkers and psychotherapists that she was too rigid and wondered what I (Arny) thought. Instead of first asking about her rigidity or her dreams, which would be a Tao which can be stated, I suggested focusing on something she had not yet said. She decided to focus upon her body experiences.

She said did not know how to do this, and I recommended that she use her "second attention," which is what Carlos Castaneda's Don Juan called attention to irrational or dreaming processes. I recommended that she just focus on her body as if it were unknown yet important. "Focus on however it feels and let that feeling unfold as if *you* were dreaming," I said.

She said that her body "feels rough, stiff," and she didn't want to feel it any longer.

I asked her if she was at an edge. That is, are the processes which are coming up too new, too unknown, too scary, or too foreign? I asked, "Is this an edge we should go over by focusing on your body, or should we drop that focus and talk about your dreams?"

I suggested that she "just give the experience a lot of time."

She responded vehemently, "It has had enough time." Then she smiled and said the rigidity felt strong.

I noticed she sat up straight when she said her stiff neck felt strong. "Would you like to go into that movement of sitting up?" I asked, thinking that perhaps her dreaming process was switching from body feeling to movement.

She sat straight up in her chair and decided to explore sitting up "straight and strong," as she said. Sitting up led her to standing up and taking a powerful stance on the floor. I saw her right foot move a bit forward and asked if her foot wanted to get more involved in the process. At this point she answered without speaking by stamping on the floor with both feet.

Suddenly she spoke so loudly she shocked me. She declared, "I am going to take a stand."

"About what?" I ask.

She looked embarrassed and said "About inner criticism." For the first time she smiled and we both cheered. Before I had a chance to ask her what her inner critic was telling her, she sat down and said, "This reminds me of a dream."

In her dream she was being chased by another woman with a gun. In the dream my client took the gun and turned it around and aimed it at her attacker. Then she awoke. We both cheered again and she told me that she understood her dream. In reality she almost never takes a stand relative to her inner critic or to the negative comments of others. She always feels wrong. Now she felt stronger and was ready to take a stand and not just listen to all that inner trouble.

The Dreambody

Let's look at this fifteen-minute process more closely. The Tao that could be said was a stiff neck and a dream about taking a gun away from an attacker. The dreaming process began when she focused upon the sensations in her neck and—using her second attention—changed channels and followed her movement. She then sat up straight, took a stand, and stomped her feet. Then she remembered a dream, something that happens frequently when people work with the dreaming process. Finally, she interpreted the dream herself. She wanted to take a stand against inner criticism. Better yet, she felt better physically.

The Connection between Process Work and Jungian Psychology

We call the connection between her symptom of a stiff neck and her dream of shooting back the dreambody. The dreaming process connects the experience of body symptoms with dreams. By getting into the dreaming process, dreams often interpret themselves. Instead of insisting that the dreamer have a "strong ego," in the sense of holding her own against unconscious contents, we recommend developing the second attention, the awareness of irrational events. This second attention to irrational processes which are distant from the dreamer's identity is like the awareness involved in lucid dreaming, except that now "dreaming' is understood as an activity happening during waking life.

The "dreamer" in this example was lucid during her dreaming process as it unfolded in various sensory channels, including visions, feeling, and movement experiences. It was also crucial for the dreamer to notice when she got to an "edge," that is, the moment where the process seemed to become blocked.

The kind of awareness that is developed in "dreaming" is similar to that found among shamans and mystics who worship, adore, explore, investigate, and unravel messages from the invisible world.

Naturally, someone's process also may involve interpretation or direct intervention from the therapist. Those clients who ask for medication or healing or who want a dream interpreted, should get what they want if we can give it. Asking a therapist to intervene with massage, medication, or an interpretation has advantages over working with the dreaming process. One of which is that it is not necessary to leave consensual reality. But the disadvantage of staying in consensual reality and receiving interpretations or interventions is that the dreamer never gets to know her whole self, since she experiences dreaming only when she is unconscious or asleep.

Each of us has our own individual process, and a process-oriented analyst takes Jung's recommendation very seriously: therapy should follow the client.

OTHER CHANNELS

The dreaming body appears in all sensory channels. To work with the dreaming process, we need to know the landscape not only of the visual channel, but also of body feelings, movements, and relationships. In other words, though dreams happen mainly at night, the dreaming process is happening all the time as it appears in our bodies, movements, relationships, and the environment. To understand this better, let us describe how this client evolved in her next session.

In her next session the client came in with one of her teenage children who had been very rebellious. This client had a very "New Age" attitude towards life, in that she spurned "negative energy" and hoped to be good-hearted and nice to everybody, including her daughter. Her fifteen-year-old daughter, however, was wild and had been enjoying late night escapades, drugs, and other inappropriate activities.

As the two sat together, I (Arny) noticed my client biting her lip and asked her and the daughter if they would mind waiting for a moment while the mother had a moment to focus on her lip. I said to the mother, "One part of you is smiling and being open to your daughter but there's another part of you, 'a double signal' which may be doing something different. Would you like to focus on that signal, namely, biting your lip?"

My client clenched her teeth, made a stern face, and said that she would like to yell at her daughter but had never done so before. To my surprise, the daughter laughed at this point and called her mother a weakling. The mother lashed back, telling the daughter she now had to obey. She had to be home by midnight and follow the rules and regulations of the house.

The daughter burst out laughing and then started to cry. She wept for a long time and seemed unable to speak. I asked the daughter what she would say if she were able to, thinking she might be at an edge.

She sniffled a few times and then told her mother, "I never thought you loved me. I thought you didn't care about me because you never took a stand about anything." The two embraced and the daughter went on, "When you are tough, I am relieved but don't know why."

The dreaming process which unfolded from the mother's stiff neck and the dream of taking the gun away from the attacker now took on a new form, creating signals; that is, double signals such as her clenched teeth which unfolded into a new kind of relationship with her daughter.

It is as if the Tao which cannot be said expresses itself through our dreaming body not only in terms of dreams and chronic symptoms, but also through double signals which occur in response to relationship situations.

We might understand the connection between the daughter and the mother not only as a relationship but as "dreaming together." Here "dreaming" is used in the sense of opening up to the unknown with another person, to the Tao which cannot be said.

What Is the Body?

So what is the body? There is a body that can be said, the body of consensual reality; it has aches, pains, a gall bladder, a neck, and so forth. Then there is the dreaming body, the body of wave functions and the experience of dreaming which becomes "real" when it is observed and discussed. However, its essence is indescribable; it is an individual experience moving outside the time and space of the real body.

Amy and Arny Mindell

The World

The idea of dreaming together can also be used in working with social and group problems. Here too, there are processes that can be said, such as business problems or social issues and there are also processes that are difficult or impossible to speak about. Again, if can we use the attitude of following the dreaming process to see what nature wants to create, new connections and consciousness often occur.

Take the example of a business that was suffering from financial troubles in part because the vice president had stolen money. Ten of the management people came together with us, and we discussed the thief whom they had fired from his job. As people spoke, it became apparent that everyone thought that the "thief" was not them. The thief was distant from the identity of the group: They were not thieves.

Since they continued to focus on the thief, we invited them to explore their ideas and projections about him, and let their dreaming go further. Most of the people said that was ridiculous because they were not thieves. One of the more courageous business people said that he had an edge to being a thief but would like to try and explore or play it first.

Then he began speaking from the viewpoint of the thief. He said, dreaming into the thief and playing the part with obvious courage but also fear, "I want to steal. I am a thief because, because—nothing is given to me. I feel I deserve more than I get."

Suddenly he touched the dreaming process and it became real for him. He wept as he spoke about his needs. Now others wanted to dream into the "despicable" thief. Stepping into the role, they said, "Nobody feels appreciated around here. Nobody gets what they want. We're all giving and giving and nobody gets enough. So we take what we need secretly."

Everyone began to speak at the same time, becoming animated as they said how they needed to be appreciated. They all began appreciating one another and formed a big, hugging circle.

What happened here? We would say this group had an edge to the thief, which was their dreaming process. They had an edge to expressing their needs and loving one another. The dreaming was trying to manifest and unfold itself through the creation of the thief and through their financial problems.

By focusing their group attention upon the unknown, they went beyond the Tao that could be said—namely, the experiences of the thief—and entered into the dreaming process. They began "dreaming together."

Dreaming together is a basic spiritual activity of all aboriginal communities. Dreaming together is not the community that can be said; nor is it just the community's goals, hopes, worldly successes, and failures. Dreaming together is the spirit that creates community; it is the unknown, the unconscious, something that is awesome, something that we are afraid of and often try to repress. With the proper focus and attention, dreaming enriches everyone's experience.

We have had many awesome experiences not only working with businesses, but also in working with native peoples, with groups suffering from ethnic tensions, with political issues, in town meetings, and with other groups and situations. Though not every process leads immediately to happy endings as with the business we described here, dreaming always leads to increased awareness. For some specific examples of this work, see Arny's book *Sitting In the Fire,* available through Lao Tse Press.

What Is A Corporate Body?

When we ask ourselves what is a group or corporate body, we run into the same problem as we do with the individual body. The corporate body has a consensual reality aspect which includes its environment: the walls, the buildings, the people, and all their aspects. But the group is also a dreaming process. Through gaining access to this part of the group, the organization gets to know itself.

There are many more details, skills, metaskills, and inner development needed to work with individuals, relationships, and large groups that we are not able to mention here. Whereas " therapist" or "analyst" is a sufficient term to describe the practitioner needed in individual work, something more like "the elder," perhaps an elder with a diverse cultural background, is needed for large group work.

Besides the skills and metaskills of eldership, one needs courage to follow the dreaming unknown. An uncanny amount of inner development is needed to withstand the stresses and strains of participating in the dreaming process when large group conflicts are involved. It requires awareness of channels, processes, and edges.

We see psychology standing at a growing edge, bringing its wisdom about the collective unconscious, dreams, and shamanism together with work on social issues and environmental problems. It seems certain to us that the next steps in bodywork and psychology will simultaneously be the next steps in physics, conflict work, and politics.

---

1. A good overview of this work is given in an interview with June Singer in the *San Francisco Jung Institute Library Journal*, volume 13, number 4, 1995. See also *Riding the Horse Backwards: Process Work in Theory and Practice*, by Arnold and Amy Mindell (New York: Viking Penguin, 1992).

Chapter Five

_____

SELF, BOUNDARIES, AND CONTAINMENT: INTEGRATIVE BODY PSYCHOTHERAPY

Marjorie Rand, Ph.D. with Gerry Fewster, Ph.D.

Editor's Note: Marjorie Rand is one of the founders and developers of Integrative Body Psychotherapy, or IBP, along with Jack Rosenberg. Marjorie and Jack's book, Body, Self, and Soul: Sustaining Integration *came out in 1985 and continues to be a primer for the field, especially in the areas of developmental process and working with physical and emotional boundaries. Their work specializes in an experiential understanding of how we can foster intimacy, excitement, and satisfaction through our ability to keep good boundaries while we contain and take care of our internal energies.*

A lifelong passionate learner, Dr. Rand has studied dance therapy, Gestalt, therapy, object relations theory, pre- and perinatal psychology and many other systems in order to formulate her extremely practical and useful work. She works with children, adults, and couples, often applying her work to developing more healthy relationships.

Marjorie also is one of our female powerhouses, doing trainings all over the world while finding the time to write, dance, and sing backup in a rock-and-roll band. A dear friend and conference companion, I can always count on some high adventure and great conversation when we get together. Though it's hard to catch her sitting down, she has the capacity to understand in a flash and empathize with a matter-of-fact clarity that leaves me honored to call her my friend and colleague.

Gerry Fewster is administrator of the Pacific North West Institute of Integrative Body Psychotherapy on Vancouver Island. He is a faculty member in the Department of Human Services at Malaspina University College in British Columbia, Adjunct Professor of Educational Psychology at the University of

71

MARJORIE RAND WITH GERRY FEWSTER

Calgary, Alberta, Canada, and editor of the Journal of Child and Youth Care. *Dr. Fewster has published three books and countless articles on children and mental health issues.*

INTRODUCING IBP

*W*ithin the broad humanistic tradition of mind-body approaches, Integrative Body Psychotherapy (IBP)[1] offers a uniquely developmental perspective. In this context, the term "developmental" refers to the focus on relatedness to Core Self and other as the primary goal of therapy, as well as the central quest in the human journey. Since the search for connectedness is a lifelong pursuit, this perspective is clearly different from the more traditional male trajectory in which bonding and separation are seen as developmental goals or stages to grow out of.

From an IBP perspective, relating to Self and relating to others are actually two aspects of the same developmental process. Hence, IBP therapists value the natural human state of interconnectedness equally with the need for people to have their own personal boundaries, a separate sense of Self, and the experience of being the center of their own initiatives. Referred to as "Relational Autonomy," practitioners work with their clients in moving toward the attainment of this mutual state of being from a foundation of body-awareness. When aliveness in the body is reawakened, the person experiences an intensified sense of self-authenticity that can be expressed through their relationships with others, leading toward higher levels of personal fulfillment and intimacy.

A particularly effective way of practicing IBP is to consider awareness as the most basic tool of change. Using the breath as the primary catalytic agent, this approach works from body to mind, honoring the client's *own experience* in each moment of the therapy session. The process involves tracking (following) the client's awareness of connection, or lack of connection, to his or her own energetic flow of aliveness in the body. While the work has no stated goal beyond greater awareness, the general intention is to increase the client's ability to stay connected to increased flows of energy and well-being in the body. In this process, the therapist simply trusts that awareness of "what is" creates opportunities for greater choice.[2] Meanwhile, the client is learning to know and trust his or her own experience.

SELF, BOUNDARIES AND CONTAINMENT

IBP BASIC ASSUMPTIONS

Working With the Whole Person

Since IBP begins with the assumption that body, mind, and spirit are experientially inseparable aspects of being, it follows that the therapeutic process must involve all of these dimensions in a simultaneous and integrated fashion. For example, we know that nutrition and exercise influence emotional well-being as well as a person's physical condition. Hence, emotional and physical experiences are both contained within the body and accessed through the senses. The cognitive processes, usually associated with the mind, are those that attempt to organize the experience of the senses, creating complex personal patterns of conscious activity and meaning. At the center of it all, lies the essence of Self, the human spirit.

Energy Containment and Self-Expansion

IBP focuses upon the energetic, somatic, and emotional experiences that form the raw material from which the mind creates its images, thoughts, and beliefs. In this way, it clearly sets itself apart from the more traditional "talk" therapies that emphasize cognitive or intellectual insight. On the other hand, it also stands apart from approaches that promote energetic discharge and emotional catharsis as their therapeutic goals. Within the IBP framework, all of these things—from the nerve-tingling aliveness of the body to the startling creativity of the mind—can be explored and experienced to the fullest while remaining contained and grounded within an expanding individual sense of Self. Along with this sense of contained expansion comes a broader range of possibilities from which the person has the freedom to make choices. In this way, the therapeutic process becomes a client-centered, step-by-step process of integration through which the body, the emotions, and the intellect become open and connected.

Body and Breath

The IBP therapist works from an understanding that the most direct access to the emotions is through the body and the most direct pathway to the body is through the breath. Encouraged to breathe and to experiment with various breathing techniques, clients are able to access and intensify the experience of the muscular and emotional patterns that, linked to particular thoughts and beliefs, have become their characteristic styles of relating to themselves and the world.

Transforming Patterns

Within the therapeutic relationship, clients are invited to explore those particular patterns, usually formed very early in life, that continue to inhibit the full experience and expression of Self. Since such patterns are often acquired at the preverbal stage of development, they cannot be accessed through cognitive or intellectual insight. From an IBP perspective, these patterns are created as a means of defending the emerging Self from potentially injurious experiences but remain held in the body even though the original perceived dangers have long since passed. Being locked in the body, they can be accessed only through the body. When, through therapy, such defensive patterns are interrupted and released, it is common for clients to "relive" the original experience. This, then, creates an opportunity for such experiences to be reexamined and reintegrated within a process of Self-directed change or transformation.

The Primary Scenario

IBP therapists regard presenting problems as symptomatic of a circular process that constantly plunges back into the crucible of early childhood experience—referred to as the "Primary Scenario." Particular attention is given to the client's relationships with parents, the relationship between the parents, and the relational "themes" that each family member brings into the family constellation. The influences of the Primary Scenario are embedded in an intergenerational history of primary relationships established long before birth and experienced by the infant well before intellectual and verbal development occurs. Consequently, the experiences and influences of this relational framework become anchored in the body, detached from the conscious reflective processes of mind. Without insight or awareness, the person is compelled to repeat anachronistic responses or patterns. While various therapeutic methods might help to relieve some of the symptoms of the presenting problem, the underlying issues can never be resolved within the current situation. For the pattern itself to be addressed, the person must return to the context of the Primary Scenario and bring it into the reality of the present. And this, by definition, is bound to be a somatic or body-centered experience.

Such therapeutic work does not mean that the experience of the Primary Scenario can in some way be eliminated or extinguished. It simply means that, through awareness, obsolete responses can be abandoned and alternatives created. In the therapeutic process, this is the examination of "what is" from which clients may create their own options and make appropriate choices.

The Energetic Self

It is important to differentiate the IBP definition of the Self from the more popular notion of "self-concept" as defined by cognitive and behavioral therapists. In IBP, the Self is not an "idea" or a pattern of known and predictable behaviors. At its core, it is energetic—experienced as a sense of well-being, identity, and continuity that is *felt in the body*. The degree to which this Self finds its authentic expression through the person's emotional, cognitive, and relational life is profoundly influenced by early childhood experience when the Self is at its most fragile and vulnerable. When the emerging Self is nurtured and supported in its authentic expression, its energetic core radiates outward, not only within the individual but also beyond the skin, forming a dynamic, though boundaried, energy field that defines the individual's place in the world. As an integral part of the cosmos, it is in constant motion, responding to its inner nature and to the ever-shifting external environment.

Energy Blocks and Disease

When the emerging Self becomes injured and defenses are established, the flow of Self-energy becomes blocked—disconnected from bodily, emotional, and cognitive awareness. This breakdown in the integrative processes of body and mind translates into specific patterns of disease that might be experienced physically, mentally, or emotionally. In IBP, these patterns are brought directly into the here and now of the therapy session. The therapeutic relationship creates a potentially powerful context in which the energy that radiates from the Core Self can be influenced. The task is one of realigning and reintegrating the intellectual and emotional energy with the natural flow of energy as it is released and contained within the body. In this way the sense of Self-expansion occurs in a complete and integrated manner—a renewed relationship with Self.

The Healing Relationship

Within the framework of IBP, all injuries to the Self occur within relationships and can be healed only within a relational context. Hence, the "here-and-now" connection between the practitioner and the client becomes the current reality for such work. Energetically speaking, the therapeutic context might be seen as a meeting of two energy fields that define the Self-boundaries of the therapist and the client. In creating a climate of sensitivity, security, and trust, the therapist's own energetic sense of Self must be present, secure, available, and contained. The therapist must be able to remain at the "contact boundary," constantly supporting the client in working through a range of somatic, cognitive, and emotional releases. Any withdrawal, uncertainty, or discomfort communicated to the client in this process could easily repeat the conditions of the original injury and recreate the defensive reaction.

The Issue of Sexuality

Since IBP therapists work directly with the aliveness of the body, the experience and expression of sexuality is an essential part of the therapeutic process. Repressed sexual energy, along with all of its emotional, intellectual, and moral associations, is part of our cultural heritage and is well rooted in most of our intergenerational histories, or Primary Scenarios. In working with bodily awareness, therefore, the pelvic area becomes a critical point of focus, even if the client chooses not to work on the more cognitive or verbal aspects of sexual experience. Therapists who are not at ease with their own sexual energy can easily transmit their discomfort around this issue. The reemerging Self of the client could then be tragically reinjured without any gesture being apparent or any word being uttered. The therapeutic task is for the client to open the flow of his or her sexual energy and integrate its fullness into an expanding sense of Self. This means that the therapist must be fully energetically present within his or her own boundary, allowing and supporting the process.

Staying Contained in the Moment

At the most fundamental level, IBP works with the body and in the here and now. From this perspective, enlightenment is a neurophysiological event—energetic, immediate, and directly accessible through the senses. The key to learning and healing is to let the event occur while containing and integrating the experience. Energetic discharge or emotional catharsis alone is not helpful or curative. Since little of the experience is actually retained, any developmental effect cannot be sustained or integrated. Release with containment, on the other hand, allows the body to retain this energy in the system, to expand, to make choices.

BOUNDARIES

Within the context of the therapeutic relationship, the goal of IBP is to establish and sustain an awareness of, and connection to, the flow of energy known as the "Self"—defined as a sense of well-being, identity, and continuity experienced *in the body*. IBP therapy contracts and expands the Self by establishing and working with its energetic parameters or boundaries.

When the Self energy flows freely, and with awareness, these parameters are sensitive and flexible, constantly shifting in response to the needs of the authentic Self and the changing conditions of the external world. In this sense, boundaries are both intrapsychic and interpersonal, making it possible to have autonomy as well as relatedness, and, above all, choice. Grounded in both body and consciousness, boundaries allow the Self to become fully present and available to engage with others and the world in a sensitive and responsible manner.

By freely expanding and contracting their own energy field, people with effective boundaries can remain present, yet determine the degree to which the Self will actually participate in any current situation. Around such people, it is possible for others to sense this state of presence and containment within the energy field, though it is most clearly seen in the eyes. When the eyes are open and clear, energy exchange can occur with the environment and with others. But it is also apparent through behavior. People with a clear sense of their own boundaries are able to claim their own physical space, identify and embrace their own feelings, be spontaneous, say their real "yes'es" and "no's," process information effortlessly, and make decisions appropriate to their own needs while remaining sensitive and responsive to the needs of others.

People who fail to develop effective boundaries cannot live in their bodies in the here-and-now. Without boundaries, there is no sense of Self. And, if there is no Self, there can be no relationship. This is paradoxical and can be confusing, since it is often believed that a close or intimate relationship is a merger involving the loss of one Self to the other. In reality, it is only by having boundaries that one can establish a relationship with another, a relationship in which both people can be uniquely themselves and be intimately related to each other *without loss of Self.* Oneness, merger, and symbiosis do not constitute a relationship that involves two people. Unboundaried associations often are considered to be close or intimate unions when, in fact, there is only one Self present, the other having given itself up through fear of abandonment.

This pattern of merging, as a reaction to abandonment anxiety, usually begins in early life when the availability of the parent-figure is a matter of survival for the infant. Later, in the adult, it manifests in clinging behaviors and a constant need to be close to significant others. Since such people continue to experience feelings of abandonment, however, the injuries continue to occur and the need for Self-protection continues to increase. On the other side of the coin, some infants experience a profound sense of invasion as they attempt to meet their early bonding needs and this anxiety can be carried into adult life. When defenses are substituted for boundaries because of invasion anxiety, a person deals with issues of closeness and intimacy by creating a wall of distance and by cutting off feelings of longing for closeness.

Since most infant/parent relationships are fraught with either abandonment or inundation injuries, these boundary disturbances are found to some degree in everyone. Very often both can exist at the same time. For example, a parent who is not energetically present and in contact with an infant may incorrectly assess the infant's distress signal and feed the child even if the child is not hungry. This creates a classic double bind. The infant's defensive solution to the injury of simultaneous abandonment and inundation, psychological or physical, is to split off consciousness from the body—often referred to as the "mind-body split."

In general, then, early childhood injuries of abandonment and invasion, contained within the Primary Scenario, prevent the development of healthy boundaries. In their place, infants construct defenses, designed to distance them from external threats and from the pain of their own feelings. As the defensive layers rigidify through repetitions of the initial injury, they become chronic, structural, and fixed in nature. Cut off from the authentic experience of his or her own body and from the responses of the external world, the child begins to identify with these defenses as the Self. Referred to as the "false Self"[3] the person continues to present this defensive pattern to the world while the true energetic Self recedes from awareness, perhaps for the remainder of that person's life. Sensitivity, responsivity, and adaptability are replaced by a set of fixed repetitive attitudes and behaviors. Where boundaries are always flexible and centered in present experience, these defensive patterns are rigid and rooted in the past. Cut off from authentic feelings and resistant to external feedback, the defensive or false Self is often presented as the very opposite: "This is who I am, what I think, and what I do, and nothing you say or do is ever going to change that."

Establishing boundaries that are appropriate for each individual, while taking into account defensive processes and injuries to the developing Self, makes it possible for the person to be available for the therapeutic relationship and for healing to take place. Within this relationship, the Self is seen as an experience that is more or less fragmented (split off and unbounded) or cohesive (contained) at any given moment. Each person is more or less connected to this energetic experience, depending upon the situation, particular defensive style (past history of relationships), degree of presence, groundedness in the body, and, first and foremost, body awareness. Awareness, in and of itself, is curative, and provides choices.

In IBP therapy, continued attention to ever-changing boundary issues in both the therapist and the client during the therapeutic process promotes both awareness and choice. The exploration and modeling of healthy

MARJORIE RAND WITH GERRY FEWSTER

boundary styles is an integral part of the therapist/client relationship and, in this, the significance of transference and counter-transference issues cannot be overestimated. Simply stated, this means that the practitioner must be aware of the client's tendency to "use" the therapist as an object figure (a parent, perhaps) in resolving personal and interpersonal issues. On the other hand, the practitioner must be sufficiently aware of his or her own needs to allow this, without becoming entrenched in the fantasy.

THE DEVELOPMENT OF SELF

From an IBP perspective, the Self is both the product and the cocreator of relationships. Its energetic core, or essence, resides in the body and can be experienced directly only through body awareness. From such awareness ("inside" as opposed to "insight") it becomes possible to truly "know" the Self and establish deep connection with others. In its fullest form, this Self is more than physical, more than emotional, and more than cognitive. It is the sum total of all our aspects, and more. It exists at the core of our experience.

When we are conceived, the energy of the Self becomes embodied and, even before we are born, traumas and injuries to the development of Self can occur. Evidence of this is increasingly well-documented through research in the field of pre- and perinatal psychology.[4] For many years we have understood how the physiological state of the mother is communicated to the developing fetus through chemical and hormonal changes transmitted through the placenta and umbilical cord. We also know that these physiological factors are profoundly influenced by shifts in the mother's psychological and emotional condition. More recently, researchers have been using the term "cellular consciousness"[5] to describe a process through which the fetus actively seeks and stores a wide range of information significant for the development of Self. Studies demonstrating the ability of newborns to recognize messages received *in utero* have become commonplace.

The evidence now suggests that the unborn child is in a state of constant communication, receiving messages from many different sources at many different levels. The manner in which this information is processed and stored has led researchers to conclude that an organized sense of Self actually begins its development *in utero*.[6] Hence, whatever is happening within and around the mother might be communicated to the unborn child, and herein lies the potential for early injury or trauma.

Physical health problems such as poor nutrition, drugs, or illnesses present obvious dangers. By the same token, however, abortion attempts, ambivalence about the pregnancy, death or divorce in the family, or difficulties in the parental relationship also could be injurious.

Developmentally speaking, these injuries or traumas to the emerging sense of Self can occur as early as conception through the first three years of life. In response to such assaults, a layer of defense is built over the injury and, over time, these defenses are transformed into styles of relating designed to protect the developing Self from further injury. In the helpless stages of intrauterine development and infancy, defensive reactions are truly survival-oriented. The problem is that these defensive styles are developed so early (even before birth) that the true essential Self gets deeply buried and is cut off from awareness.

The critical point to remember is that this happens so early that it is a nonverbal, preintellectual event and, as such, it can be recovered *in no other way* than through the body. When Reich stated that "Remembrances must be accompanied by appropriate affect," he was making essentially the same point—that early traumatic experiences are held in the "muscular armoring" of the body and cannot be reached by talking alone.[7]

CONTAINMENT

With its emphasis on "containment," IBP takes a step beyond Reich and most cathartic body therapies. The goal is not to simply release the repressed trauma held in the body but to connect to the energetic core of Self. Boundaries are both the goal and the vehicle for achieving this. Staying with a feeling, sensation, or emotion, simply watching its natural flow without attempting to increase or decrease it, enhances awareness and clarity. In this process, the holding patterns are released, opening the body to expand and contain more aliveness, rather than to discharge feelings and lose energy from the system.

The IBP energetic model of containment is much like tantric yoga in which sexual energy is heightened through breathing and exchanged through genital and eye contact. The goal in tantric yoga is to raise the level of energy to spiritual consciousness, not to discharge it through orgasm (ejacu-lation). In IBP, the holding patterns in the body are opened, not to release energy but to expand the container (body) so the system can tolerate more energy (life force, Self). Releases of holding patterns in the body and breath-ing techniques serve to spread the energy and circulate it throughout the system rather than discharging it through emotional catharsis. The more aliveness a person can contain in the body, the more a person can deepen and support the experience of Self.

CONTAINMENT VERSUS CATHARSIS

If the flexibility of boundaries is substituted for the rigidity of de-fenses, it becomes possible for the injured Self to be both protected and revealed. In IBP this is done without confronting, attacking, removing, or otherwise taking away defenses from the client. Boundaries are introduced in the very first session and over time (often in that first session), they take the place of defenses. Beginning with the physical distance from the thera-pist, the client is invited to become aware of his or her boundaries as a felt sense in the body and to use this awareness in making choices. Over time, the body and energy field expand, allowing the therapist to touch quickly the true essence of a person in a noninvasive, safe, and supportive way.

When this experience is repeated over time within the context of a therapeutic relationship, deep early injuries are no longer feared. Rather, they are faced and relived with a connection to internal Self-support. Defenses then open by choice, having been replaced by boundaries which protect the Self and care for it appropriately in the present circumstances.

Conversely, the cathartic model of body therapy would see the re-lease of the underlying repressed pain as the goal of therapy. Consequently, defenses are confronted, either verbally or physically, to get at the feelings underneath. Many body therapists believe that it is necessary to directly re-lease the chronically tense holding patterns of the body by deep massage techniques. This may work initially, but because it is being "done to" the client from the outside, the patterns usually return even stronger than be-fore.

This seemingly powerful and effective cathartic model is outdated, since its invasive techniques often repeat the injury that caused the defensive holding pattern in the first place. There is initial relief when feelings are released, but when the holding pattern in the body returns, it is much like scar tissue over a wound. Repeated discharges in this manner actually strengthen muscular armoring and make it tighter. Even worse, the core Self doesn't seem to be reached, remaining buried and estranged from both the client and the therapist. Energy is discharged out of the system in a dramatic catharsis, rather than contained within the system and transformed into Self-experience.

BOUNDARIES WITHIN THE THERAPEUTIC PROCESS

When clients first enter the room, the IBP therapist notices their body attitudes, energetic presence, positions they take in the room, and quality of their contact with the practitioner. Given this information, the therapist will work with the client's awareness of experience in the body, while bringing boundary issues into consciousness. The therapist may, for example, work with physical distance or closeness, eye contact, tension or relaxation in the body, breathing, and connection of these experiences to early relationship issues.

The IBP therapist often will help clients to set appropriate boundaries through experimentation and body awareness, thus teaching them how to do this for themselves. The practitioner also may convey parenting messages by setting his or her own boundaries, thereby providing a container for the therapeutic relationship.

The following is a transcript of boundary work conducted with a new client at the beginning of a session. The therapist and the client are seated on cushions on the floor, facing each other.

Therapist: How do you feel about working with me?
Client: I feel nervous.
T: What do you feel in your body and where do you feel it?
C: My stomach is tight, my heart is beating. I'm not breathing and my hands are sweating.
T: Notice where you're sitting in relation to me—how does that feel? (Client is sitting about three feet away.)
C: It feels OK.

T: Would you be willing to experiment with moving a little further away? (Client looks worried.)

T: What just happened?

C: I felt rejected.

T: What did you feel in your body?

C: I feel sad.

T: Where did you feel that?

C: In my chest, throat and eyes—like crying coming up, but I stopped it.

T: So you are anxious if you are close and sad if you move away.

C: Yes, I guess.

T: Would you try moving a few inches back and see what happens?

C: OK. (Client moves, looks at therapist, takes a breath.).

T: I noticed you took a breath. What did you feel in your body when you moved?

C: I'm calmer.

T: Where do you feel that?

C: My shoulders and stomach are more relaxed.

T: Look at me—what do you feel in your body?

C: I can see you better.

T: So when you move just a little further away, you are less tight and scared and our contact is better.

C: Yes. (Breathes again.)

T: It seems like you have an idea that being close means that you feel connected, but our connection is actually better when we are a little further away. Is that true?

C: Yes, it's amazing—I'm tingling in my chest and arms now.

T: You're becoming more alive as you become more relaxed. Would you be willing to draw a circle around yourself on the floor?

C: (Becomes tense again. Tentatively takes chalk from therapist, and draws circle very close to body.)

T: What happened? What do you feel in your body?

C: I got scared again. I didn't want to do it.

T: What is the fear?

C: That you won't be there.

T: If you have your own space, you're afraid you'll be alone. You're afraid I'll abandon you.

C: I guess so.

T: Where do you feel that?

C: Sadness again in my chest and throat—my throat is tight.

T: Would you be willing to do another experiment?

C: OK.

T: Erase your circle without moving—make it a bigger circle.

C: OK. (Draws a bigger circle, breathes.)

T: I noticed you took a breath.

C: Yes, I relaxed again.

T: When you have more space, you are more relaxed.

C: Yes.

T: Can you see me and hear me?

C: (Looks at therapist.) Yes.

T: If you have a boundary and enough breathing room for yourself, I won't go away. I won't leave you.

C: (Cries.)

T: What's happening?

C: No one ever said that to me before.

T: So you couldn't have a separate Self in your family because you would be abandoned.

C: (Crying) Yes, that must have been true.

T: What do you feel in your body?

C: My chest and throat are more open. I can breathe and I can see you better.

T: Now I'm going to draw a circle around myself. (Draws a circle at about arm's length.) This circle means that I will be here for you. I will not cross your boundary without asking permission.

C: (Breathes again.)

T: What are you feeling?

C: Grateful.

T: Where do you feel that?

C: In my heart—I feel open and safe. I trust you.

T: So, when we both have boundaries, we are closer and more trusting, and have better contact.

In this particular session, the therapist is working with breath and boundaries to promote physical, emotional, and cognitive awareness. The work is taking place in the here and now, with one reference back to the experience of the Primary Scenario. To assist the client in recognizing these patterns, most IBP therapists will explore this history of early relationships within the first few sessions. Some therapists keep a diagrammatic outline of each client's Primary Scenario, in the form of an intergenerational chart, and have this available in each session.

While IBP therapists might use a variety of other techniques to intensify body-awareness, working with boundaries ensures that the process remains non-invasive, with the client always in charge. Breathing, stretching exercises, and self-release techniques are often taught and practiced within the sessions. Some practitioners may use light acupressure, but the guiding principle is that any method that might be perceived as something being "done to" the client is simply unacceptable. Constant attention to, and respect for, boundaries ensures that this principle is upheld.

A GROUP BOUNDARY EXERCISE

The following is a group exercise that allows people to experience and experiment with boundaries as a felt sense in the body:

> Sit on the floor across from another person. Notice what the contact between you feels like in your body. Now take a piece of chalk (or yarn, string, or something similar) and draw a circle around yourself to represent your boundary. Notice how large or small you've drawn it. Does it feel like the right size in your body? Make a boundary statement to the other person, something like, "This is my space. Please stay out of it unless I invite you in." What happens in your body as you say this? Notice that you now have a boundary and the other person doesn't. How does that feel? Now have him or her draw a circle and make a boundary statement. What do you feel in your body? Is your experience of the contact between you the same as before the circles were drawn, or different? Are your boundaries distant, touching, or overlapping? Who decides what space each of you gets? For most people,

having a boundary not only makes them feel more secure, it actually enhances the contact. The other person is experienced as a separate individual with whom one can connect without needing to fuse. You may feel, "I know where I am and I know where you are." For some people, usually those who have a fairly high level of abandonment fear, making the circles is scary; it brings up the fear of being isolated. Others feel secure when they have drawn two or three circles around themselves and delivered their boundary statements in a threatening tone: these are usually people with a fear of being engulfed by others. In any case, this simple exercise can be very revealing and diagnostic.

SUMMARY

At its essence, IBP is a body-focused psychotherapy that works developmentally with the Self and relationships. The therapeutic relationship is the vehicle through which the Self is brought into the here-and-now, as well as the framework in which healing can take place. In IBP, the core of Self is energetic, residing in the body, while the broader concept of Self is holographic, incorporating body, mind, and spirit. Working with the energetic parameters, or boundaries, of Self, practitioners support their clients in moving developmentally toward enhanced experiences of relationship, separateness, containment, groundedness, presence, and awareness.

This form of therapeutic alliance is achieved through a boundaried therapist-client relationship that consistently generates a climate of trust and safety. This makes it possible for both therapist and client to become fully "present," having effective energetic contact while remaining grounded in their bodies. These are also the conditions in which the therapist can experience and express the authentic, empathic understanding that supports the work and validates the client's Self. Taken together, these ingredients constitute the therapeutic climate in which it becomes possible for the client to open to his or her own experience, expand and elaborate the sense of Self, establish effective Self-regulatory mechanisms, create options, and make life-enhancing choices in relationship with others. This is the state of "Relational Autonomy."

1. Rosenberg, J., M. Rand, and D. Asay. *Body, Self and Soul. Sustaining Integration.* Atlanta: Humanics, 1985.

2. Beiser, A. "Paradoxical Theory of Change" in Joen Fagan and Irma Lee Shepherd, eds. *Gestalt Therapy Now.* New York: Harper Books, 1970.

3. Winnicott, D. W. *The Maturation Process and the Facilitating Environment.* New York: International. Univ. Press, 1965.

4. Chamberlain, D. B. "How Pre- and Perinatal Psychology Can Transform the World," *Pre- and Perinatal Psychology Journal* 8:3, 1994.

5. Verny, T. and J. Kelly. *The Secret Life of the Unborn Child.* Toronto: Collins, 1981.

6. Stern, D. *The Interpersonal World of the Infant.* New York: Basic Books Inc., 1985.

7. Reich, W. *Character Analysis.* New York: Farrar, Strauss & Giroux, 1961.

Chapter Six

THE BODY WE ARE

Richard Strozzi Heckler

EDITOR'S NOTE: *I first encountered Richard's work through his ground-breaking book,* The Anatomy of Change. *I remember well what it was like to read this accessible book; I felt moved by his stories of how he related to clients and was transfixed by his simple yet powerful explanations for how change could occur. As it happened, we both ended up teaching at The Naropa Institute in Boulder, Colorado, and have met there briefly. Richard's is the finest voice I know that joins the deep wisdom of an Eastern contemplative martial art, namely aikido, with the more Western concepts of healing and psychotherapy. To have access to someone who is an acknowledged master of both these forms is a rare treat. Richard has an instinct for taking the essential principles and techniques of both these traditions, seeing their deep correspondence, and vividly articulating the resulting whole.*

I come from the tradition of the martial arts, meditation, competitive athletics, and body-oriented psychology. In these disciplines I learned fundamental principles that profoundly influence my work today. In martial arts dojos, meditation halls, and track stadiums, I saw that I am my body and that I am more than my body. In my somatic practice with individuals and groups, it was revealed to me that we are a living process in which we are shaped by our experience and that our shape forms our experience. My studies, especially aikido, revealed a world of energy to me. When, as a young boy, I first saw men in belted *gis* throwing each other over their hips, I was caught as if in a spell. It was beauty in much the same sense as the poet John

Keats meant when he spoke of beauty as truth. There was a grace in their throws and a redemption in their falls that captured and expanded my imagination. Waves of energy shaped a field potent with feeling and action. In the directness and simplicity of their movements I saw that the body we are *is* the life we live. Energy and the body are intimately linked and as a unity they become the cause of our life.

We are connected to others and to the world through an energetic process that promotes new relationships and ends others. Pulsations, vibrations, streamings, expansions, and contractions of one's bodily life build boundaries, express emotions, shape attitudes, and generate a process for living. I saw that life was formed from life and that there were cycles of beginnings, endings, and in-betweens. I learned how to organize this energy, or *ki*, (as the Japanese call it) to build an identity and a structure for taking care of what mattered to me. I also learned how to surrender to this vast, resonating field of excitation and let it organize me. This taught me to trust the territory beyond the self and to dissolve into the yearning that reaches beyond the dominion of the personal "I." This energy simultaneously seeks balance and disruption, homeostasis and growth, becoming and dying. To live in the center of this contradiction is how we continually form, contain, release, and re-form the body we are.

Through these disciplines I also discovered that the body we are goes beyond the physical form. While we are in a living process of becoming different selves and different bodies, there appears to be a parallel process in an entirely different domain. The first time I became experientially aware of this phenomenon was when I was running for the United States team in the pre-Olympic meet in Mexico City in 1967. In one particular race I suddenly found myself above the track watching myself and the other competitors in the 200-meter dash. I was both running and watching myself run. A mantle of calm had settled over me and my concerns about competing and winning had completely vanished. While I was seemingly powerless to affect anything, I was powerfully joined to everything by a pulsating, unified field. A few steps past the finish line I reentered my track body. I was both perplexed and fully refreshed. I could see by the way the judges and other competitors treated me that they were oblivious to my experience. Although there was no one to talk to about this experience, it initiated my inquiry into the nature of expanded states of awareness.

THE BODY WE ARE

Years later during aikido training a similar episode occurred. During an exceptionally fast and powerful throw by my teacher, I again stood apart from my physical body, watching everything with lucidity, including the expressions on the faces of the other students, the teacher's technique, and my body hurling through space. I wasn't afraid and I wasn't concerned, nor was I particularly ecstatic. The personal "I" through which we normally act and perceive simply wasn't present. I felt part of something much larger than what I was normally accustomed to. I wasn't bound by the self. I was a member of a community whose scale diminished vanity and generated compassion.

Regarding these experiences and others that followed, I wasn't satisfied with explanations that I was out of my body. Rather, I conceived that I was simply in another body; a body which has its own organizational structure for perceiving, acting, and feeling. Further experiences in dreams, intuitions, and meditation states supported the existence of a time/space domain that resides beyond the physical form. Our common sense and historical tradition of language hasn't embraced this phenomenon, and thus doesn't offer a structure to support it. I believe that not only are we many bodies over a lifetime, and even over a day, we also live in bodies that can't be reduced to our standard assessments of analysis and inspection.

When I speak of the body, I'm referring to the shape of our experience, not to the collection of fixed, anatomical parts as in the Cartesian interpretation. The body is not a machine, its boundaries are not clearly defined. Our experience is subjective, self-responsive, and at the same time constantly responding to the world. We are self-contained *and* we merge with others and the environment. We are our bodies when we're engaged with the air, our neighbors, the landscape, making promises, planning our future, or thinking of our loved ones. The body contains and expresses our thinking, actions, emotions, and perceptions.

The way we expand towards warmth and recoil from pain is too complex to understand in a diagram or mathematical formula. Moreover, our bodies produce a language and a thinking by which we coordinate with others to build a mutually committed future, or not. When we allow ourselves to be touched by the rhythm of life, by sensations, streamings, waves of excitation, and fields of energy, we grasp the possibilities of becoming self-healing, self-educating, and self-generating.

RICHARD STROZZI HECKLER

The rationalist tradition that portrays the body as a machine is the foundation for the present-day psychological language of insight. This way of thinking reduces embodiment to understanding, which relies on gathering information. In addition, the body as machine metaphor is currently extended to equate the mind with a computer, another machine. When this machine metaphor determines our life, we feed ourselves information in order to form a theory about living and acting. Our decisions and choices, then, are based on this theory, not from the embodiment of our ethics, values, and stand in life. To its credit we owe many of our advances thus far, in both science and technology, to this way of thinking. I say "thus far" because it is now producing more breakdowns than breakthroughs in our capacity to take meaningful action in our personal and professional lives. The vast amounts of information to which we have access have not made us more fulfilled, effective, or peaceful. For all of our understanding we still live in fear, anxiety, and uncertainty. Our labor-saving devices and material wealth haven't salved the wounds in our families or communities, nor have they helped us evolve to a more satisfying way of being. How can a machine live the richness of an incarnate spiritual life?

To highlight this distinction between information and embodied knowledge, consider this example: I'm in Latin America having a conversation with two acquaintances from North America. There is a disagreement about the meaning of a particular Spanish word. Dictionaries and phrase books are brought out. One man is adamant about his position and gains ground in his claim by repeatedly referring to the texts. The second acquaintance, who has been working in this country, is not convinced but is acquiescing under the weight of the other's argument. Unexpectedly, the doorbell rings and a man says something to us in Spanish. The first man shrugs, uncomprehending. The second man replies in Spanish, and there's a brief conversation before the Latino thanks him and exits.

Embodied knowledge is the skill to act appropriately at the appropriate time. Embodied knowledge has a historical and rigorous formal training behind it. It lives in the present time in its immediacy, availability, and directness. It anticipates and corrects for breakdowns in the future. Skillful performers such as athletes, dancers, equestrians, teachers, musicians, and pilots are exemplars of embodied knowledge. The man who helped the Latino at the door was the embodiment of knowledge. He was an actor in the world in that he was able to engage and respond.

Information is not instantaneous. It is formless until it is organized. While embodiment is alive, information is static. Information is stored in computers, books, fiber optics, and theories. It is not interactive, self-forming, or responsive. You program and access information. Embodied knowledge acts to take care of the concerns of living.

The difference between information and embodied knowledge, we might say, is like the difference between knowing a word in a Spanish/English dictionary and speaking Spanish.

This point was consistently and faithfully brought home to me in many dojos, schoolyards, and playing fields. When a newcomer would show up at the dojo bragging about his prowess or why something we were doing wouldn't work, somebody, in due time, would offer, "Put it on the mat. We'll see what works." Inevitably, the pretense of the boaster would fall to the embodied expertise of the trained athlete.

Don't mistake this example as an endorsement for physical strength or machismo. Often the winner was smaller, not particularly strong, and perhaps even younger. The difference was that he or she had been training rigorously with equally rigorous training partners under a qualified teacher. This person embodied a certain domain of knowledge. The other was a repository of information for this domain.

I you want to produce new behaviors or competencies—in short, if you want to evolve or improve yourself—it isn't sufficient to be knowledgeable only cognitively about a subject. It is necessary, however, to have a teacher, to commit to a practice, and to practice and study with a community of learners. This notion shifts learning from understanding information to embodying actions.

In my opinion one of the failures of contemporary psychology is that it doesn't provide practices that lead to fulfillment, new competencies, and the satisfaction of taking on that which is difficult. Most talking therapies offer possibility for insight, which can be valuable for orienting historically to our present-day situation, but they drive inward, away from the larger world of social sensibility, the politics of care, and stewardship of the natural world. Their reductionist bias rigidifies and fortifies a self that ultimately becomes isolated from others and the environment. This, of course, can also occur in somatic therapies, though it comes dressed in a different cloak.

Many somatic therapies emphasize feeling states that are disconnected to any meaningful activity. While it is meaningful to expand one's capacity to sense and feel, I believe it's only a beginning point and not the conclusion for living a life that embodies actions for taking care. If we are seduced only by sensation or only by our stories, we remove ourselves from membership in the larger community of humans, animals, and landscape. If we don't outgrow a self that is defined only by how we feel or what we know, we become part of the narcissistic plague that is now a national epidemic.

Human beings live in bodies, and they live in language. When I work with people, I look to see how and where life has been lived in their bodies, and where life has been shut down. I listen to how they live the stories they tell themselves or how they live in a gap between their stories and their actions. I look at how they have allowed their energy to express aliveness and where they are rigid and lifeless. I listen to the stories they tell about their lives, and I listen to how these stories live in their bodies. I'm interested in how they've shaped themselves around their stories and how this shaping brings them satisfaction or restricts them from acting on the future for which they long.

Listening to people this way includes their past, present, and future. We embody a history that is constantly influencing us; we act, feel, and perceive only in the present. We are like a radar screen that is always scanning for the best future we can imagine. I don't see minds, bodies, and spirits. I see in each person an identity, biology, history, a certain bearing, and a future-forming language that expresses the unique quality of aliveness we call the Self. I see a life of becoming that is formed by a process of intertwined events, images, actions, emotions, and a thrusting into the future.

I am alert to what wants to come to life in the person, that which has been long buried. For some this may be withheld grief; for others, rage; for some the capacity to declare their mission in the world. It might be the yearning to freely receive and express love. Whatever it is, I am interested in *how* it is withheld, both in the patient's body and in the story the patient has about his or her life. I work with patients' resistance and their becoming through touch, movement, breath, expression, and practices that support a new way of being. The following study exemplifies this approach.

Carol came to see me at a transition point in her life. She had just turned thirty-three and had recently been promoted at work. In her new position as a supervisor, she was being asked to manage people for the first time. She had been divorced for more than year and was just beginning to date and consider being in a long-term relationship again. In her new professional and personal identities, she found herself trapped in ways of being that were no longer useful to her. She "understood" cognitively what was happening, but found herself helpless to take new actions.

As we began working, Carol quickly assured me that she had "taken care of most of her stuff." When I inquired about this she informed me that she was in Alcoholics Anonymous and through that process had set her life in order. She had come to see me because recently she had been given to inexplicable bursts of anger at work. These incidents had been increasing over the past few months and were now showing up in her relationships with the men she dated. Her boss, who knew me through a course I had presented on embodied learning in the workplace, recommended that Carol see me. This produced a certain degree of trust in me as she trusted her boss; at the same time she made it clear that she wasn't interested in therapy. This meant not engaging at an emotional or intimate level. She simply wanted to understand something so she could fix it. I asked her how she would know if what we did together was successful. She replied that she wanted to be effective at work without having to be angry and that she wanted to be in an intimate, committed relationship.

Carol was a warm, outgoing person who expressed vibrancy and aliveness in her face and gestures. She considered herself a "people person" and enjoyed the company of others. Because she had always thought of herself as having a cheerful, positive outlook on life, she was disturbed by her recent outbursts of anger. Her eyes reflected a warm, receptive style of relating. Yet her buoyancy appeared forced and unrelenting as though she were trying to convince others that she was an "up" person. Behind a smile that seemed permanently fixed on her face was a tightly held jaw.

The aliveness in the upper part of her body did not have a place in her pelvis and legs. When she stood, her legs were stiff and immobile, like wooden posts on which her torso balanced precariously. Her pelvis was pulled back like a cocked trigger and the tissues in her hips and lower abdomen were dense and unyielding. While her hands moved gracefully and flirtatiously, her walk was heavy and plodding. The life in the upper half of her body had no correspondence with the lower half. It was as if they expressed two different views of the world. Her upper body was requesting contact and acceptance; her pelvis and legs were guarded and unresponsive, declining intimacy. Her belly, which separated the top and bottom, was like putty, unformed and childlike. It was a no-woman's land in which there was little possibility for coordination between the two halves.

In our initial sessions the work centered around Carol directing her attention to where and how she held herself. As she sat, stood, or walked I would tell her what I saw and would ask her to describe what she felt in that area. She had had little experience in becoming consciously aware of her body sensations, and much of our early work was educating her in this domain. From the beginning it was clear that she had little feeling in the lower half of her body, and while there was the capacity to feel in the chest and face there was rigidity there.

In one of these sessions I pointed out that when she spoke to me she never looked directly at me, but rather angled her head off to the side and looked at me out of the corners of her eyes. She was unaware of this and when I positioned her head so she looked straight at me she blushed and her head automatically rotated away. She told me she felt too vulnerable in that position; that people would be able to look straight through her.

At this stage of our work I gave her two practices. The first was to set aside some time every day simply to feel the sensations in her body. We folded this practice into the daily walks she took through a park near her office. Her original motive for walking was to lose weight. It was a rather mindless activity in which she sped along in much the same way she drove herself in life. I suggested she could do the same walking, but now pay attention to the sensations of weight, temperature, contraction, and movement in her body. The second practice was to notice the position of her head and eyes as she spoke to people and to bring her head back to center when she observed she was angling away.

Her initial reports on these practices were that she had a difficult time remembering to attend to her body and posture in this way. This made her realize how much she was "in her head" and that when she did feel her body she immediately became uncomfortable and sometimes frightened. As she continued, however, her capacity for being with the life of her body increased. She could make new distinctions of warmth, stiffness, openness, and contraction. In the practice of directly facing someone she began to see her mistrust and guardedness. This produced a gap between her perceived image of being open and how she was actually guarding herself in relationships.

We added to this practice by teaching her how to center. This is a practice appropriated from aikido, without the martial context. It produces the distinctions of being aware in the moment, present to others, and connected to the body. We did this by having her balance and align along the somatic dimensions of length, width, and depth, and then drop her attention to her center of gravity. In this practice, she was learning to be straight without being rigid and relaxed without being slack. She reported that this produced a stronger presence and deeper calm at work. In addition, she saw it was a place from which she could more easily observe her reactions to people and events.

It was still difficult for her to stay with the sensations in her pelvis, but she had more resolve and less fear. As she became more aware of her body through our sessions and the practices in daily life, a pattern of behavior began to unfold. It became apparent how difficult it was for her to make a clear request. She could clearly formulate it in her head, but when it came time to speak, her body simply wouldn't do it. She understood the importance of asking for what she wanted, but she wasn't able to embody it. She hadn't developed the body for making a request. The result of this was that Carol took on the work that she should have been delegating to her subordinates. In addition, she never told her boyfriend what her concerns were and what she wanted. This made her resigned and resentful. As the frustration escalated, she would reach a point where she could no longer contain herself and would suddenly lash out angrily at those close to her.

In the next phase of our work, we uncovered Carol's embodied story of being the good girl, the pleaser. Raised in a fundamentalist family by an authoritarian father and submissive mother, Carol learned to do the right thing to gain approval and love. The right thing in this case was not asking for too much, if anything at all. It meant always having a smile on her face and being grateful for what she did have. There was no room for desire, exploring new ground, or expressing pleasure and joy. She was never given permission to ask for what she wanted. She became permissive and let men use her. Her pliancy was a way to appease others and distance herself from her concerns and desires. This narrative lived in Carol's body as a deadening in her legs and pelvis and an over-boundedness in her chest that restricted her from expressing any emotion other than a superficial mood of gaiety. Now that she was managing people and seeking a committed relationship, she was having to face her inability to make personal and professional requests. The more she faced this the more she touched the years of anger held under the surface. And below this was a deeply held grief at never allowing herself to fully experience satisfaction and intimacy.

Uncovering this allowed us to invent practices for her to develop a body for making requests. As we began, she saw the commitment involved in making a request. There was the commitment to be sincere in what she asked for and the commitment to the other in her listening to the other's ability to fulfill the request. In this commitment there was an intimacy that she both feared and desired. In learning to ask for what she wanted, she had to look at what mattered to her. She also had to face her fear of rejection. In the beginning this was daunting to her and she would collapse in despair. She was unable to contain the excitement of this newly forming self. As her excitement increased, she was unable to hold and allow it to come to form. It was like blowing up a balloon halfway and then letting it go. It was important to mobilize the energy of her anger to fuel the newly-forming self that was learning commitment.

At this point I had Carol lie down and breathe in a way that increased sensation in her body. We did this in order for her to expand her capacity for being with and containing her excitement. She began to see how she ran from feeling. She saw that she lived in a story that feeling was dangerous. She believed that if she allowed feeling she would lose control, look foolish, and be rejected. In one particular session, her legs began to move as if they wanted to run. Carol reported a prickly feeling in her thighs that made her uncomfortable. I asked her to engage with the sensation and movement. With encouragement she allowed the warmth to move through her pelvis and into her legs. Her legs began to push, and I offered resistance at her feet. As the pushing increased, her entire body became involved. She began to kick, pound with her fists, and spontaneously shout, "Get off of me!" After a while her excitement naturally subsided and she reported that she felt warm and alive. She was somewhat concerned that I might have negative judgments about her anger. I answered her that I didn't and she allowed herself to experience the satisfaction of being deeply relaxed and

THE BODY WE ARE

alert. Her chest opened to deeper breaths, there was the flush of aliveness in her legs, and her face had taken on a completely different countenance. In this session Carol opened to the possibility of being someone who could take authentic action for herself.

During the course of our work together I tried to show Carol that knowing something and embodying new actions are not the same thing. I revealed that it was necessary to commit to practices in order to embody new actions. We discovered that there's a plasticity about the body that allows us to transform and be different observers of ourselves and the world. I tried to show her the link between our behaviors and the stories we have about our lives. Carol saw she could partner her excitement instead of defending herself against it. Working with her excitement, Carol became more assertive and more relaxed. In her new capacity for being self-generating, she overcame her pattern of acquiescence. In her new way of being in the world, she fell deeply in love and advanced in her career path.

My study of somatics has been guided by a number of remarkable teachers. Maharaj Charan Singh, my spiritual teacher, exemplified the enduring power of love. Chogyam Trungpa Rinpoche, the Tibetan meditation master, demonstrated the relationship between emptiness and form. Dr. Randolph Stone, the founder of Polarity Therapy, revealed the power of presence and the life we live as an energy field. Saotome Sensei, my aikido sensei, taught me how to stand and interact in the world. Doris Breyer and Al Bauman, both students of Wilhelm Reich, introduced me to the interface of breath, energy, and emotional states. Magda Proskauer, who was a student of Elsa Gindler, showed me the relationship between the breath and the psyche. Tom Hanna and Eleanor Criswell mentored me through my Ph.D. and were important supporters of my somatic vision at a crucial point in my life. My partnership with Robert Hall at the Lomi School, and Wendy Palmer and George Leonard at Tamalpais Aikido Dojo, enabled me to explore and bring these ideas to fruition.

Chapter Seven

THE MOVING CYCLE

Christine Caldwell, Ph.D.

EDITOR'S NOTE: *As far back as I can remember, I have been a synthesist. I love looking at many different systems and finding their commonalities and divergences. I fervently hope that in my lifetime, unifying theories about the way the world works will arise and connect all the various sciences and arts. I am one of those dreamers who feels sure that if you study any discipline deeply enough, all of the organizing principles of the universe will be revealed. This passion to commingle systems is what recently led me to edit this book and what has moved me all my life to study such disparate fields as geology, anthropology, dance, physics, and evolutionary biology.*

My work, called the Moving Cycle, also reflects this history. I have studied the work of many, and have not been content in any one area. I have looked deeply into bodywork, movement education, dance ethnology, psychology, Buddhism, Darwinism, and cosmology, and I have come up with what I believe is their unifying principle—movement. It is in the understanding of movement, in all its personal and universal manifestations, that we find the inspiration to heal, grow, and evolve towards greater wholeness.

INTRODUCTION

The words "The Moving Cycle" represent the deepening spiral of human experiences that are central to the processes of healing, growth, and conscious evolution. To move is to be alive; this principle is echoed in every beat of our heart, every breath of our lungs, and every gesture of our hands. Our attention to the interior rumblings and rhythms of our bodies forms the deepest and most abiding sense of self that we will ever have. Our ability to express (press out) our experiences, to make ourselves known in the world, relies completely on our ability to move our bodies through space, to vibrate our vocal chords, and to posture and gesture; all of these are the fundamental components of communication.

This form of body-centered work studies, recovers, and celebrates our inherent movement processes and, by doing so, facilitates, first, a return to our essential nature, and second, a commitment to a creative response to life. I birthed this work out of the influences of dance, bodywork, and contemplative psychology, which is to say that its ancestors include art, engineering, and spirituality.

HOW THE MOVING CYCLE WORK DEVELOPED

My initial training was in dance therapy. I had entered school (UCLA) in the early 1970s as an anthropology major, and found that I was fascinated with the dance rituals of primal cultures and how they used many dance forms as a method of healing. I was fortunate at this time to meet and study with Buckminster Fuller's daughter, Allegra Fuller Snyder, a dance ethnologist with interests in healing rituals. She helped me to combine my interests in anthropology, dance, and healing, and encouraged me to become a healer myself. While I was getting my master's degree in dance/movement therapy, I also studied verbal therapies, early body-centered psychotherapies, and bodywork.

After graduating, I worked for four years with severely disturbed people in state mental hospitals in the Washington D.C. area. By seeing the extremes of human behavior, alongside extremes in body distortions, I was able to learn a tremendous amount about how our human nature can warp. At the same time, I studied Aston Patterning with Judith Aston. This exquisite form of bodywork and movement education helped me to assess postural and movement behaviors and to use massage-like manipulation and movement coaching to restore mobility and grace in my private clients.

In 1980, I moved to Boulder, Colorado, where I still live today. I began teaching at the Naropa Institute, a small private college founded by a Buddhist teacher and dedicated to experiential and contemplative education. I founded and directed their dance therapy department and, in 1990, expanded the master's program and renamed it the Somatic Psychology Department, which gives degrees in dance therapy and body psychology. It was here that I developed the Moving Cycle work, using my students, clients, and colleagues as inspirational sources.

The Moving Cycle work began to take shape in the late 1970s, when I became dissatisfied with the predominant models of therapy and healing. I felt that many therapeutic systems often recapitulated the woundedness of patients by assuming that the system knew what was wrong with them, knew how to cure them, and would control their experience until they fit its definition of "healthy." This largely unconscious attitude even permeated many body-centered forms of healing. Many body practitioners felt sure they knew how healthy and adjusted a person was merely by looking at his or her body. This subtle arrogance, which I engaged in myself, deeply disturbed me. As I moved into the gentle, nonaggressive environment of the Naropa Institute, I was determined to drop this approach. I vowed to develop a way of working that arose from the natural forces of healing. I spent the next few years simply observing my clients and students, and noticing what processes seemed to occur spontaneously when they healed.

What I found was that healing is not a series of moves toward a goal, but a process. Regardless of what was being healed, whether the healing was physical, emotional, cognitive, or spiritual, a recurring and ordered *process* seemed to be involved. An action rather than a result seemed to define and create healing. I could see ordered stages in healing, and it seemed that if I could somehow support the natural flow of these stages, I truly would be facilitating the natural healing of myself and others.

There are four stages in this healing process. They come in sequence, and they all have to be present for healing to be complete. The first stage is *Awareness*. The journey begins with sensing, identifying, and waking up to something that I was not paying attention to before. This might be an awareness that I feel feverish, or noticing that my jaw is clenched every time I visit my ex-husband, or realizing that my thoughts are moody and blaming. I first have to wake up, to become aware of my current experience and name it. Often this takes the form of acknowledging that something is wrong, off, or painful. The Awareness phase is a body experience, in that awareness of physical sensations forms the keystone of my ability to pay attention and wake up. Awareness recovers my ability to know what is actually occurring, to assess what *is*.

The second stage is *Owning*. After I wake up to what is going on, I then take responsibility for it. It is only when I say to myself and others, "This is me feeling this, this is me doing this," that I access the ability (the power) to change what is occurring. If I blame my anger on others, I require them to change in order to take care of my feeling. I then need to spend my energy trying to control someone else's experience. If I blame my anger on my own character defects, I spend my energy making myself out to be bad and wrong, and then lose the energy needed to heal. The key features of the Owning phase are to relearn how to tell the truth, and to disentangle blame from responsibility. In the body, it requires that I tolerate and commit to continuing to feel and to being curious about feelings and sensations that I was disowning before. It means staying with my experience, and letting it move me. Owning recovers my personal power, and this power is necessary for my continued healing journey.

When I stay with the process of Owning, things can get intense. Whatever needs healing will surface. What surfaces is often an incomplete and therefore repeating experience from childhood that drags my energy away from my being fully myself in the present moment. When I find this unhealed place, and I greet it and take care of it, I enter the *Appreciation* phase. Appreciation recovers my ability to be unconditionally accepting of myself. I cease trying to get rid of some experiences and hold onto others. I allow the flow of life to pass through me. I get back my ability to love myself in this phase, and this love is not conditioned by any rules or strictures. In my body, I relax into myself and physically can both move and be moved by life with just the right amount of effort and grace.

The process is not complete, however. I must engage in an *Action* phase in order to achieve healing. By actually taking my experience out into the world and manifesting it in relation to others, I make my inner changes real and meaningful. No change will be permanent unless I do something with it in my daily life. Otherwise, I merely have pleasant or even fascinating experiences that do nothing to alter the results I get in life. My action may involve simple acts of learning to breathe more deeply while under stress, or to look a person with whom I am in conflict in the eyes. Whatever action it is, my healing won't "stick" until it is practiced, and it is my body that must first and foremost engage in action.

The Moving Cycle

Observing these four phases consistently and repeatedly in myself and others formed the basis of the Moving Cycle work that I teach today. Since discovering these cyclic phases, I have experimented with ways of teaching these techniques and attitudes to myself and others.

The Body of the Work

When looking at the body of the Moving Cycle work, I can see that it departs from many types of therapy in that it is not overly concerned with what went wrong. Though we all need to honor our history, our real opportunities lie in moving differently. This is paradigm shift that involves a transfer of our creative energies from illness models of change to transformative models of change. By focusing on the inner resources I want to awaken to, reclaim, recover and use in my daily life, I don't have to restrict myself to only healing my wounds. I also can have the life I want by moving myself through it with integrity, curiosity, creativity, and generosity.

Healing systems rest on assumptions, and the Moving Cycle arises from five basic statements about how the world works. Some of them have been stated before in other systems. I believe in making these value statements up front, so that the work can be completely visible:

1. We are inherently whole; innately just fine as we are. This inherent wholeness is called embodiment.

Our nature as human beings is revealed in how we have specialized as a species; in other words, in what we are good at. What we appear to be specialized for, what our ecological niche involves, are self-awareness, on-the-spot learning, and tool use. Self-awareness is often called consciousness and is sometimes called the observing self. It means we enjoy a great capacity to witness ourselves and to reflect upon ourselves and on the external world. We can discern patterns in events, and we can determine causality because of our ability to contemplate patterns.

A related aspect of our nature is that we can learn from what we observe. We can change our programming about how to operate in the world at the drop of a hat. This ability to learn on the spot is the source of our cleverness as a species. It is also how we access our adaptability.

Because we are good at learning, we also like to modify things. As a result of our ability to reflect, we constantly harbor urges to change things. This began eons ago as tool use—making a rock sharp-edged so it would cut better—and has evolved to massive building projects, complex resource use, and sophisticated technology proliferation. We also have turned our tool-using skills inward on ourselves. We have developed medicine to alter our physical well-being. We have learned to put a creative twist on our experience through humor and art. We have even developed the ability to observe ourselves pulling all this off, through meditation.

This nature of ours is a given; it is our birthright as humans. Anything this basic, this universal, exists without judgment. It just is. It is in judging any part of our nature as wrong that we beget our suffering. In this light, we can see that by deprecating our self-awareness, we create craziness. By making our tool use wrong, by thinking it is someone else who pollutes through technology, or that technology itself is somehow wrong, we treat our material creations just as badly as we have our own bodies, and we set ourselves up for environmental catastrophe. And by devaluing our spontaneous learning, we rigidify ourselves so that our adaptability plummets.

When we cooperate with our natures, we are happy, feel healthy, and evolve as individuals and as a species. I call this state of cooperation "embodiment." Our true nature is felt in and expressed through our bodies, which are our true homes.

2. We are many bodies.

When I use the term "body," I refer to not just our physical material selves, but to all that we are. One way to avoid the hazards of the body/mind split is to see oursleves as all body and only body. Body in this sense is our form, our shape and size. I have a physical body, an emotional/energetic body, a cognitive body, a spiritual body, as well as other bodies. We exist along a continuum. We are physical mass, we are waves of feeling and emotion, and we are abstractions called thoughts.

One of the dictionary definitions of body is "the main or central part of anything." From this perspective the physical body is the central or main part of our existence. It is the reference point that contains the rest of our experience. As such, the physical body helps to define and shape such nonmaterial events as emotions and thoughts. It is the vessel in which they can arise and be experienced. This is the body that bashes into chairs, that touches another person. The laws of mechanical physics apply to this body. This is also the body that has tangible and immediate needs for nourishment.

We are also an energetic body. Our energetic body is that aspect of our being that changes things, that regulates our homeostatic balance, and that provides the fuel for transformational experiences. It manifests as waves of excitation that travel through our physical bodies, and it frequently is experienced as emotions. Emotions are actually excitations mixed with thoughts. Thus the emotion "anger" is an energetic effort to regulate our power; we often become angry as a direct result of disempowering ourselves, and the emotion is an effort to get our power back. Likewise, sadness moves us to realign ourselves after we experience loss.

In our energetic bodies, a more relative world exists. Energy molecularly vibrates mass and, in so doing, can change its structure and properties. This ability to change ourselves with energy, from our physical structure to our thoughts, presents the possibility that we can change the way we experience the world. Each emotional happening can be an opportunity to align my form more closely with the external world so that I maximize my contact with it. Events become relative to the energy we put into experiencing them directly.

We are also a cognitive body. In this body we experience the ability to transcend regular space and time through thought. Its vibrations manifest as cognitions, brain waves of massless energy. We can remember the past, imagine the future, and create whole worlds that exist only in fantasy. We can grasp and work with abstractions. The life of this body can be quite limitless. This lack of limits is tremendously freeing, and also tricky. If we allow this body to operate separately from the physical and emotional bodies, we can come to live in a world further and further removed from the nourishment that we need from physical, consensual reality.

We have other bodies as well, all of which live through our material body. The transpersonal body deals with space and the creative void. It is revealed in the gap between our thoughts when we meditate and in the spontaneous creative act. The movement of this body exists in the experience of communion with that which is outside of our selves. It is a resonant pulsation with that which is outside our physical container but is essentially similar. It dances with all life.

The spiritual body is the part of ourselves that can transcend any form and completely occupy space. It is at one with all that is because it *is* all that is. In the spiritual body there is no separation from anything.

Each of our bodies has value and function. None can exist without the other. All contribute to form our essence. If we cultivate one more than another we become out of balance and get sick. As our physical, emotional, cognitive, and spiritual needs are met, a connecting bridge of relatedness is formed from one level of development to the next. A chain of interdependent influence arises and is maintained by movement. This capacity for movement to constantly nourish inner connection to all aspects of ourselves is the basis for the Moving Cycle.

3. Creativity is inherent and necessary in all our bodies.

We all need order, stability, and constancy in our lives. Without it we wouldn't remember how to brush our teeth each night. Our nervous systems function not only as information processors, but also as information eliminators, so that we are not overwhelmed by the wealth of stimuli available to us. We need predictable patterns. We also need a way to escape them, a way to dance with the changeability of life. In this sense, our lives are a constant balance between constancy and creativity.

Creativity embodies and celebrates our highly adaptive natures. When we create, we cause something new to exist. Whether it is an idea, a sculpture, a song, or a new kind of bread, life requires us to be creative, or we fail to be human. Creativity is evolution on the spot. By owning our creative natures, we make conscious evolution possible.

Creativity coalesces in our body. We create when we drop a habitual pattern of behavior, thought, or feeling, and opt instead to dance without the reference points of the way we have always done it, seen it, felt it. This dropping and dancing creates open space and allows options of bringing something new into form. I have repeatedly noticed in my life and in the lives of my clients, colleagues, and friends that when we fail to take creative opportunities in our lives, our lives stop working properly. Life requires us to be constantly and unconditionally creative, or we become less fit and cannot succeed in life.

4. Movement is the common feature of all creation.

From the spectacular explosion of the Big Bang to the spontaneous wiggles of an infant, creativity and all creation are made manifest through movement. Movement is the *modus operandi* of life. If we look at the nature of movement in the universe, we can see that it occurs either in spirals or waves. That is, the cosmos breathes, life pulsates. The pulsatory nature of our bodies is what the Moving Cycle seeks to celebrate and restore. Our organs expand and contract, our emotions and energies ebb and flow, our thoughts wax and wane. By recognizing and following this natural movement, we can consciously access our creativity, our part in creation.

5. Stopping movement takes us out of creativity and out of our bodies. When we move with what is, we reestablish embodiment, and we recover our creativity.

The Moving Cycle defines illness as an interruption of our natural spiraling or pulsing movement. When we stop moving with our environment, stop dancing with both our inner and outer worlds, we become out of synch with them. We can't be in our bodies at this point, and we can't participate with our creative capacity. We stop pulsing out of fear. If we look at our history as animals, we can see that in situations of danger, animals either go still, rush to attack, flee at top speed, or play dead. (We call this the freeze/fight/flight/faint response.) This can save our lives, but if we engage in it too often, we habituate to these interruptions of normal movement flow. Our behavior then organizes around movement that is either held back or depressed or exaggerated. When we move this way consistently, we cannot experience life normally. Our behavior become stressed and exhausted, and we become ill physically, emotionally, mentally, and spiritually.

By reestablishing natural movement, we recover our bodies, our health, and our creativity. The Moving Cycle is designed to return us to our natural flow, our individual signature of self-pulsation. In this way we become reintegrated with life.

These five assumptions guide and inspire the Moving Cycle paradigm. This system is client-centered and process-oriented. It seeks to recover flow, and so it operates within a context of flow. It has been used successfully with people who are severely disturbed and folks who simply want to fine-tune their creativity. It can be applied to groups, couples, and individuals. The next section looks at how sessions occur and gives case studies as examples of how movement flow is recovered and practiced.

How the Moving Cycle Works

Because the Moving Cycle likes to undulate and spiral in creative ways, a Moving Cycle session can look very different from one client to the next, one session to the next. It can involve a lot of talking, or none. It may take up a big room in all its movement antics, or it may occur quietly in a chair. It will, however mysteriously, flow along the sequence of Awareness, Owning, Appreciation, and Action.

A session usually begins with checking in. Checking in often includes the relating of various events that have happened (whether in the close or distant past) that feel important to the present moment. Checking in is not complete, however, without turning the attention inside and doing a body check. The question is, "What am I feeling right now? What kind of sensations, energies, feelings, thought patterns are happening in me right now?" Without this reference point of how and where I am now, I cannot adequately house or hold any issue I may want to work on. So this first phase is a blending of what is occurring right now in the room with my growth and recovery interests. This blending gives me vital information. If I identify a tensing of my brow that occurs as I talk about a fight I had with my boss this week, I am carrying my whole being into the session.

The next task, the Owning phase task, is to empower myself completely to resolve any way that I may have obstructed my flow around this issue. In other words, I get to the source of how I am creating any illness I feel or any way in which I have failed to own my creativity. By taking responsibility for the experience I am having, I access the fuel, the power to change it. If I do not take ownership, I create a body that makes others responsible and then manipulates me to get others to give me what I think I need. This is a costly affair and requires me to practice defense strategies that will protect me against the effects of my blaming, in other words, the various forms of protest that people will engage in and direct towards me when I make them or myself wrong.

In the body, this Owning phase occurs as a deepening of my direct experience. If I have furrowed my brow, I furrow it further, consciously. I let myself really feel the muscles in my face that create the furrow. Perhaps a frown shows up. Maybe it brings up a feeling of disapproval, and I find myself also wanting to point my finger in accusation. As I go ahead and do that, a memory may come of how my mother used this gesture, and I discover that I am reenacting a relationship dynamic that is very old and rooted in my unfinished feelings about my mother. As I allow this movement gesture to go wherever it wants to go, perhaps all the way into a rigid, accusing stance, it may access a feeling I had been hiding from myself. The act of hiding it has obstructed my movement flow. At this point, I allow my body to take over, for it knows exactly what I need to do to complete this feeling, and the feeling is completed in the body's only language, movement.

I can simply keep moving, alert to the moment when I begin to obstruct my flow, or I can choose to *move* the obstruction by doing the obstructing consciously. In moving the obstruction, I actually embody it, I own it. In the case of the furrowed brow, I might find myself embodying a Wicked Witch of the West character, cackling and accusing and actually owning up to how judgmental I can be. By playing with her consciously rather than running her on people unconsciously, I turn a maligned energy into a playful one. Or I might consciously feel the physical tension it takes to stop myself from being so blatantly judgmental (the tension it takes to merely furrow my brow rather than rant full-blown as the witch), and access feelings I may have hidden since childhood about not being able to speak up, disagree, or call a spade a spade. In either option, I am moving with what is; I am realigning with life. This dissolves any way in which I have abandoned my body, my self.

When I keep moving with the accuracy of what I feel, I reach a complete appreciation and acceptance of myself. This fundamental act is the process of healing made manifest. I reoccupy my creative nature, and I access my ability to problem solve, adapt, grow, and evolve. It is important in this phase to *keep moving*, to explore, like an astronaut, this open space, this creative void. What is life asking us to do when we have removed our obstructions to movement? It is not enough to heal; we must reoccupy and reassert our creative core. The Appreciation phase is where this occurs.

The last phase, that of Action, is an application and practice phase. As I move into my creativity, what do I create? Do I recreate my relationship with my husband? Do I commit to new ways to relate to my boss? Do I finish that short story I always wanted to write? Whatever creativity we have reclaimed, we must complete through creative contribution. In this way, I assert myself in the world as a contributor rather than a taker. And all creation progresses apace, with us riding on its back.

In the body, the Action phase often involves a moving back into my daily life with new movement sequences to practice. Maybe I will breathe more deeply when I talk to my spouse, and take a less confrontational stance. Perhaps I will be able to look people in the eyes and let myself be moved by the depth I see there. Whatever creative space our bodies have accessed we can use to transform our world.

Below are two short case studies, examples of the various surgings and cavortings that occur in the Moving Cycle.

Clara is a successful interior designer, who works ten-hour days, six days a week. She came to see me because she wanted to address her "workaholism," which left her keyed up for much of the day and exhausted at night. We had done some work with her history of feeling she needed to produce at all costs, as well as her feelings around a consistent deficit of play she had experienced as a child. She was currently working on recovering play in her life. This particular session she came in and stated that she had had a good week, except for the fact that her boyfriend had gotten drunk twice and had passed out on the couch both nights. Her chest began to sink as she told the story.

I asked her to describe these incidents as dramatically as she could, using her body to make her point. She showed me his slumped posture on the couch as he "sucked brew" and channel-surfed in front of the TV, only grunting at her attempts at communication. She then let her body go limp and acted out how he had collapsed onto his side and begun to snore loudly. She began to laugh at how well she was portraying him and noted how fun it was to act out his drunk. She began to look more alert and present, though I sensed there was still more to do. I asked her to play out how she had acted towards her boyfriend as he drank. She tensed up, and showed me how she had become anxious, hyperalert, and whiny, trying to cajole him out of his position on the couch. She paced about the room and reported feeling uptight, angry, and scared.

I asked her to concentrate only on the body movements of these two dynamics, and to do each alternately, as fully as she could. She let herself go back and forth between these two extremes, her body going heavy and limp, and her body shaking with tension and moving in a bursting, jerky manner. After ten minutes of this, she stopped and began to cry. She had come literally to feel her own lifestyle of work, work, collapse, work, work, collapse, being acted out in her love relationship. The dominant pattern, that of tense working, she had unconsciously chosen to act out, while her boyfriend obligingly (and equally unconsciously) took on the collapsed, exhausted pattern.

I asked her to keep moving, now that she had identified these dynamics. If she befriended these two extremes by moving in them as accurately as she could, what would happen? For a few minutes, her movement continued to oscillate between the two extremes. I asked her to pay attention to the transition points between the two dynamics, and to let herself luxuriate in the transition phase. An amazing dance ensued, in which she experienced extended moments of blended effort and relaxation. Her arms began to describe lyrical circles in the air, and her pelvis circled in a undulating manner. She started to laugh softly as she moved. She continued this dance for several more minutes, until she found a satisfying completion.

As we talked about her process, she marveled that even though she had intellectually known about finding the middle ground between overwork and collapse, she had never *experienced* it before. As self-assigned homework, she committed to each night turning on some music and dancing freely to it.

In the following sessions, she reported that she now had a reference point in her body for knowing when she was overworking and when she was exhausted, and that if she let herself dance during the day, in small ways, she was able to find the middle ground she sought. She also was able to talk through this issue with her boyfriend, who had finally confessed that he sometimes got exhausted and irritated at all her uptight ways, which reminded him of his harping mother. She committed to doing her dance, and he committed to telling the truth instead of withdrawing and projecting.

The second example is a man named Bob, who suffered from headaches, usually after work, just before dinner. Doctors had determined that there were no neurological, dietary, or physiological factors involved. He was referred for psychotherapy to "that body person," myself.

At first, Bob was a bit put-off that I didn't ask him a whole lot about his childhood. He thought the headaches had something to do with his feelings about his mother, with whom he used to fight at the dinner table regularly when he was a young teenager. I told him that this sounded like an excellent theory, but that we needed to test it out. I asked him to give me the most minute details about the sensations he experienced before, during, and after his headaches. As he did so, I noticed that he would often rub his closed eyes with his fingertips. I asked him to repeat this gesture and be curious about it. As he did this, he reported that it felt soothing. I remarked that by definition, he couldn't see while he was soothing himself in this way. I asked him to simply close his eyes and let me know how this felt. Here is what ensued:

> Bob: It is a great relief not to see sometimes.
> Christine: What are you not seeing?
> B: (quickly blurting) My dad.
> C: What is he doing?
> B: Nothing. Just sitting there at the table, ignoring me and my mom (begins to cry).
> C: Stay with how your body wants to move as you feel that feeling.
> (Bob lets himself really cry, while shaking his hands and finding a pushing away motion in his arms. He lets this pushing move him for some time, as it goes into other parts of his body as well.)
> C: How do you feel now?
> B: Strangely, OK.

The session ended, and Bob decided he would sit and close his eyes each afternoon before dinner and see what came up. Over the next few weeks he shared the result of his practice. At first, the headaches went away. Then, they began to come back. As he now knew to do, he stayed aware and curious about them. After a few days, he arrived at the intuition that he needed to ask his mother about this, that there was something she wasn't telling him. He phoned her, and asked her about these dinner incidents and specifically if there was something she wasn't telling him. After some hedging, she revealed that it was during this time of his life that she had found out his father was having affairs. Her own mother had advised her to ignore it as the best means to make it go away. She tried. Then her arguments with Bob started and they only stopped after he moved away to college. The dinner table was the time and place where the tension of deceit and withholding was at its peak, and it was Bob who bore the brunt of it.

Still, the Moving Cycle was not finished. Bob's headaches only stopped after he committed to clearing up the massive amount of withholding he had been doing with his friends and coworkers, withholds large and small. He also began a daily ritual of a few minutes of quiet, eyes-closed contemplation just before dinner.

The Moving Cycle work is done in many formats, from individual to couple to group. The work takes on areas of specialization, applications that can speak to people's different learning styles. Some programs are run as intensives in the deep wilderness, in conjunction with canoeing, sea kayaking, horse packing, or scuba diving. The wilderness environment can provide an atmosphere that allows our natural movement processes to emerge more profoundly and mindfully.

The Moving Cycle work can also be specialized for addictions recovery contexts, from substance abuse to repeated failures of creativity. It also can be applied to the transitions of birth and death in special workshops, using the power and grace that lies inherent in these states as a framework for movement exploration. Lastly, it can be focused on the phenomenon of play, offering intensives on our biological need and imperative to play throughout our lives.

Moving from Retreat to Recovery to Recreation
So That All Can Benefit

Twenty years ago, when I began to ask myself what healing looked like in its natural state, I wanted to find an answer that would apply to all healing, in all people. Ah, the ideals of youth! Though I believe the Moving Cycle approaches this universal, I was surprised to find out something else. The sequence that I was witnessing resisted being restricted to healing. It seemed to actually describe the way change works. I realized then that healing is only a small part of our biological imperative on this earth. It is not enough just to repair ourselves when things go wrong. What other plant or animal just contents itself with fixing its boo-boos?

All life grows, and all life must engage in metabolic activities (eating, digesting, secreting) in order to grow. How can we cooperate with the growth imperative in all our bodies? What kinds of nourishment do we need in order to support this in all our bodies? Growing also replicates the Moving Cycle. The Zen master Thich Nhat Hanh is fond of saying that what we pay attention to will grow, that attention is like sunlight and water to a plant. By attending, by cultivating awareness, we grow ourselves into new forms. By owning our natures, we fuel the process of growing beyond those natures. By appreciating our creative longings, we break out of old patterns and grow into new forms. By acting in the world, we help it to grow beyond its previous limitations.

All life reproduces. We create offspring that we hope are just a bit more adaptive, a bit more creative than even we have been. Sometimes the offspring are children, sometimes they are powerful ideas, inventions, a lifetime of sharing joy, or a capacity to be at peace. Our imperative to reproduce is strong and cannot be denied for long.

The Moving Cycle is designed to give us a road map for all these possibilities. When we commit to movement in every aspect of our lives, we don't require life to whack us upside the head with illness and heartbreak in order for us to move into healing, growing, and transforming. Our evolution can take place right here, right now. We can commit to our creative movement cycles, and they will take us into all these realms with inherent rhythm and grace.

Chapter Eight

PBSP—Pesso Boyden System Psychomotor

Albert Pesso

EDITOR'S NOTE: *The Pesso Boyden System Psychomotor was discovered/founded by Albert Pesso and Diane Boyden Pesso in 1961. Thus it is one of the earliest "second generation" systems in somatic psychology. Both Al and Diane started as dancers interested in the way movement and the psyche related, both within an individual and within groups. Since that time they have devoted their energy to refining their process and improving and expanding long-term certification training programs in Norway, Denmark, Holland, Belgium, Switzerland, Germany, and in many cities throughout the United States. Their careful and thorough articulation of how we come to feel ill and how we can move into health is a standard for others to follow. The Pessos specialize in creating experiential "structures" or activities that remediate past developmental deficits that are dysfunctionally driving one's current life. Through enacting need-satisfaction in a supportive coaching environment, we truly can come into the present moment.*

I once had the pleasure of watching Al demonstrate his work with a workshop participant. I was moved by the power of his presence and his ability to create an invitation for another to heal. He is a perfect example of the art of practicing psychotherapy, and this chapter illustrates the dynamic blend of Al and Diane's two powerful minds and two compassionate hearts.

I write this from the perspective of thirty-five years of exploration and experience using Pesso Boyden System Psychomotor (PBSP) procedures with thousands of group members, trainees, and — more recently—managers and top industry executives. More than ever, I am impressed with the long-lasting influence that memories of early-life events have on people's experience and understanding of present-day events, and further, how memories of those early-life events limit the range and quality of options available to people as they prepare for and anticipate future events. I am equally impressed with the general lack of attention given to understanding and working with these phenomena.

It should be more widely recognized that (1) the experience of the present is always seen through the "lens" of past memories, (2) an appreciable portion of what appears to be transpiring in the present is actually a recollection and reexperience of the past, (3) memories of the past directly influence and modify present-day actions and interactions, and (4) anticipations (expectations) regarding the future are based largely on assumptions formed on experiences in the past. Simply put, the past is embedded deeply in the experience of the present and woven into anticipations of the future. Without awareness of these phenomena and—more importantly—without techniques which allow control and modification of the storage, retrieval, and influence of memories, people are not likely to escape the "fate" predicated on—and predicted by—their early history. The common wisdom is that the past is over and done with and has little to do with one's present life. It further holds that all one can do about the past is realistically accept its "facts," and as to the future—that is in the hands of the gods.

The past is neither such a permanently fixed constant, nor is the seemingly inevitable unfolding of the future so shrouded in mystery. Memories of the past are not absolute facts, but are subjective experiences, combined with assessments of interpersonal events, which are encoded in our nervous systems in ways that affect the appearance of present events and influence future plans and interactions.

A memory is not a mere copy or a simple internalization of interactive events; more accurately, it is a translation of those events. Thus, a memory is not a fixed thing; it is a neural record about many things. People digest events in their minds and convert them into meaning stored in neural patterns. We are a living record of the past. Each moment of the present, we tap into the database or library of living knowledge that memories of past events have deposited in our beings in order to determine how we should respond to the latest challenge or opportunity presented from the outside world.

One might conclude that I think there is no intrinsic meaning in life and that meaning is only formed individually and subjectively—that individuals only create meaning for themselves as they face an essentially unknowable, booming, buzzing, and meaningless external world. That would not be an accurate conclusion.

A person is not born into the world as a *tabula rasa*. Indeed, by being born, we inherit a virtual treasure trove of meaning packed into our genes. This meaning can be externally observed in the determined-to-live purposefulness of our biological organization. It can be internally experienced in the not-to-be-ignored, felt presence of our deepest emotional needs, longings, and tendencies. In every cell we have maps, blueprints, and inclinations that can lead to a life of pleasure and fulfillment. Our living flesh and nervous system—born of our genes—is a virtual database and library which "knows" beforehand those experiences and interactions which will result in the continuity of our individual life and the continuity of the human species.

This genetic information stored everywhere, inside every part of us, knows—and has successfully played—the game of life from the beginning of time. We call that gene-carried information pool—that living record which knows how to keep life going—"evolutionary memory." It is not memory in the sense that we have personally lived its history. But it is memory in the sense that our genes contain the record of successful living organisms from the beginning of time. We human beings are the living-generation stewards of this precious, time-tested "life-knowing" and should be conscious of that awesome responsibility.

This adds a new wrinkle to the understanding of how memory plays a part in every moment of our lives. From this standpoint, the "now" of a present moment is not only filled with the "then" of our personal memory of past events, it also is full of the "way-back-then" evolutionary memory of gene-captured, life-enhancing ways of perceiving and acting. Seen in this way, a moment in time is quite a dynamic thing.

Like all memory, evolutionary memory influences our experience of the present and our anticipations of the future. Evolutionary memory is not value-free. It is invested in—and indeed, it is literally responsible for—the continuity of generations to come. It has knowledge of all that has lived successfully before us. It contains information about the yet-to-be-fulfilled yearnings and present requirements of our evolutionary past. Evolutionary memory is alive in us and can supply us with the basic materials and information needed to meet and create our personal and evolutionary future.

Memories should help us cope successfully with the present and guide us to a happy future. For what good is memory if it does not promise to help us handle the present and improve the future? Then what about personal memories that do not support the goals of evolutionary memory? Many remembered past events result in attitudes that are antagonistic to the fulfillment of life. Remembered negative life lessons promote dreadful experiences in the present and prepare the mind and body for wretched events in the future. Why do we experience such life-denying and future-killing events, and what can we do to keep those memories from wreaking their havoc inside and outside us. These questions are the stimulus behind the creation/discovery and evolution of PBSP.

Not every individual encounters conditions that sufficiently satisfy the developmental needs and longings of life. There are wars and famines, social and natural disasters, all of which make it impossible for parents to provide their children with what they are genetically primed to anticipate. Memories of need-frustrating events encountered in difficult times inevitably leave their negative imprint and prepare people for more of the same in the present and in the future. People with unsatisfying early histories are less inclined to provide their offspring (should they even conceive them) with what they themselves never experienced. They are likely to pass on to the next generation a taste of their own personal culture of diminished hope in life (with perhaps a compensating belief in perfect satisfaction in the afterlife—gene expectations for satisfaction have to show up somewhere).

Though these event-injured people do manage to exist (albeit while suffering greatly) in the world as they find it, all people are genetically prepared to be able to more than simply exist. People can flourish (flower, mature, and metaphorically bear fruit) when provided with conditions that fulfill their innate, geared-for-satisfaction, genetic requirements.

By the very nature of existence, people long to have pleasure, satisfaction, meaning, and connectedness in their lives. When genetic requirements for maturation are satisfied at the right age, by the right providers, those happy states are the natural outcome of existence. When they are not, the opposites are experienced: not pleasure, but pain; not satisfaction, but frustration; not meaning, but despair; and not connectedness, but alienation.

PBSP—Pesso Boyden System Psychomotor

Note that I emphasize the conditions required for appropriate satisfaction of genetic maturational needs. Am I saying that once the appropriate time has gone by that those genetic maturational needs are never truly satisfied? Practically speaking, yes. But, the search and longing for fulfillment of those requirements, though frustrated, does not go away nor appreciably diminish over time.

Though we are no longer children and our parents may be long dead, those genetic aches tirelessly seek relief and lead us to desperately search for (and sometimes think we have found in our spouses, friends, mentors, and others) those necessary, soul-satisfying interactions that would provide the "click" that our evolutionary memory has prepared us for. We justifiably hunger for that glorious sense of relief, that finally-felt rightness that would let us move more joyfully in the world and be more able to confidently face the next stage of our development.

If, metaphorically speaking, we missed the boat, what can we do to alleviate the discomfort that negative history produces? How can we finally get a glimpse of—and a ticket to—that heaven on earth that our brain/body organization is prepared to encounter? We do not believe it is possible to literally satisfy developmental deficits in "real time," at one's present age, with people in one's present life—nor do we attempt to do so.

We have developed a technology in Pesso Boyden System Psychomotor that enables people to experience the symbolic satisfaction of genetic requirements for maturation in a precisely-designed event that we call a "structure"—a highly organized and client-controlled activity. In a structure, the client remembers, and simultaneously reexperiences, the emotional/body state when those needs should have been met in the client's actual past. In that sense, the client is at the right age. Then group members selected by the client role play "Ideal Mother," "Ideal Father," "Ideal Grandmother," and so on, who—had they been back there in the client's "personal memory" of the past—would have responded in ways the client's "evolutionary memory" had anticipated they would. In that way, the group members become the right providers, for they move, interact, and speak with the client in ways that provide the "click" of long-awaited and internally anticipated satisfaction and relief.

These ideal figures are not constructed out of elements of the client's real parents; they are new parents designed to behave in ways that are most consistent with the client's "evolutionary memory" expectations. We have learned to gather information about those expectations from the client's emotional reactions, facial expressions, posture, body sensations, and also from the client's more conscious thoughts and ideas about what would be best.

The kinesthetic, sensorimotor, and cognitive recording of this symbolic counter-event then is designated and stored as if it had actually been experienced in a more distant past. These new-map "virtual memories" serve as alternatives—not replacements—for the negative, actual memories. Thus, structures can be transformational experiences which free people from the prison of their past and help them escape from a lifetime of pain, frustration, despair, and alienation.

Later in the chapter I shall describe an actual structure, but first I will outline the basic theories and techniques of PBSP so that readers will readily understand the technical steps taken in the procedure.

The work of building life-enhancing structures is based on four important concepts:

1. The longing for fulfillment of the basic, genetic developmental requirements is experienced bodily and emotionally and inclines us to look and move toward the outer world in specific, need-based ways. Each need has its own shape.

2. The interactions which optimally fulfill these longings for satisfaction must precisely meet and match the interiorly driven longings, and they include sensorimotor, kinesthetic, verbal, and conceptual need-specific responses. Each need satisfaction has its own countershape.

3. These needs are most fully satisfied when provided by the most appropriate family members. Each need satisfaction has its own satisfier(s).

4. There are specific age levels that must be recalled and reconnected to when virtual memories are constructed. Each need fulfillment has its own time frame.

PBSP—Pesso Boyden System Psychomotor

To sum up, our genes dispose us to anticipate the satisfaction of basic developmental needs necessary for personal development and maturation. They also provide us with hard-wired, sensorimotor "templates" that enable us to recognize and pleasurably respond to those outer conditions, people, shapes, and interactions that most optimally meet those inner requirements. We also have stored within our nervous systems the categories of basic family relationships, such as mother, father, sister, brother, grandmother, grandfather, aunt, and uncle. Further, we have the innate capacity to register and respond with different kinds of behaviors and expectations at different ages to those in different categories of kinship relationship.

In Pesso Boyden System Psychomotor, we attend to five genetic maturational needs that we are internally driven to satisfy. We need to:

1. Satisfy the basic developmental needs for:

   ◆ Place

   ◆ Nurture

   ◆ Support

   ◆ Protection

   ◆ Limits

2. Integrate and unify the polarities of our biological and psychological being:

   ◆ Sperm/Egg—own and comfortably identify with mother's and father's antecedents and gene pool

   ◆ Neurological—integrate and have good communication between left and right hemispheres of the brain

   ◆ Sensorimotor—be comfortable and skillful in all combinations of perception and action

   ◆ Behavioral—have an easy acceptance and comfortable use of all body apertures involved in "putting-out" and "taking-in"

◆ Symbolic—be at ease with one's metaphoric androgyny of combined maleness and femaleness (animus and anima) while able to identify with one's biological gender

3. Develop our consciousness—increase subjectivity and objectivity, with a well-developed interior world of images and concepts combined with a strong sense of individual identity and ego

4. Develop our "pilot"—have a strong, active, self-organizing, self-initiating center (akin to taking our rightful place as the "president" of our own "united states of consciousness")

5. Realize our personal uniqueness and potentiality—come to maturity, ripen, and bring the precious fruit of our existence to the world

I will go into each maturational need in more detail.

SATISFYING THE BASIC DEVELOPMENTAL NEEDS

The basic developmental needs for Place, Nurture, Support, Protection, and Limits must be met in three stages: first, in a concrete, literal way by the appropriate satisfiers; second, in a metaphoric or symbolic way by the appropriate satisfiers; and finally, these needs must be met by ourselves.

I will use Place—the most fundamental need—as an example to illustrate these stages. In the first stage, we need to experience being literally inside a safe place that communicates to us that we are loved and wanted, and where we are provided with the room to exist, protected by the ones of whose stuff we are made. Before birth, we have a place inside the uterus. After we are born, we have a place inside the loving embrace of our parents.

In the second stage, we need to experience being metaphorically or symbolically inside a loving, life-sustaining place. After our birth, we can feel the pleasure of living inside the metaphoric place of our parents' hearts, lives, gazes, and, most importantly, their minds. We can experience—by how they look at us—that we exist in their image of us, inside their minds, surrounded by love. Their consciousness of us enables us to be conscious of ourselves.

After the successful completion of the first two stages, we can model/ internalize the place-giving behavior and attitudes of our parents and feel literally "at home" inside our own bodies. We can feel metaphorically "at home" inside our own minds where we have created an image of ourselves, surrounded by the remembered love of our parents, supplemented by our own appropriate love for ourselves. In this final stage, we have gained a firm sense of belonging, so we can feel "at home" anywhere in the world, with full rights to existence.

I will not go into detail regarding the other basic needs except to say that these same three stages also must be completed for them. We must first be literally nurtured, supported, protected, and limited and then metaphorically nurtured, supported, protected, and limited in order to be able confidently to do these tasks for ourselves.

If there are major flaws in the provision of the literal and metaphoric satisfaction of those needs, one's capacity to be comfortably self-reliant is damaged. Memories of need-frustrating interactions distort the way people experience the present in predictable ways and diminish hope for fulfillment of future life-goals.

Integrating and Unifying the Polarities of Our Biological and Psychological Beings

We are genetically drawn to take full and conscious ownership of the entire range of our bodily and mental capacities. To be true to our organismic integrity, we must explore, discover, and own the living being that we are and learn to take pride and mastery in all of our natural functions. In an optimal upbringing our parents would support this endeavor and not prohibit us from awareness and ownership of any parts of ourselves.

We must own and comfortably identify with our mother's and father's antecedents and gene pool—with both the sperm and the egg. In an optimal upbringing, we would not be given any reason to want to tear out, discard, or not love those parts of ourselves that remind us of our parents or their antecedents.

However, there are many not-so-optimal families in which the mother or father derides or despises the other parent to the dismay of children who identify with and look like that parent. There are many maternal or paternal grandparents who make disparaging remarks about the "other side of the family." Children who hear these criticisms are inclined to disown that part of themselves that is descended from the "wrong" part of the family.

We also must be integrated neurologically, that is, we must integrate and have good communication between left hemisphere and right hemisphere of the brain. Although the brain functions as a single unit, each hemisphere has its own special features and functions. We need to be raised in an environment that licenses the fullest use of both hemispheres—the right, generally regarded as emotional/spatial, and the left, generally regarded as intellectual/linear. Neither hemisphere should be characterized as "male" or "female." Children, regardless of their gender, should not feel that use of any part of their cortical capacities is "off-limits."

Some families and cultures teach children that being emotional or artistic is not masculine and discourage boys from expanding or exploring those capabilities. Even in recent times, girls have been discouraged from being too intelligent as it would hinder them from getting a good partner. Such cultural and familial restraints result in a psychological numbing of capacities and restrict the fullest use and experience of mental and emotional faculties.

We also must be comfortable and skillful in all combinations of perception and action, in other words, in our sensorimotor capacities. We should be brought up in an environment which encourages us to explore moving in all the ways our nervous systems allow. We can move reflexively; we can move volitionally; and we can move emotionally. While children are growing up, they experiment, in play and other interactions, with the entire range their systems allow. Some parents get annoyed or irritated with elements of such play. They might not like to see certain behaviors and find them unacceptable, crude, or frightening. Such messages, whether verbal or nonverbal, will result in children inhibiting those "unacceptable" forms of behavior. In extreme cases, parents may be saying to children in indirect ways, "Parts of you are unacceptable. I will kill all those forms of action and being in your body."

Children are naturally curious and want to use and "play" with all their senses. They touch everything, smell everything, taste everything, and want to see and hear everything. How often are children told, "Keep your hands off that," or "You poke your nose into everything," or "Get that out of your mouth," and so on. The admonishments may be given in the interest of safety or order, but in extreme cases there may be underlying messages, such as "I can't stand you being a living, sensing being—stop being a curious, reacting, living creature."

We must have an easy acceptance and comfortable use of all body apertures involved in "putting-out" and "taking-in" behaviors. We have many different kinds of fluids that come out of the openings of our bodies. These have a life-maintaining function and should be accepted as a natural part of the rhythm and beauty of life. But in many cultures and family settings, they are not. Children are significantly influenced by how they are responded to and described when they sweat, salivate, urinate, and defecate, when they have mucous coming from their nostrils or tears coming from their eyes.

When children reach puberty, parts of their bodies start to grow hair or enlarge. These events must be normalized and accepted without humiliation or derision, or there will be detrimental effects on their future capacities as adults to accept and enjoy these parts of their nature. When fluids like semen, lubricants, and menstrual blood flow from them, children must be told honestly and respectfully about the place of sexuality in life. Then, as they mature, they can freely and joyously take part in the continuity of the human species.

Women have breasts that produce milk after they give birth to children. Breast feeding should be a normal, accepted activity, but just today I read in the *International Herald Tribune* that a woman in Philadelphia was arrested for disorderly conduct for nursing her baby in a food court. Clearly, we also need to develop a society that appreciates and supports our genetic nature.

We also have apertures for intake that are necessary for maintaining the individual self and the species. Our noses breathe in air and our mouths take in sustenance—activities essential for the continuation of our individual lives. When children make movements and sounds connected with those life-fulfilling functions, these movements and sounds should be normalized and not made to seem strange or ridiculous.

Women have vaginas that are designed for the "intake" of a penis and its sperm. Women should be honored and respected for this species-sustaining capacity and not be seen as less worthy than men because they have an organ that is made to "take in" sperm and to "output" a baby.

Being at Ease with Our Metaphoric Androgyny

We are born male or female (with some mixtures occasionally occurring, recent research tells us), but we all have "male" and "female" hormones. This may explain why we all have "male" and "female" characteristics regardless of our gender. Whatever our sex, we live best when we live what we are genetically organized to be. But what if we are born a girl and our parents wanted a boy—or vice-versa? And what if our culture has very limited ideas about what is "natural" for boys to do and "natural" for girls to do?

What happens to our understanding and integration of our maleness and femaleness when one parent is not sufficiently present in our lives before we can successfully model and internalize their caretaking? We have found that the death or early disappearance of either parent has a profound effect on our behavior in this dimension.

When a parent dies, other outside figures usually fill in for that parent, but a less-observed phenomenon is that a part of our own psyche tends to take over the place and function of that missing parent. Regardless of our biological gender, we become our own "magical, omnipotent, interior father" or our own "magical, omnipotent, interior mother," depending on which parent is gone. This has a profound effect on our psychological orientation and outer behavior.

Further, children tend to form a "magical marriage" with the surviving parent, which produces behaviors that reflect cultural, mate-differentiated roles. Put simply, the "magical husband" child tends to be "harder"— more protective and assertive with his or her surviving mother, and the "magical wife" child tends to be "softer"—more nurturing and caretaking with his or her surviving father. "Magical marriages" tend to interfere with actual mate-choosing and commitment to marriage later in life. This may explain why some wives and husbands bitterly complain that their spouses are far more "connected" to their own mothers or fathers than they are to them.

PBSP—Pesso Boyden System Psychomotor

Developing Our Consciousness

We are able to exist in the world and also able to know that we exist in the world. We have the nervous system capacity to subjectively stand in the center of our experience and also to stand back and "look" at ourselves as objects in the world. This kind of self-consciousness can enhance living and should not result in the inhibition of the fluid experience of "being in the world." Although we have glass mirrors to see ourselves with, the real mirrors of the self are the people who are around us as our personalities are formed—our parents and other members of our family. It is their "image" (and treatment) of us that gives us the materials to make our own "self-image." We become "self-conscious" in the negative sense—paralyzed and unable to be "in the flow of life"—whenever we become aware that our present behavior is akin to those behaviors we exhibited in the past that were "unacceptable" and brought shame and humiliation.

In an optimal upbringing, our parents would nurture an image of ourselves that was core-validating so that our developing consciousness would contribute to our capacity to live in the world with more pleasure, satisfaction, meaning, and connectedness.

Further, our nervous system is organized so that we can construct a micro-universe in our minds that is an inner, sensory equivalent of the outer, macro-universe. As we live in and experience the world, we see it as it actually is in our brains, and we simultaneously make a mental image of it for later use when we want to recall it and see it in our mind's eye. Now there are two universes: one, the outer world "as it is" that we see with our physical eyes; the other, the outer world (which includes ourselves) constructed in our minds that we see with our mind's eye. (When people have a far-away look, they may have stopped seeing with their physical eyes and may be absorbed in seeing with their mind's eye what is on their minds.)

Not only can we see the outer world as we have remembered it in our minds, but we also fantasize and make those images in our minds do things that we may never have seen done in the outer world. Thus, by using the pictures we have created in past events as the raw materials for our creativity, we are able to play with the world in our minds and construct imaginary events. Since we have our bodies represented in our minds, we can also feel and react to those remembered or imaginary events in our "mind's body."

We use this faculty to good advantage when we construct new, "virtual memories" in structures.

Consciousness includes a third element. We have the brain-supported ability to apply verbal symbols (names) to all that we see in the outer world and in our mind's eye. We also name what we feel in our actual body and in our mind's body. We can then remember the linkage between the name of the thing, the thing itself, and our image of it in our mind's eye. Putting it all together, we can remember the link between the name of the actual feeling, the feeling itself, and the feeling in our mind's body.

Thus we have a verbally-represented universe in our minds that we can manipulate, using words, just as we have a visually-represented universe in our minds that we can manipulate using visual images. It is important that our parents assist us in our drive to accurately portray the world in our minds.

Developing Our Pilot—A Strong, Active, Self-Organizing, Self-Initiating Center

We have the neural capacity and the right to self-regulate and self-organize. All that we see and feel in the outer and inner world arrives at a point of reference that we call the "pilot" aspect of ourselves. It is where "the buck stops." It is not another term for the observing ego, for it includes the executive aspect of the self. The fully developed pilot can see, feel, and understand all that is happening and endeavors to choose the optimal course in each circumstance. The pilot then implements that choice in the best interests of the self and the species. Thus the pilot not only is influenced by personal memory but also by evolutionary memory.

Parents should cultivate and support the pilot capacity in their children as they develop. However, some families, institutions, and cultures suppress self-initiated behavior. Children may be discouraged from thinking and deciding for themselves. They may be told, "I know what is going on in your mind better than you do and I know what is best for you." Some institutions and cultures teach that simple obedience and suppression of the self is the highest value, placing the pilot function out of the individual's reach and into the hands of a few selected others.

Children who grow up in families that support the development of

PBSP—Pesso Boyden System Psychomotor

the pilot will develop competence and confidence in their own decisions and actions. When such children grow up, they are more able to cope successfully with difficulties they encounter in the real world.

The pilot aspect of the client is constantly addressed in therapy, so that control of the structure is always in the hands of the client and not in the hands of an "expert who knows best." An important function of the PBSP therapist is to enrich the client's pilot with information arising from his or her evolutionary memory that can be seen from the outside as behavior, posture, and facial expression, or heard from the outside as emotional tone.

Realizing Our Personal Uniqueness and Potential

Each of us is conceived with a unique set of coiled genes primed for realization. We are born with a desire to develop our resources and contribute our matured talents to the pool of human resources. This unfolding and becoming of an individual self is not only a biological activity, it also is a spiritual one. When we bring to life our unique personal contribution, we are active, local participants in the endless cosmic drama of the creation of ultimate meaning as the universe, itself divine, unfolds. We must allow our precious fruit to mature and ripen, and we must bring it into the world.

If we do not find our calling or determine what we were meant to do in this world, we are left with the bitter taste of meaninglessness and despair. It is the greatest misery imaginable to find, as we near the end of our days, that we have missed being active, meaningful participants on this one-and-only stage of life because we had neither found nor developed our special part to play in the extraordinary drama of physical existence.

Parents always should treat their children with the full knowledge that children carry the treasure of existence. Parents should provide opportunities for their children to explore all their native capabilities so that they can discover for themselves what it is within them that they most love to do. Parents who dampen children's natural enthusiasm and curiosity about themselves and their lives imprison their spirits and virtually prohibit them from stepping on the grand stage of life where they can proudly and confidently "strut their stuff."

This completes the short survey of what people need to have experienced in their past in order for them to live a life of pleasure, satisfaction, meaning, and connectedness.

Obviously, there are few people who have the good fortune to have had all those elements successfully attended to in their pasts. It is our belief that the unmet requirements of our genetic nature and the painful memories of their frustration underlie and are interwoven with the suffering and desperation that people experience in the present. This is not to say that people who have had histories of evolutionary memory satisfactions, or who have successfully undergone a therapy that attends to that, do not experience troubling times—certainly they do—but they are in a much better position to cope effectively with life's difficulties. Most importantly, they are much more ready and able to respond to other's feelings and needs, to enjoy living with other people, to love and be loved—and if they choose—much more prepared naturally and joyfully to be a parent.

Now I shall describe the technology, concepts, and practices we use to help people contact what is going on inside their bodies, emotions and thoughts as they face the issues that concern them in their immediate present.

These procedures are typically followed in a PBSP session called a "structure":

- ◆ offering the "possibility sphere"
- ◆ helping the client be in the "center of truth"
- ◆ developing the "true scene"
- ◆ developing the "historical scene" and
- ◆ developing the "healing scene" (antidote)

A structure typically is done in a group with the understanding that other group members (clients or trainees) will play the necessary roles. Clients in individual therapy sessions designate objects in the room to represent the various roles and figures relevant to the work. The goals of a structure are to help the client discover and attend to:

◆ the memories, emotions, and attitudes of the past that are embedded in their experience of the present and prevent them from successfully coping with what is going on in their lives

◆ the expression of buried emotions connected to those past events

◆ the satisfaction of needs that were not met originally in those past events

◆ establishing and experiencing the appropriate age level when those needs should have been met

◆ the satisfaction of those needs with the gene-anticipated appropriate satisfiers of those needs

◆ the construction and accurate storage of the "virtual memory" (new map) in association with the literal memory

I will now elaborate on these five steps.

Offering the Possibility Sphere

The "possibility sphere" is the name given to the literal and metaphoric space that the therapist extends to the client in PBSP. It is called the possibility sphere because it proffers the nonverbal message that life is possible and that the unfulfilled possibilities of the client will be allowed to emerge and find what is necessary for their fullest expression in this setting. It provides a safe, respectful, highly-structured environment where clients can consciously attend to the meaning of verbal, nonverbal, cognitive, and emotional information as it rises to the surface of their minds and bodies.

Before the session begins, the therapist connects with his or her therapeutic center—out of which all therapeutic moves and interventions will arise. The "possibility sphere" is empty of the therapist's needs, hopes, or expectations and filled only with his or her consciousness and awareness of the client. The PBSP therapist has trust in the self-organizing power in the client as well as in him or herself and depends on the inner, motivating force of evolutionary memory to provide the impetus and pathways to healing.

This attitude defines the client-therapist relationship. The therapist recognizes that the client is most knowledgeable about what he or she feels, thinks, and longs for and only takes responsibility for providing:

◆ the capacity to understand and decode literal and symbolic body expression

◆ technical interventions based on knowledge of human interactive processes and psychological theory

◆ mature, non-needing caring

The therapist is not the healer but uses his or her caring to sustain belief and trust in the possibility sphere.

Although the possibility sphere is empty at the start of the session, the therapist certainly is not idle. Even before the client begins to talk about whatever he or she might be thinking, the PBSP therapist has taken a "snapshot" of the client's appearance in the moment to get a picture of what might be forthcoming. The therapist assesses the client's posture, gestures, facial expressions, facial color, gaze, and voice to get a clue as to what kinds of feeling states, situations, needs, and ages might be present or on the threshold of emergence. The therapist runs this data past his or her grid of theory regarding evolutionary requirements to prepare possible future structures.

HELPING THE CLIENT BE IN THE CENTER OF TRUTH

This simply means directing clients to attend to their centers of information about how to live life—namely, their emotions and their thoughts. The question "What are you feeling in your body and what are you thinking in your mind?" typically is asked to elicit this information. The idea behind that instruction is to help clients attend to the two vast databases of information within them that they can tap into for guidance in making decisions as they face the world and its opportunities and frustrations, moment to moment. What is felt in the body is connected to both personal memory and evolutionary memory.

Personal memory has an emotional aspect because we have emotional, body-felt reactions associated with pleasurable or painful events in our past. Evolutionary memory has an emotional aspect because the as-yet-unfulfilled longings of the unborn self will show up as emotional drives and longings as we talk about events in the present which have evoked genetic unfinished business.

Personal memory has a cognitive, verbal side because our thoughts are the constituent parts of the verbally-based interior world we have constructed out of the values, ideas, beliefs, and injunctions gleaned from our personal experiences with life. As far as I understand it, evolutionary memory leaves no cognitive traces in individuals. However, individuals may consciously construct scenarios of what they think would have been an optimal upbringing and use their cognitive functions in the service of their evolutionary memory which communicates with us primarily through body language.

Developing the True Scene

The "true scene" is constructed for an audience of one, the client, who is directed to begin the session by talking about what he or she is thinking or feeling (emotions, body sensations, and impulses) about disturbing people and events in the client's life. The true scene provides a client with a unique perspective that illuminates the architecture and organization of his or her psychological and physical processes in the immediate present—moment to moment. For, the fabric of the present is woven mostly from threads spun out of personal memory and evolutionary memory.

The presenting symptoms of clients who come to Psychomotor therapy for help and relief are always observed against the backgrounds of the clients' lives. PBSP therapy seeks to relieve the symptoms by releasing their energy as behavior and by changing the history which caused them to emerge.

In the true scene we isolate those threads by "microtracking" the ebb and flow of the client's emotional state, cognitive stance, personal memories, and evolutionary longings. We trace the strands of personal memory back to the events, emotions, thoughts, and life-rules the client encountered in the past; and we follow the subtler fibers of evolutionary memory to determine what interactions are still longed for in the client's life-journey toward self-fulfillment and maturation.

We employ two types of role-played hypothetical figures to facilitate this process. The therapist listens carefully to what the client is saying and tries to take in the client's overall state of being from his or her posture, gestures, and facial expressions in order to be prepared to use the appropriate figures. We use a "witness figure" to track the client's emotions as they become evident in changes in gaze, facial expressions, and vocal tones. We use several different "voice figures" who are called by a variety of descriptive names, including the "voice of truth," the "voice of negative prediction," the "voice of warning," the "voice of judgment," and so forth, to track the client's thoughts, attitudes, and injunctions. The title given to each voice is dependent on the type of message it delivers.

We posit the "witness" as a caring, compassionate figure who sees, names, and implicitly licenses (just as our parents should have done when we first learned that everything has a name) whatever emotion the client is feeling. People have emotions that have never been named accurately or sanctioned and therefore do not exist in the client's verbally-represented universe. The witnessing process provides the client's pilot with a model or template for seeing, naming, and licensing the client's emotions and thus facilitates the entrance of those unspoken emotions into verbal consciousness.

The formula statement by a "witness figure" runs like this: "I see how (affective word) you feel as you (use the words the client used to describe the situation that he or she is talking about)." For example, if the client looks pained as she speaks about her father not coming to see her school graduation, the therapist might say, "If there were a witness present, the witness might say, 'I see how hurt you feel when you remember that your father did not come to your school graduation.' Would that be correct?" The therapist always checks whether the affective term used is accurate and strikes a chord of recognition and receptivity in the client.

The "witness figure" is posited in the present and does not speak as if he or she had seen what had happened in the past. That is why the figure says "as you remember," making it clear that the client is having a memory and has not drifted out of the present time frame and landed somehow in the past. This helps anchor the client's pilot in the present.

Though the therapist is the source of the words given to the witness to say, the therapist is not the witness, nor does the therapist role-play the witness. Through extensive testing we have found that the client experiences less dependency and more autonomy and inclination to master his or her own inner process when the witness figure is either posited "in the air" or role-played by another group member.

The witnessing procedure tracks both personal memory and evolutionary memory. The witness, noting the client's hurt about the absence of her father at her graduation, tracks the personal memory of disappointment. Hidden beneath the hurt may lie the longing for the father's presence at the ceremony that publicly validated her intelligence. Later in that session, the client might say, "I wish he would have put aside his business appointments and put me first."

Then (if her face showed an appropriate expression) the therapist might say, "If a witness were present the witness would say, 'I see how much you long for your father to have put aside his business appointments and put you first.'" The witness procedure which observes her longing for validation of her intelligence thus tracks her evolutionary memory requirement for the integration and unification of polarities, that is, the need for ownership and blessing of both cerebral hemispheres.

Further in the session, the client might say, "He came to my brother's graduation but just couldn't make it to mine. If I had been a boy, he would have been there."

That would be a cue for the therapist to suggest using a "voice" figure and say, "That sounds like we could posit a 'voice of truth' that would say, 'If you had been a boy, he would have been there.'" Notice that the therapist changed the pronoun from "I" to "you," taking her thought and presenting it back to her as if it were a statement of fact coming from an outside "truth-speaking" figure. That helps the client's pilot to feel the full impact of what first had been taken as a simple thought and to begin to see and feel the life-controlling lesson contained in that part of her history. In this way, the use of the voices tracks the cognitive aspect of personal memory.

Developing the Historical Scene

When clients have strong emotions as they speak of a figure, we surmise that they are not only accessing information from their verbally-represented universe but also from their visually-represented universe, for we assume they are seeing that figure in their mind's eye. That condition is a cue for the therapist to attempt to create a similar figure in his or her own mind in relation to their already-created image of the client. Thus, two inner arenas should operate in tandem, playing essentially the same show.

When the client has intense feelings and seems to be in a dialogue with the figure the client is talking about, the therapist can say, "You seem to have a very vivid picture in your mind of your father, as you remember feeling so angry with him; why not have someone role-play your negative image of your father?"

If the client agrees and chooses a group member to role-play that negative image of her father, the group member says, "I will role-play the negative aspect of your father." That group member has agreed to be an "accommodator"—the name given to role players in PBSP. Accommodation means the role-player will not invent his or her role but will be instructed by the client to respond to the client's emotions in ways that provide maximum satisfaction to the feelings or needs expressed. The client then is free to construct a visual representation, in the therapy room, of the scene in her mind. This representation becomes a third, physical-space arena that is running the same show as the two previous mind-space arenas. As soon as that charged figure is represented in the room, the intensity of feeling that the client had in relation to the figure in her mind's eye is transferred to the figure she sees with her actual eyes. She still sees the memory in her mind's eye and uses that inner scene to perfect the projection process so that even though she knows that a group member is role-playing her father she virtually sees her father's characteristics and persona in the role player and reacts with authentic emotions to that combined inner and outer image.

The function of the historical scene is to bring to the client and therapist the clearest picture of the past event and its significance. It gives clients the opportunity to feel the impact it had on them, but in a safe, controlled setting. When people have a powerful memory, it is as if they had inserted a videotape into some part of their brain—their entire being becomes the monitor as they feel and perceive the outside world very much as if they were in the original event. Now, with the aid of their pilot, they can attend to all the body sensations and emotions that they may have not adequately experienced or expressed in the original event.

If it were possible to simply and without consequence eliminate disturbing body sensations, it would perhaps make life more comfortable for the client. However, it is questionable whether it would serve the client well in the long run when one considers that buried in the symptom might be the first step of a healing, self-realizing sequence.

PBSP—Pesso Boyden System Psychomotor

Those disturbing physical and emotional sensations are called "energy" in PBSP. In this phase, we follow the formula of: energy which presses toward action—which means that the outward expression of what is felt inside (shape) seeks an interaction with the appropriate object that would give that expression satisfaction (countershape). The result is meaning—the learning that is drawn from the event and then internalized as thoughts and memory.

The client may have felt fear, rage, disappointment, or other painful feelings in the original event and determined then that there was no way to openly, or safely, express those feelings. Now, in the structure, the client can vent those emotions that are still in the client's body, as evidenced by the symptoms of trembling, pain, quickened heartbeat, constricted breathing, and so on. We encourage the client to follow whatever might emerge from those sensations, aided by the role-playing figures (accommodators) who are instructed to respond to the action directed toward them in ways that would provide the satisfaction not available in the original event.

It is a relief for the client to process feelings that have lain dormant so long. Sometimes it is fury, sometimes terror or despair, sometimes even love that has been kept from full expression. The therapist oversees the accommodators' "countershaping" function to ensure that they properly carry out the client's wished-for responses. Although this expression is necessary to reduce symptoms, it is nonetheless not the most important change agent. It is the healing power of believable, new memories that produces deep and long-lasting change.

A secondary value of the historical scene is that it provides clear details about what was most significant in the original, deficit-ridden, wounding events. The memory of those details must be brought to light so that the behaviors of the healing ideal figures can be organized properly to neutralize and repair the damage of the original events. This is attended to in the last phase of the structure process.

Developing the Healing Scene (Antidote)

The "healing scene" refers to those moments in a structure when a "new memory" can successfully be constructed. There is a technology in this process requiring specific and clear procedures. We have found that to insure that the new memory has the most long-lasting effect, it should be recorded in association with vivid recollection of the original, damaging memory.

Therefore, during the healing scene the client should be aware of:

◆ the age when he or she had anticipated that those needs would be met

◆ the active and conscious desire for the satisfaction of that unmet past need (shape)

◆ the places in their body (there are location-specific, receptor sites determined by evolutionary memory) primed and ready to experience the satisfying interaction (countershape)

◆ the appropriate satisfiers that would minister to those needs

The healing scene experienced by the client in the therapy room should simultaneously be seen in the mind's eye of the client in combination with vivid, emotionally-laden images (memories) of the client in the past event. The healing scene is constructed using the client's adult body, linked with the memory of the client's childhood body-experience in his or her mind's body.

It is imperative that the client operates from the pilot position (with the assistance of the therapist) so that the client can monitor the situation and see to it that all these elements are present and in proper order. Otherwise the situation could become chaotic, with little distinction made between present age and childhood age—between what is happening and who is participating in the "here-and-now" and what should have happened and who should have been present in the "there-and-then." Therapists who follow these procedures avoid the pitfalls of literal regression and acting-out, neither of which has much therapeutic benefit.

Therapy is not simply a matter of deciding that the client needed support in the past and then having the group, as themselves, carry the client around the room, in real time, whether or not the client longs for it at that moment and whether or not the client is in touch with child-level desires for that kind of interaction.

The healing scene should never be posited as an actual, literal event in the present that would provide literal satisfaction of a childhood need. That is not possible. The healing scene is a hypothetical event that is composed for the mind to accept as real enough to construct a virtual memory of an interaction that should have taken place in the actual past.

Therefore, the ideal figures are instructed to preface their statements with the phrase, "If I had been your ideal father (or mother) back then, I would have given you" whatever was needed

Sometimes the statements of the healing figures need to recount negative actions that had been carried out by the original figures so one might say, "I never would have done. . ." whatever negative action affected the client. The healing figure continues, "If I had been back there then, I would have done. . ." and then adds what would have been the opposite behavior. That is why the "healing scene" is sometimes referred to as an antidote in the sense that it gives the opposite of what was toxic.

There is no predetermined time to construct an antidote in a structure. However, there are situations which sometimes precede the moment when a healing scene might arise. If a client is in the midst of a historical scene, trembling and sobbing in the vivid memory of abuse or abandonment, it might be the time to introduce a contact figure who is posited as being in the immediate present (as is a witness figure). The contact figure is available to hold the client in ways to support the distressed areas of the body involved in the expression of grief—the heaving shoulders, chest, and belly—while saying, "I'll help you handle how much grief you feel." This means, "I am here now in the present, helping you handle the pain you feel as you see yourself in your mind's eye in that distressful situation."

At some point, the client might remember that she had hidden in the closet when she had to stay at home by herself at night and might cry the same bitter tears she had cried then. She might say, "I was so alone and there was no one there to protect me if anyone wanted to hurt me."

That is a moment when their evolutionary memory is activating the longing for protection. The therapist could then say, "Would you like to have the contact figure expand their role to be an ideal mother (or ideal father, depending on the gender of the contact figure) who never would have left you alone and would have given you protection when you felt the need of it?"

If the client agrees, the contact figure then says, "I will change my role to that of the ideal mother (or father)." Thus the category of kinship relationship shifts both in the client's mind's eye and in the therapist's mind's eye as the accommodator moves from the designation of contact figure—a peer in the present—to the designation of ideal mother or father—a parent in the past. Also, the time frame shifts and the client can now experience in their mind's body (facilitated by the actual, immediate sensations in their adult body) and imagine in their mind's eye how it would have felt to be held and protected in the arms of a loving parent in that past situation.

With agreement from the client, the ideal mother can say, "If I had been back there then, I would never have left you alone and would have given you protection when you felt the need of it." This is a crucial, ego-preserving statement. In effect the figure is saying, "I am here with you now in your symbolic experience of being parented, but if I had been with you then—as you are imagining it in your mind in conjunction with your memory of what it actually was like when you longed for such protection—this is what I would have done and this is how it would have felt."

This kind of precise clarification—and conscious combination and reorganization of memory and experience, past and present, physical eye and mind's eye, physical body and mind's body—is what it takes to construct a virtual memory of the past. Without such critical attention to consciousness of time and body states, the client would be left with only a literal memory of a happening in the immediate present with the actual people in the room.

There are times when the therapist may perceive that the client has not made the inner shift of taking in the healing scene in terms of the past—for the client seems to be basking in the arms of the ideal parent while the client is in his or her adult consciousness and adult body. That is akin to an adult eating the sweets intended for a child. Though it feels pleasant, the remembered child is not getting the benefits it has waited for and dreamed of for so long. It is impressive and illuminating to see the dramatic changes in the quality of satisfaction that occur when the client is helped to make the necessary shift.

To assist the client in making this shift, the therapist can say, "Can you remember how it felt when you were a child and did not have that protection you so longed for? Try being that child-self in your mind's eye and in your mind's body and let that part of you experience the protection you are getting now in your adult body."

When the shift occurs, it is astonishing to behold. The client's expression as the experience is processed this other way is ecstatic and wonderstruck. Often this is followed by intense grief, for the client has finally felt what was longed for. By seeing the contrast, the client can feel the full impact of what the client had missed. Clients often will say with great amazement and wide eyes, as if they were seeing in their mind's eye how it might have been, "My entire life would have been so different if I had been loved like this when I was a child. The whole world would have looked safe to me and I wouldn't have been scared all the time."

Thus the new memory is already the base for making new predictions about the remembered child's future. Later, the adult, with this virtual memory, may be able to look at the present through the lens of this new past and see less danger and then forecast a future that is less fraught with threat.

A Structure[1]

I will now describe a structure from a workshop for practicing, professional psychotherapists. There was some question as to who would have the next structure. One of the women in the group raised her hand. I looked about and saw that no one else had raised their hand, so I said it was her turn.

She turned red, looked a bit anxious, smiled with a look of surprise and dismay, and said, "I didn't expect to have a turn or that I would be the one to have a turn. I was sure someone else would get it."

Moving directly toward creating the "true scene," I said to her, "If there was a witness here now, he or she would say, 'I see how shocked, surprised, and unsettled you are that you were the one to get the turn.' Is that right?"

"Yes," she said. "Things aren't supposed to come so easily."

"That could be posited as the voice of your truth saying that," I said. "It would say, 'Things aren't supposed to come so easily.'"

"Yes," she said. "You have to work for what you get in this world."

At my suggestion, she enrolled both the witness and the voice of her truth and the scene was created. The witness saw how surprised the woman was, and the woman flushed again remembering that feeling. She said, "I really didn't expect that I would get it."

"That implied a voice of negative prediction that would say, 'You shouldn't really expect to get it,'" I said.

"That's true," she said. "My sister always got there first. My mother preferred her and she was always the favorite."

She said she was an adopted child and her eyes filled with tears as she told how she was taken from her biological mother on the day she was born and given to her adoptive mother.

I asked her if she wanted to enroll her adoptive mother in the structure. She then asked a female group member to play that role and placed her further away in the room.

"My mother never really wanted me or liked me," the client said.

The adoptive mother was instructed to reflect that statement back to her.

Hearing what she said, the client looked forlorn and slumped as she sat on the couch. I suggested that the witness could say, "I see how forlorn or dejected you feel when you remember that your mother never really wanted or liked you." The client agreed.

"How does it feel in your body to hear that?" I asked.

"It hurts in my chest," she said.

I instructed her to contract the muscles around the feeling and see what movement, sounds, or emotions arose from there. She made a sound that gave me the impression of a wounded animal, or a very small, injured child calling weakly and hopelessly for help.

"How does it sound to you, hearing that?" I asked.

"I heard it, but it didn't seem like it was coming from me," she said. "It didn't feel like it came from my body."

I suggested that the feeling was split away from her or she was split from her feelings and that this might be the time to enroll a voice of dissociation, which would say, "Don't feel that it came from your body."

"Yes," she said. "I often dissociate. It is an old habit and problem of mine."

I suggested that it was normal for people to dissociate when encountering feelings that are too powerful or uncomfortable.

Then she looked at the adoptive mother and said she was angry at her for rejecting her and favoring her sister. She spoke forcefully and made gestures emphasizing her aggressive feelings. I asked her if she wanted her negative mother to act as if the anger had struck her. She said yes, and the accommodator did so. The client was pleased to see the effect of her anger, and then directed the accommodator to fall as she aimed blows in her direction. The accommodator fell to the ground.

Seeing that, the client suddenly began to cry. "I feel so alone," she said. "Now I have nobody."

The witness said that she could see how sad the client was now that she had nobody. The client wrapped her arms around her body and tightly gripped her own shoulder and leg, her fingers digging into her flesh.

I asked her if she wanted to have someone other than herself whom she could hold onto like that.

She chose a group member to enroll as a figure she could hold onto. In my mind I was associating that clutching, penetrating gesture with my understanding of the child's wish to be embedded in the flesh of another and I imagined the client was doing it to herself in the absence of having someone to do it with. But at the moment I did not say this to her.

She held on to that figure and began to smile and look happy. The witness duly noted this. Then the client began to move her pelvis. I asked her to find a way to move that part of her body in some way that would produce a satisfying interaction with the role figure. She maneuvered her body and the accommodator's body in an interesting fashion. For a moment it even looked like she was about to separate the legs of the accommodator as if to climb into her. Then she began to rock together with the role player and a look of pleasure and delight came over her face.

"It is as if we are on a boat together and sailing. It feels wonderful," she said. She continued rocking for some time with a look on her face that was nearly ecstatic. I saw a combination of infantile feelings and sensual feelings showing on her body. But mostly I imagined that the water metaphor had to do with the wish to be rocked and be safely intimate with a female figure.

All at once she stopped and said, "It can't last. Nothing good lasts." She separated from the figure and lay crumpled on the couch. The voice of negative prediction was instructed to say, "Nothing good lasts."

The client agreed with that statement and her body got more and more shrunken. She said, "I feel like I want to shrink until I disappear."

I told her to follow that feeling and give movement to it. She wound up in a little ball.

"I feel a tension in my throat," she said.

"Tighten the muscles around that tension and see what comes of it," I said. "Make the sounds that would seem to come from there." Once more she made those helpless sounds, this time they escalated until she began to cry with bitter desperation.

"Do you want a contact figure to hold you while you cry?" I asked softly. This is an intervention I often make when there is deep grief that seems unbounded and without sufficient physical support to handle it.

She said, "No, I have to be alone. I have to take care of myself."

This attitude was underlined by the voice of her truth.

She stretched out on the couch. She was limp and looked helplessly upwards as if to an absent god. Once again her pelvis began to move and she reached up helplessly.

I said, "What do you need that would bring some satisfying interaction?"

She said, "There is nothing and no one that I can turn to."

When people make that kind of statement I assume they have projected satisfaction somewhere and I asked her if she had such thoughts. After some time, she said that in the afterlife she knew she would be happy, but not in this one.

I said, "Create a place in the room where that afterlife condition would be, and then place someone there to be the voice or the spokesperson of that place." She chose another woman in the group as that figure.

The client said that in this place she knew she would find peace. The accommodator was instructed to say, "Here you can find peace."

On hearing that, the client began to cry, saying, "There I wouldn't have to do anything to get things. I would just have to be myself."

The role player said back to her, "Here you wouldn't have to do anything to get things, you would just have to be yourself."

I asked her if she wanted to be in contact with that figure. She said yes, but looked puzzled. She said, "Does this mean that I am suicidal or that I want to be dead?"

I reassured her, saying that she could be in contact with that figure, knowing that she had projected peace and relief there, and that it would be a symbolic process and not an expression of a wish for literal death.

She asked the role-player to sit on the couch and then moved her and herself until she found a way to climb into her lap, pulling the arms of the accommodator around her.

Being held in that position brought up a great well of sadness, longing, and relief, and she began to cry deeply in a way that was very moving to the group as several members began to weep.

While sobbing, she began to clutch desperately at the figure and at an appropriate moment I suggested that perhaps the wish that had shown up before was again being expressed and that she should try to squeeze that figure as tightly as she wished. She said she was afraid to do that, thinking it would hurt the role-player. It was not that she wished to hurt the role-player, but that she felt the wish to clutch was so great she was certain it would be too much to bear.

The voice of her truth could then say, "Your need to clutch someone so tightly is too much for anyone to bear."

She cried desperately at that and buried her head in the shoulder of the accommodator.

I asked her if she wanted that figure to say that she could bear how much the client was clutching her. On hearing the figure say this, the client dared to hold the figure tighter, and her crying this time included the relief that bespoke the possibility of having the new license.

Here I thought it useful to point out to her that this was no longer merely a figure from the next life but was functioning more in the style of an ideal mother. I suggested that we change the enrollment of this figure into the ideal mother category, for that was what the client had wished for in the first place although she had not expected to experience such a mother until the next life.

She agreed and began to feel the pleasure and relief that had surfaced with the earlier figure of contact, but this time she was not holding the figure as if to ride on the waves but clearly as a little child holds onto a mother.

After some time she said, "This won't last either."

Here was the latest expression of the pattern established early in her history—that all good things come swiftly to an end. The voice of negative prediction said, "This won't last either," and she agreed with it.

I thought this would be the appropriate time to provide an antidote. I felt sure that her life had been one long, continuous series of losses, the root of which was the first loss of being plucked too early from her biological mother. Therefore I suggested that she construct this figure as an ideal biological mother who would not have given her up for adoption as her original mother had, but would have raised her herself.

The remembrance of the pleasure of a few moments before, coupled with the possibility that it could last with this ideal mother who would never have given her up, lit up her face. Clearly, this new thought presented hope and she began to return to the peace and satisfaction she had felt when she first contacted that figure as someone representing the next world.

To cement the connection between the two images, I asked her if she would like to hear her ideal mother say, "I would make you feel as wonderful as you expected to feel in the next world." The client agreed and thus linked the two experiences.

Now she settled into the embrace of the mother. Her breathing became deeper and slower, and her body visibly relaxed.

She said, "I could stay here forever."

I asked her if she wanted to hear from her ideal mother that she could stay there forever, meaning that on the feeling level she need never leave this state of bliss with the mother.

The ideal mother said, "You can symbolically stay here forever."

I asked the client to make an image of herself at that age, including all the blissful feelings she was having, and then to make another image of the ideal mother providing those feelings. That way, she could internalize that composite image within herself so that when the structure was over it would not be as if the ideal mother was leaving. Her pilot could note that the structure had come to an end.

She stayed some time in the arms of the ideal mother, consciously establishing and recording the feeling of acceptance and bliss. She said she wanted one more thing. She wanted to hear the ideal mother say that the client didn't have to do anything special to have attention or have her needs met, but that the mother would be there for the client just as she was. The ideal mother said that, and the client smiled with her eyes closed, nodding her head as if saying "Yes" as she included that feeling in the image she created.

After some moments she opened her eyes, having the look of peace and satisfaction that people have when they have come to the end of a structure. I asked her if she had the images firmly in place.

She said, "Yes."

I asked her if she was ready to de-role the figures.

She said she was. She first de-roled all the negative figures and ended with the de-roling of the ideal mother.

The accommodators returned to their places and thus the structure came to an end.

Afterward the client told me how much she appreciated the work. Although it was only one structure, it did give her new perspective, and the healing, reconditioning nature of the antidote gave her some of the means, as well as the hope, that she could effect positive changes.

Some Personal History

Diane and I grew up never taking things for granted. We both wanted to understand how things came out the way they did. Diane never took other people's explanations for how things were at face value. She had to find for herself why this way and not that way was more or less useful in all things. She was never satisfied to simply repeat what she was told and would never accept a "fact" until she understood the reality of it for herself.

I was very curious as a child. I would take things apart so that I could learn how the parts related to one another and then see how to put them together again.

These inborn attitudes directly influenced the development of the essential features of Psychomotor. We never began with pre-formed theoretical or technical assumptions. Each step in the evolution of the process was the outcome of this attitude in tandem with the information we gathered in reports people gave us in our early psychomotor and dance groups. We also learned much from the experiences we personally had in the exercises we devised. Only after we saw what worked and understood how it worked did we formalize it into a theory or a technique. We tried never to take anything for granted.

We believed people had the right to know, experience, and accept whatever emotions or impulses came into their bodies. I am sure that attitude came from our dance backgrounds. But we discovered by trial and error what made it possible for people to accept and feel better about what came welling up from their insides.

We met at Bennington College in 1949, where we were both on dance scholarships. The educational policy at Bennington, the learning atmosphere, and encouragement from faculty to follow our own bent were major influences in the development of our own attitudes and views on life.

After leaving the dance mecca of New York City (to better raise our growing daughter), we opened a dance studio in a Boston suburb and took upon ourselves the task of redefining dance. We looked at every aspect of dance technique and examined whether it was the best possible way to get knowledge across.

We continued in that spirit as Diane taught dance at Wheaton College in Massachusetts and also at Sargent College of Boston University and Emerson College in Boston. I also taught at Wheaton and then at Emerson College, where I became a tenured associate professor and was appointed head of the Dance Division of the Theater Arts Department.

Being dancers, we knew how good it felt to be totally integrated and move exactly and directly as we felt. Although our dance backgrounds were quite different, we entirely believed in the value of emotionally based dance and were devoted to living the truth of our inner experience through movement. Dance was not superficial, ornamental, or frivolous for us. It was—as it was for artists like our teachers, Martha Graham and Jose Limon—a precious art form that we loved because it brought us exquisite awareness of life and was a medium that communicated life's deepest meanings to both dancer and audience.

When Psychomotor was not even a gleam in our eyes, we were busy developing exercises for our students so that they might better improve their technique, creativity, individuality, and emotional expression. Those exercises had a profound effect on their lives as well as on their dancing skills.

Our intentions, as artists, were to find ways for our dance and choreography to communicate to audiences more precisely what we intended. This desire led us to explore the fundamental relationship between emotion and motion. We wanted to find out how we moved, what different ways of movement there were, and what moving in those different ways communicated to and affected the viewer. We wanted to find out how our emotions became actions and how they affected our bodies if they did not. We looked for answers as we examined our own dance process and watched our students' performances and choreographic experiments. We had endless discussions about the nature of all things. From constant observation of emotional action we hypothesized the cerebral organizations that must underlie them—even then trying to make a model of the brain from a deep understanding of how the body worked.

Teaching these theories, exercises, and techniques to large numbers of students and particularly to members of our performing company had important results. It gave our students the capacity to be more relaxed as they expressed themselves freely, and it developed in us a fine sensitivity to determine emotional states from facial expression, posture, gesture, and movement. It also taught us to recognize the disparity between what people verbally told us about their feelings and what our sensitivity to their bodily state told us nonverbally. We were fascinated with these discrepancies and grew more interested in the path of personal development in preference to the path of artistic development.

After seven years of exploration, we began to call what we had discovered Psychomotor therapy, for we had led our first structures, and the unexpected journey to the domain of psychotherapy and personal growth had begun.

Back to the Present

People come to Pesso Boyden System Psychomotor to work on many problems, including depression, anxiety, abuse, addiction, and problems with work; as well as crisis situations such as divorce; death of a spouse, parent, sibling, or child; loss of job or home; or moving to a different country or culture. To benefit from PBSP, a client must be motivated and able to respond to symbolic images and situations, must have access to emotions and body sensations, and must be able to distinguish between role-play and reality.

Certification Training in PBSP for Practicing Psychotherapists

Leading and helping create effective and believable structures is not a casual or simple undertaking. It takes much training, discipline, and the good and timely use of a large number of theoretical and technical procedures.

When we interview a practicing psychotherapist who is a candidate for training in Pesso Boyden System Psychomotor, we look for someone who is mature; in touch with his or her own feelings, trusting of his or her emotions and organismic/emotional intelligence; unafraid of strong emotions in others; capable of teaching a group; and who also is empathic, creative, playful, realistically optimistic, and protective of others' rights. A candidate also must have a sense of inclusiveness, the capacity to learn, a sense of humor, respect for life and others, and a good sense of boundaries.

SHORT-TERM TRAINING FOR MEMBERS OF THE HELPING PROFESSIONS

Training in PBSP elements has been found to be useful for medical doctors, teachers, social workers, counselors, nurses, occupational therapists, physical therapists, and others. PBSP theories and exercises are valuable by themselves without direct application in structures. Workshops are held during the year at Strolling Woods, New Hampshire and in other locations throughout Europe and the United States.

---

1. Descriptions of structures by two other authors can be found in *The Fragile Bond* by Augustus Y. Napier, New York: Harper & Row, 1988, pages 21-33; and *A Time to Say Goodbye* by Mary Goulding, Watsonville, Calif.: Paper Mache Press, 1996, pages 121-123.

Chapter Nine

Hakomi Integrative Somatics:
Hands-On Psychotherapy

Pat Ogden

EDITOR'S NOTE: *Hakomi Integrated Somatics came into being because Pat Ogden had an extensive bodywork background and knew the value of somatic experiencing, especially through the use of touch. She took the principles of Hakomi, which she had helped develop and popularize, and channeled them into a form of work that has profound implications for the healing power of touching and being touched.*

Pat has always been one of the unifying members of our field. Her straightforward kindness, her keen curiosity, and her ability to study and appreciate people's differences has made her one of our finest networkers. Her focus on professional standards, deep respect for clients, and clinical accuracy has also made her a powerful spokesperson for the use of touch in psychotherapy in general and in somatic work in particular. She is a dear friend and a brilliant colleague, and I feel proud to include her work in this volume. This chapter showcases one of the first forms to grow out of another body-centered form, while at the same time remaining philosophically and professionally related to its predecessor.

INTRODUCTION

*T*he union of bodywork with psychotherapy is a complex and multi-faceted endeavor, as rich with healing potential as it is fraught with complications and hazards. In the hope of avoiding the hazards (unworkable transference, overt or covert sexual abuse, misinterpretation of the intention of touch, real or perceived boundary violations, to name a few) some legislative bodies have banned the use of touch in psychotherapy practice alto-gether, and so have sacrificed the unique benefits of this synthesis. When psychological and physical issues are addressed concurrently through bodywork, physical changes are more lasting, and information is often revealed that would have remained unconscious in conventional therapy. Clients report feeling more integration between body and mind, a fuller sense of embodying all parts of themselves. Yet, while the advantages can be profound and enduring, the blending of these two disciplines is delicate work, requiring more knowledge and skill than does either of the two separately. Over the last twenty years, Hakomi Integrative Somatics has developed a synthesis of psychotherapy and body therapy, including movement, body awareness, and hands-on bodywork. In this ongoing process, we have gleaned numerous insights, techniques, and maps that speak to the effective melding of the two distinct approaches to healing. What follows is the story of how the integration of hands-on bodywork and psychotherapy came about, including a presentation of our guiding philosophy and a session description to demonstrate how the work is applied.

THE BEGINNING SYNTHESIS

In the 1970s, prevailing therapeutic practices had psychotherapy separated from hands-on bodywork. As both therapist and bodyworker, I found that I maintained essentially a distinct private practice in each discipline, with very little overlap. In addition, my own personal therapy consisted of psychotherapy one week and bodywork the next. I remember that when emotionally charged memories or autonomic nervous system activation (such as sweating, trembling, or increased heart rate) surfaced during bodywork, my practitioner and I joked that now I would have something to talk to my therapist about. But by the time I saw my therapist, neither these memories nor the activation were accessible experientially, and the possibility of discovering their significance was lost. Conversely, during psychotherapy I noticed various physical postures that were rich with emotional content, particularly a mobilization in my chest that occurred automatically when I felt insecure or threatened. I felt keenly how my physical structure held in place the pride and defensiveness I was working so hard to relinquish in psychotherapy sessions. But by the time I got to my bodyworker, the mindbody connection was no longer salient. As I struggled on my own to bring my emotions and belief systems together with the energy, structure, and movement patterns in my body, I began to ask: why not forge these two disciplines into a simultaneous process?

A prime opportunity to experiment with just such a synthesis soon presented itself. A counselor at the University of Colorado requested that her clients see me for bodywork. These clients, all participants in either private or group therapy for pre-orgasmic women, became among my first teachers in blending bodywork with psychotherapy. As I worked to help these young women reconnect with their body sensation and energy through hands-on work, I found that our goals could not be accomplished without addressing the psychological components that sustained their disconnection from their bodies.

My task became one of attempting to translate the techniques used to process psychological material into techniques that would interface with bodywork. The first technique I applied was simply making verbal contact with the emotions, memories, and thoughts that emerged spontaneously on the table. I had learned the art of bodywork as a primarily nonverbal activity; massage and deep-tissue work were performed in silence, with perhaps a few verbal cues from the practitioner or reports from the client. Reflecting feelings back to my client and commenting on the changes I tracked in the body throughout the bodywork process encouraged awareness, as well as emotional release, and helped reveal patterns and beliefs that had been unconscious.

At first, I approached these sessions as I had been taught in my bodywork training, by making my own decisions about where to begin and how to proceed with bodywork. The pelvis, full of both tension and numbness, was my prime target, for I figured we could get the most benefit from working in this area. How wrong I was. My clients would return the following week, often with no improvement, sometimes with increased fear and dissociation. Soon, I abandoned the part of my bodywork training that said "the practitioner should know what to do," and began seeking specific and precise guidance *from my clients* as to the direction and type of bodywork indicated. I asked clients to sense the body, to feel where was the right place to be touched, and to tell me how they wanted to be touched. The effects of facilitating the client's guidance were remarkable. These women slowly went from bodily dissociation to curiosity and interest, from fear to the feelings of dignity, empowerment, and satisfaction that come from being in control of where and how one is touched. I soon discovered that most of my clients had been sexually or physically abused, so the choice about how they were touched had been violated. The bodywork session became an arena to restore this simple choice to its rightful owner.

As these explorations progressed, my clients and I discovered that a physical correlate exists for every psychological phenomenon, and vice versa. For each memory, thought, image, or emotion, a corresponding body sensation, movement, or posture can be felt. And, for every body sensation, movement, or posture, a related memory, emotion, image, or thought can be revealed. The bodymind interface became more and more apparent, as did the interventions suitable for exploring it. The work became highly experimental and mindful as we delved into the intricacies of bringing this interface to consciousness where learning and change, both psychological and physical, could happen.

During this time period, I was an apprentice to Ron Kurtz, who was to become the founder of the Hakomi Institute in 1980. As a founding member of the Institute myself, my desire was to blend the Hakomi methodology with bodywork. The Hakomi Method is a form of body-centered psychotherapy based upon self-study in mindfulness. We teach clients to become mindful, to turn attention inward so that they can notice the spontaneous emergence of feelings, thoughts, body patterns, and images. With a client in this state of heightened awareness, we instigate "little experiments" in a process of self-discovery. A phrase such as, "You are safe here," may be stated by the therapist, and the client, in mindfulness, notices her automatic reaction to this sentence. These automatic reactions reveal valuable information about the state of the client's internal psychophysical landscape. The techniques of bodywork soon became a source of these little experiments. Instead of employing bodywork to change the structure, relax the body, or accomplish any of the other usual goals of hands-on work, the purpose became one of simply bringing inner experience to consciousness. I began to ask my clients to "notice what happens as I work on this tension." I asked this question as I worked on shoulder tension in one of these early clients. As the bodywork brought about relaxation in her shoulders, she remembered being sexually molested by her father and wanting to push him away with her arms, but stifling the impulse. The connection was made between her tense shoulders and a long-held defensive impulse, which is valuable information in effecting release of the tension and restoring an active defensive response. I could actively evoke psychological issues relevant to a particular body pattern, through hands-on work with the body pattern itself, by setting up the bodywork *as an experiment* for self-study. This technique of experimentation became essential to the synthesis of bodywork and psychotherapy. It was a most exciting discovery, and is a major cornerstone of Hakomi Integrative Somatics, reflecting a guiding philosophy at the root of the method.

A GUIDING PHILOSOPHY

This guiding philosophy holds three points to be essential: one, that the practice of activating the healing potential is one of honoring its mystery, without the need to know in advance the details of how this mystery will unfold; two, that we can trust the organism's capacity for self-regulation, meaning that we, as living systems, *form* our behavior and perceptions in accordance with available information, and by the same stroke, *change* our perceptions and behaviors in response to new information; and three, that we assist clients best in their healing process by helping them bring mindful attention to their own inner world, so they can perceive how they organize their own experience in the present moment. In this section I will elaborate on the interrelationship between these three points and try to illustrate how they are woven into the actual style of working we use in Hakomi Integrative Somatics.

Activating healing powers involves guiding a client to turn inward toward her own true experience, with trust that the mystery of healing will evolve, which it does in surprising, unpredictable, and often wondrous ways. It requires faith: Faith in the unique and intelligent unfolding of each human being. Faith that, given the right circumstances, each one of us will gladly progress in her own evolution towards wholeness. Faith that we hold a healing power within, sometimes hidden, but ever-present. The job of the therapist, then, is to help this inner wisdom unveil itself, rather than to provide advice or answers. In this way, a client learns, not to depend on an external authority for her own evolution, but to tap the resource of healing capacity inside herself.

The job of the therapist becomes both simpler and more complex, simultaneously. Simpler because it is no longer essential for the therapist to know the solutions to the multitude of ailments that clients present. With skillful guidance, clients will find their own answers and solutions. What a relief! Yet, it's also more complex, because guiding clients inward to their own healing potential requires subtle, sophisticated, and refined techniques, and lots of experience.

This experience and skill are reflected in the therapist's ability to discern a conditioned response from true bodymind wisdom. Our bodies and minds will develop patterns over time that may on the surface appear spontaneous, organic, and intelligent. For example, as a result of bodywork, a client may dissolve into a cathartic release, both emotional and physical. At first glance, the expression appears to reflect a healthy release. Upon deeper examination, however, we may discover that this pattern is more the result of a cycle of activation and release that repeats itself periodically, but does not actually resolve. The system enters into a habit of building up emotional and autonomic nervous system charge, which demands eventual expression, but this expression only serves to strengthen the pattern itself rather than to heal it. This particular phenomenon is a common response to trauma. One widely experienced symptom of post-traumatic stress is the inability to modulate arousal levels, and therefore frequently feeling overwhelmed by the intensity of one's own activation. Knowing this to be true, the therapist can watch for the beginning signals of such arousal (skin color change, increased heart rate, slight anxiety) and use the bodywork to titrate the client's response so that such energy can be expressed without becoming overwhelming.

In any case, the overall approach remains one of the client signaling the direction of the process, through words, affect, and physical patterns, while the therapist works to recognize and follow these signals, even if they are faint or obtuse. A signal may be as subtle as a slight movement in the neck, a fleeting comment, or facial expression. In one instance, a client complained of all-over tension and stress, and in the course of conversation mentioned going home to her parents for the holidays. A barely discernible frown appeared momentarily on her brow. I sensed the relevance of the signal (the thought of going home, accompanied by the frown) and gently brought my client's attention to it. When she resonated with curiosity and interest, the exploration began. The signal was used as a jumping-off place for deepening my client's level of awareness, to delve into her unconscious where the healing potential lies.

Once this deepening process begins, the therapist must then allow and direct the client toward discovering for herself, through her own experience, the significance of the signal. Restraint is called for on the part of the therapist, who must refrain from interpreting or explaining the signal, even though she may have a good idea of what it implies. Rather than providing the answers, the therapist constructs experiments to help the client learn from the signal. This initiates a process that is based in the body and in experience rather than in rationale. In the instance mentioned above, I asked my client to mindfully notice what happened in her body when she thought about going home. The frown came back, and the tension increased, particularly in her belly. (This client also harbored a peptic ulcer.) As we began the bodywork on her belly (the client's choice), childhood memories emerged of trying so hard to be "good" but never feeling she had achieved the goal. This young woman, raped at age eight, was a perfectionist, never satisfied until she was at the top of every class, and even then she gleaned no real nourishment from her accomplishments. We found that the initial signal was connected to a deep-seated belief of not being "good enough," a belief activated more strongly at the prospect of returning to her family home. This belief, previously ambiguous and defended, proved to be the psychological key to her stress and tension. Her body's fleeting frown had given us the clue on how to find that key.

Through the therapeutic process, a client is taught mindfulness as a tool for her own self-discovery. The qualities of mindfulness, as we teach it, include focusing one's attention on the spontaneous emergence of such things as feelings, thoughts, memories, images, and body patterns. These phenomena are ongoing occurrences within every human being, but are often unconscious. A client learns how to interpret them as signals of underlying issues, and to use them as a springboard to deepen awareness of experience. This style of working reflects the basic tenet of Hakomi's information theory (self-regulation), which holds that a living system will spontaneously reorganize in the direction of health when enough of the right kind of information becomes available. Healing potential is activated by bringing previously unconscious information to consciousness. This is why so much emphasis is placed upon *awareness* in the overall set of techniques and approaches that this method employs.

For example, in mindful attention to her own inner experience, my client made the connections between her tension and her belief; memories and body organization became clear, and she felt the emotional pain of this belief. Eventually, she was able to appreciate, through her experience rather than her cognition, that this belief was not true. This was "new" information for her; she had previously been operating from the premise that she was not quite "enough" as she was. As she had the inner sense, in therapy, of trusting her own sufficiency, her tension naturally lessened, as did the extreme pressure she had placed on herself to achieve. This is the essence of self-regulation, which holds that a person will naturally adapt both perceptions and behaviors in accordance with the information from inner and outer environments.

In the instance of working with clients suffering the effects of trauma, we can especially see the need for a skillful blending of encouragement for the client's process along with informed guidance from the therapist. In one case, a client began to exhibit a symptom of slight trembling in his chest, along with increased heart rate (both common signals of autonomic nervous system activation). He also felt an anxiety and a sense of imminent danger that he feared would turn into full-blown panic, as it often had before. On the basis of my knowledge and experience of teaching clients to modulate their arousal levels, I asked him to just notice what happened if he kept his attention on this trembling, rather than focusing on the anxiety. To his surprise, the trembling spread to his arms and his anxiety lowered. This client had suffered post-traumatic stress (he had served in the Vietnam war) and had till now felt at the mercy of his own over-activation, which usually manifested as panic attacks. Through his own mindful attention to staying with his body sensation rather than the anxiety, my client gained an empowering tool for modulating his own arousal, thus restoring a self-regulatory capacity that he had lost.

In its natural state, the self-regulation mechanism is fluid and flexible, effecting creative and progressive adaptation to variables in a unique and individual manner. Our perceptions are altered as incoming information is received, and subsequent behaviors are also modified. It's as simple as when a small child who wants a toy yanks it forcefully from his playmate's hands. The parent disapproves, his playmate cries, and eventually the child adapts to the displeasure and distress by modifying his behavior. It's a response that chooses his parent's approval, his playmate's well-being, and his own good inner feeling over his first impulse. If all goes well, he learns to treat others kindly, and to expect the same. He continues to adjust his perceptions and behavior based on his outer environment and his inner well-being. His self-regulation mechanism is functioning effectively.

CORE ORGANIZERS: A MAP FOR SELF-STUDY

In the course of our development, we form habitual, automatic attitudes (both physical and psychological) by which we generate patterns of experience in the world. This is a natural function of what we call our "core organizers." The core organizers are a medium through which we perceive and understand. We notice, absorb, digest, and understand stimuli from our external and internal environments through these various aspects of being. These core organizers *organize* fragments of our experiences into coherent gestalts; they take over the function of doing this for us automatically, usually without our conscious awareness. They are a fundamental way in which we self-regulate. We need them to do a good job for us, to function effectively and creatively, but unfortunately this is not always the case. In another scenario, perhaps with a somewhat harsh-mannered parent, the above child could interpret the entire incident as meaning he is a "bad" person for yanking away his friend's toy. Instead of his body and psyche being relaxed, his belly could tighten with this belief; he may have self-punitive thoughts, and negative feelings. Instead of freely giving and receiving kindness and respect, his experience is clouded with confusion and painful feelings about himself. From the conviction that he is a "bad person," he develops unsatisfactory patterns of relationship with others. His ability to creatively respond and adapt is hindered by this belief about himself.

A belief like this is not simply a construct of the mind; it is accompanied by distinctive physical and emotional patterns, in the form of bodily tensions, constrictions of movement, and recurring sensations, images, thoughts, and feelings. These patterns, composed of our core organizers, are seldom conscious, dwelling instead in the deeply unconscious and involuntary recesses of our internal organization. From there they exert a major influence over our belief systems, with the complexity of feedback dynamics at the bodymind interface. The therapeutic key becomes one of helping this critical information from within become accessible to the conscious bodymind, where it can be examined, understood, and resolved.

CORE ORGANIZERS

COMPLEX EXPERIENCES

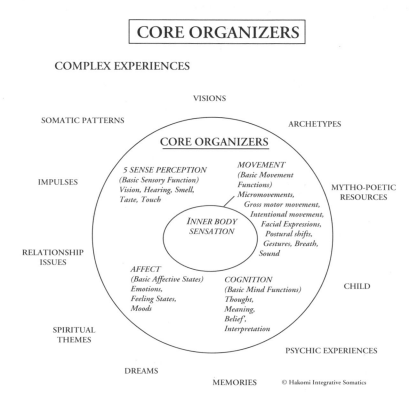

The quality of our life, and the creativity of our self-regulation, are strongly influenced, if not determined, by our ability to be connected to our core organizers and to respond appropriately to the information they furnish. We illustrate the dynamic relations among the core organizers by the use of a map, with sensation at the center (see Core Organizers chart). In order to study the organization of our internal experience, we utilize a model, wherein five basic organizers are identified, as described below. The relationships among the core organizers are not linear, but quite complex, with intricate feedback dynamics among them.

1. *Inner body sensation* refers to the actual physical feeling that is created as the various systems of the body monitor and give feedback about inner states. The realm of sensation extends to the proprioception of the cells and tissues of the body, to a sensing of its structure, energy, and function, and to how the process of being alive feels in the body. Inner body sensation pertains to the flow of physical feelings that are continually created by movement of all sorts within the body: movement of muscles, ligaments bone, fluids, organs, breath, biochemicals, and energy.

2. *Five-sense perception* refers to the basic inner and outer sensory functions: smell, taste, sight, touch, and hearing give information about the outer world, and internally-generated smells, tastes, images, and so forth contain information about the inner world.

3. *Movement* refers to the actual movement of the body and can range from micromovements to gross motor movement, including posture change, facial expression, gesture, locomotion, trembling, twitches, and so on.

4. *Affective states* include emotions such as fear or joy, along with more subtle nuances of feeling tones and mood, such as a sense of peace or slight irritation.

5. *Cognition*, the functioning of the mind, contains thoughts, meanings, our interpretation of stimuli, and beliefs about ourselves and the world. Cognition can range from relatively innocuous thoughts like "I think I'll go shopping" to charged beliefs that influence the overall quality of our lives, such as, "I don't deserve to be alive," "I'm not good enough," or "I'm a bad person."

The core organizers relate to one another as they continuously communicate with and influence each other. In optimal functioning, they are congruous; they go together, yet are open and responsive to change and variables. They are not a closed, fixed system but rather an alive, fluctuating, mutable system, like the movement of life itself. When we have full access to each core organizer, and when they are appropriately connected and vital within us, we experience integration, creativity, aliveness, and wholeness. When our feelings match our thoughts, when the information we receive from our senses is congruous with our sensation and movement, we feel at one with ourselves. Our path is clear. Our inner experience constitutes an integrated whole, and our behavior emerges from a sense of alignment and integrity, appropriate to our current inner and outer reality.

You will notice on the Core Organizers chart that this map also includes what we call "complex experiences," which are represented outside the circle of core organizers. Complex experiences are constructed by the five core organizers working in concert. For example, a memory (a "complex experience") occurs through the interaction of affect, body sensation, thoughts, images, and so on. If a client talks about a memory, we can discover how the core organizers give rise to the memory in the present moment by asking a question like, "How do you experience the memory right now?" or "What happens inside as you remember this event?" The client may say, "As I picture my mother, I feel sad, my chest tightens, I remember focusing on her red face and fighting the impulse to run away." In this way, we elucidate the dynamics between the complex experience (the memory or dream, issue, theme, idea, etc.) and the core organizers.

Sensation is our body's primary language, which we experience through an awareness commonly called the "felt sense." Whenever we experience any one of the other four core organizers, we have an accompanying body sensation. If we have an emotional response, we can feel it in our inner sensation; if we move, the movement itself creates a body sensation; as we have thoughts their impact is registered in this deeply instinctual aspect of the body's knowledge system, and so on. We can experience an emotion without a thought, but we cannot experience an emotion without a corresponding sensation in the body. Sensation is a link that connects all other aspects. It's the hub of the wheel. Because of this it can have an especially *integrative* influence in the overall scheme of relations among the core organizers.

It is important to understand the distinction between awareness of sensation and awareness of other core organizers like cognition and affect.

The sensate realm is perceived and described through its characteristically primal and distinctly physical qualities, like trembly, warm, buzzy, tingling, numb, clammy, energized, etc. In this way, it differs from the realm of cognition and meaning, which would be described with words like safe, unsupported, important, etc., and it differs from the realm of affect, described with words like sad, angry, calm, joyful.

Teaching awareness of sensation is an indispensable tool for supporting and expanding one's connection to the body and for reinstating healthy functioning among the core organizers. If we spend enough time in sensation, we can begin to have a direct perception (the "felt sense") of the movement of our own intelligent life energy, which is both vital and informative. Through simple awareness of sensation we often feel closer to a sense of who we really are beyond the conditioning and limitations we have learned. We gain access to the myriad ways of knowing that are not rooted in cognition, but in a deep body knowing, an inner knowing that is informed by sensation. Tapping into sensation may access inner states that existed before self-identity and the formation of psychological beliefs, or that continue to exist beyond these realms. In addition, awareness of sensation in indispensable in learning to modulate our own arousal, a skill and function so often lost as a result of trauma. As in the above example of the Vietnam veteran, cultivating the ability to experience pure sensation, distinct from emotion, is an empowering tool in healing traumatic response. When we work to integrate the raw data from the sensation level of our experience with other aspects of our overall reality, we develop a strong resource for knowing and expressing who we are and a strong resource for healing.

DISSOCIATION: RELATIONAL DYNAMICS AMONG THE CORE ORGANIZERS

We can utilize the map of core organizers to talk about dissociation as the outcome of a profoundly disturbed relation with or among the core organizers. Some instances of dissociation are common and natural in human beings. For example, we may dissociate mildly from sensation when we're driving along the highway, listening to a favorite piece of music, fantasizing, or daydreaming. Alternately, we might dissociate away from our thoughts and emotions and really appreciate the fresh information our senses deliver to us as we watch the beautiful scenery in an engrossing movie. These usually harmless forms of dissociation can actually enrich our experience, allowing us to bring a higher degree of focus to a singular aspect of our experience, enabling us to expand a specific perception. However, when we engage in forms of dissociation with the intention to distort perception, and when this form of dissociating becomes strongly fixed into unconscious patterns, we can disrupt the optimal relationship among core organizers, thus diminishing the overall quality of our experience.

An example of this is seen in the "over-achiever" client I mentioned earlier who took certain situations she encountered as a child to mean that she was not "good enough." One significant memory that surfaced in therapy was of coming home from kindergarten with a painting she was proud of, which her parents then criticized. Immediately prior to the encounter with her parents, she had felt a sense of congruity among her core organizers — a feeling of joy and confidence, a thought about what a great picture she had made, a sensation of excited anticipation in her body as she rushed home to show her painting to her parents. As she experienced their criticism, her core organizers shifted. Recalling the scene in therapy, she felt an immediate hardening in her chest, a sinking feeling in her belly, confusion in her feelings and thoughts as her own perceptions were so unkindly challenged approval she needed so much. She remembered concealing her hurt feelings, pretending the criticism did not bother her, and tightening her chest and belly as she resolved to make a better picture next time. A pattern became more fixed as her core organizers conspired to support a bodymind conviction that she needed to try harder to be good enough. The pattern manifested in the relationship among core organizers: the concealment of feelings, the rigidity of opinion, the tightening of muscles. This event was one of many that led to a lifelong pattern of striving, characterized by dissociating from sensation and emotions.

The above example illustrates the typical pattern of a "developmental wound," expressed by a particular belief ("I'm not good enough") that pertains to a developmental learning task (confidence in oneself) that was obstructed or arrested in childhood. Interference with effective learning of these tasks can occur through unfavorable family and social dynamics, and through the meaning or belief systems an individual develops out of these dynamics. Developmental tasks present themselves naturally as we mature and contain such things as: learning to get our needs met, to be autonomous, to esteem ourselves and hold ourselves as worthy. When there is an obstacle to the effective learning of these tasks, the functioning of the core organizers is disrupted, leading to patterns of dissociation.

More pronounced habits of dissociation can be caused by traumatic events, arising out of situations which are perceived as life-threatening. Such events cause a person to instinctively mobilize a tremendous amount of physical and energetic resources for the purpose of self-protective action, typically called the "fight or flight" response. If it is not possible to escape or overcome the source of the trauma, the next line of defense is called "freezing," which requires profound dissociation from various core organizers. For example, a child who is beaten or sexually abused may "leave" the body—dissociate nearly completely from the physical sensations—so she or he does not feel the pain. When a painful stimulus is greater than the individual's ability to tolerate, understand and integrate, a natural and salubrious response is to dissociate from feeling the full impact of the provocation. This happens frequently through dissociating from body sensation, as in the case of a friend of mine who walked away from a car accident, only to discover a few hours later that he was severely injured.

Dissociation also occurs among other core organizers. An abused child may dissociate from the meaning of the situation (that her perpetrator is wrong for abusing her, for example). Or, she may be "frozen," unable, literally, to move. She may be numb to the horror, fear, and emotional pain of the abuse, cutting off her affective response. She may alter the perception of her five senses to cope, like a client of mine who hallucinated her perpetrator as a cartoon character. In this "buffered" condition of dissociation, there is the chance for the organism to more slowly absorb the effects of the stimulus, bit by bit and over time, especially if there is proper support in the environment, such as someone to turn to for help. Gradually, as the person assimilates what has happened, the feeling returns to the body, the emotions are felt, the true meaning of the situation is experienced and understood, and movement and sensual perception are restored. In a flexible system and supportive environment, dissociation is only temporary.

This innate mechanism of dissociation is nature's way of providing us with an extraordinary means with which to cope with overwhelming stimuli. Trying to assimilate such painful, staggering, and complex experiences, such as a traumatic event, immediately or all at once could be extremely fragmenting and disintegrating to the system. The disadvantage is that dissociation often turns from a temporary coping mechanism into a lifelong pattern of disconnection. The same abused child who failed to comprehend the meaning relevant to the abusive situation may exhibit an overall diminished capacity for reasoning, and a diminished emotional capacity that extends to all of her intimate relations.

A main method of our therapy is to first discover patterns of dissociation, through the study of the core organizers and then to help a client learn to "reassociate," to reestablish the appropriate functioning of and connectedness among core organizers. The dynamics of dissociation are multifaceted, and take a variety of forms which overlap and feed into each other. Following is an enumeration of the most commonly seen patterns of dissociation.

1. We can disconnect from a particular core organizer, severing awareness of that aspect, restricting its function and expression. In this dynamic, some other core organizer becomes dominant and the individual quite often depends upon it and uses it excessively, to the exclusion of the others. A common example is that a person who is disconnected from emotional experience may become quite skilled cognitively and analytically.

A variant of this kind of dissociation is sometimes found among those with a special attunement to their physicality, such as athletes, dancers, movement therapists, and bodyworkers; we may allow the sensation or movement of the body to become dominant. We may be exquisitely connected to our sensation, but *not* to the accompanying emotional quality, for instance. We can actually use our ability to be in contact with sensation to dissociate from other core organizers, thus limiting the full richness of our own capacity to perceive and experience. We usually think of movement as something that will bring us into deeper contact with ourselves and our feelings, and I think that in general this is true. However, I recently spoke with a friend who had done an improvisational dance with someone she did not really want to be physically close to. She talked about getting into the dance, and cutting off her feelings of aversion, overriding her boundaries through accentuating her movement. She consciously used movement to disengage from other core organizers, but regretted it later and walked away from the dance with a diminished sense of connection with her feelings and her sense of self.

2. The core organizers don't relate to one another in a coherent or sensible way. Peter Levine calls this form of dissociation "undercoupling" when evidenced in trauma survivors. The channels of communication among them may be too open, too fluid, so that impressions flow too easily and chaotically. When sense perception doesn't adequately inform affect, when affect doesn't inform movement, and so on, then the person's experience is incongruous and actions may be inconsistent. When a person smiles, all the while telling you how sad she is, we see that movement (the facial expression of smiling) and emotion are incongruent. There is a fragmentation, or splitting, among the core organizers. They do not constitute an integrated, coherent whole.

3. Core organizers may also be over-connected, forming a closed system, like a feedback loop. The various components become locked together in a fixated, rigid way that excludes incoming information. For example, affect, cognition, and movement may all be looped together, with no fresh information received, such as: "I feel sad, because I'm all alone, which makes my body collapse, and then I feel even sadder and more alone, etc." The relationship among the core organizers is predictable; if you start with the belief (I'm all alone), the remainder of the organizers manifest as expected. Or, you could start with the collapse in the body. Anywhere you enter in this dynamic leads to the anticipated outcome. Levine calls this over-association "over-coupling," when applied to traumatic dissociation. This pattern was evident in the Vietnam vet described above. He felt trembling (inner body sensation and movement), anxiety (affect) and a sense of danger (cognitive meaning), which formed an escalating closed system that eventually turned into a panic attack. Interrupting

this cycle required his staying with sensation alone.

4. The core organizers as a whole may dim or shut down alto-gether. This pattern is commonly revealed when clients describe simply "leaving" or "not being there," particularly during a trau-matic event. One client reported that her way of coping with sexual abuse as a child was to stare at the pattern in the wallpaper until she became entirely numb. She didn't know what she was thinking, seeing, or feeling, and she had no body sensation. This form of dissociation is a way of "leaving" an unbearable situation without actually removing oneself physically, thus tempering the impact of such an event. My client had effectively shut down her core organizers while remaining physically in the situation.

The strength of any of these dissociation dynamics is always a mat-ter of degree. For instance, we may disconnect from a core organizer a little, or we may do so nearly completely. The dominance of a core organizer may be expressed powerfully or more mildly. The strength of overconnection between core organizers may be slight or profound. And even when the core organizers are connected in a meaningful, cohesive way, there is still the pos-sibility of a weakened or tenuous connection among them, as well as the possibility of any degree of "dimming down" of the entire system's overall functioning.

Other important considerations in the patterns of dissociation are the timing and frequency of the occurrence of these dynamics. They may be triggered by such things as environmental stresses and cues, by shifting inter-nal states, or by maturational life changes. Our personal triggers will be closely linked with our developmental and traumatic histories. When we encounter situations that resemble or remind us of past woundings wherein dissociation was called into play, a similar dissociation is likely to be trig-gered again. The duration of dissociation may be related to the duration of the stressor. When the stress is over, the core organizers usually return to a more healthy functioning. And, some people take only a slight degree of stress to trigger dissociation, while others with more internal resources can tolerate higher levels. Those triggered more easily will, of course, dissociate more frequently.

EXPLORING THE CORE ORGANIZERS THROUGH BODYWORK

Bodywork can be used to access the functioning of the core organizers, to detect and observe the individual's particular patterns of dissociation, and to restore the self-regulation mechanism to its full creative potential. Rather than seeking to *change* the body (relax it, bring it into structural alignment, increase its energy, etc.), we endeavor to use bodywork to bring the operation of core organizers to consciousness, all the while studying the bodymind interface. This of course requires active, mindful participation from the client and the skill of the therapist to assure that the information is coming from the client's present *experience* rather than from preconceived notions of core organization.

To illustrate the synthesis of psychotherapy and bodywork, I have included a client's description of how a session developed for her, with comments on the application of the techniques and core organizers map. This is a session that took place in a Hakomi Integrative Somatics training, with an advanced student as therapist, a thirty-eight-year old woman as client, and myself supervising. We will call the client Meg and the therapist John.

> I came to the session wanting to find out about a long-standing ache in my left groin. This ache had bothered me since I was a child, when it used to keep me awake at night. My mother had said it was just a growing pain and that I should forget about it. John asked me to feel the ache and notice what it felt like. I could tell exactly where it started, and it went through the whole side of my hip. It sort of throbbed. I got sad as I began to feel it. I felt kind of weak and alone, and felt like it was difficult even to stand. I began to feel a lot younger.

The exploration begins with the "signal" the client presents; in this case it is a bodily sensation—the ache in the groin. The questions John asks simply turn Meg's awareness into the ache, to glean information from this signal itself. The form of his query is to say, "Take all the time you need to just feel that ache right now. What kind of sensation do you notice? How deeply does it go into your body?" and later, "Just stay with the throbbing, feel it—maybe you notice feelings, thoughts, movements, or images connected with it." John invites association to core organizers, by asking first for a description of the sensation, going with Meg's strongest signal, and then inviting affect, movement, thoughts and images (one of the five senses). His questions require that Meg access her core organizers to answer. His soft tone of voice and slow pacing are additional keys in calling forth Meg's mindful attention, which in turn, evokes a wealth of information.

> We had been standing, but now I wanted to explore further with hands-on bodywork, so we moved over to the table. I lay down.

Beginning with the client standing (rather than lying down or sitting) is an option which can make structural and other body patterns more apparent to both therapist and client, for the effects of gravity on the structure are more obvious. It's a way of raising the signal slightly. When both the physical and the psychological components are evident, and when the client is ready, then we move to the table.

> John asked me to notice what happened as he began to contact this ache with his hands. He pressed lightly with his fingertips into the area, trying to meet and match the sensation I'd described. At first the pressure was too light; I wanted a really deep pressure. I was surprised that I could tell exactly what kind of touch was right for me, and John made sure he got the place and the pressure the way I wanted it. It felt great that he responded so precisely to my needs.

John elicits Meg's guidance here, using the bodywork as a means to teach her about the wisdom of her own body in telling him exactly what kind of touch is right for her. In this process, Meg receives the subtle message that she both knows and can follow her own inner direction. John does not impose his agenda upon her process, but evokes her own inner acumen.

> As he pressed into this ache, I first felt only relief. It felt so good to have him contact the pain. I had been alone all my life with pain. John continued to work physically, all the while asking me to share what was coming up for me. The tension released a

little, and I could suddenly see myself as a little girl, trying to deal with everything alone, trying to be strong in an emotionally and sometimes physically abusive family. I began to cry when I saw this image. In my image, I looked (and felt) so young and vulnerable, and so alone. John was very compassionate which made me feel OK about feeling so weak and sad. I cried for what seemed like a long time.

All along, John is evoking Meg's core organizers by simply asking her to study how she organizes her experience in response to the bodywork. As the tension shifts, a memory emerges that contains the elements of a visual image (five-sense perception), a belief about needing to be strong (cognition), and an emotional response of sadness (affect). When a physical holding pattern releases through bodywork, the issues that the pattern is protecting frequently emerge, in this case a certain childhood aloneness and vulnerability. This is one primary way that bodywork interfaces with psychotherapy: as the hands-on work helps to change the patterns of the body, underlying issues come forth and are also available for change. Of course, John's authentic and compassionate presence with the childhood pain Meg carries is imperative in creating a healing environment that encourages the client to enter a depth of contact with herself.

Finally, my tears were spent, and John asked me what his hands might be saying to this younger part of me. I could feel that the hands were offering help, help I never had as a child. An unfamiliar sensation of warmth and release swept through my body and for once I felt the possibility of having support.

The quiet, receptive inner space available after emotional release is the favorable moment for John to ask Meg for the meaning (the core organizer of cognition) of his physical contact. "Translating the language of touch" is an effective way to bring unconscious beliefs or thoughts to awareness. As Meg is able to "hear" John's hands speaking to her, she experiences "for once" what she had not experienced as a child: that help is, literally, at hand. This is a wonderful technique for bridging the mindbody interface and stabilizing an experience that was absent in Meg's childhood. Through translating the nonverbal language of touch into words, an additional option is accessed cognitively: Meg's belief shifts from one of not expecting help to one of knowing that help has arrived. Mindfulness is deepened by this point, and Meg is also able to notice the parallel body sensations.

We continued to explore more deeply with hands-on bodywork. As the pressure of John's hands went deeper, my whole feeling changed. I could feel that the deep muscles in my groin were pushing back. John asked me to go ahead and push back as much as I wanted, and see what happened. I immediately felt angry, and a memory came up of having been punished by being made by my mother to sit on a chair when my older brother and I had fought. He was mean and abusive, but I always got blamed. I saw and felt what it was like to sit on the chair, something I hadn't thought about for years. I was furious and wanted to kick with my left leg, but as a child that would only have gotten me into more trouble, so I didn't do it. I realized that I had been taught to never get angry, especially at my family.

Having dealt with the first issue of being in pain and receiving help, the tissue in Meg's groin is more open, and John can go deeper with body-work. During the continued exploration, John again asks Meg to just be aware of her experience as his hands contact a deeper layer of tension. By helping to release the physical tension through bodywork, he's awakening a long-held, healthy impulse to express anger. Something new begins to hap-pen as Meg unexpectedly and spontaneously pushes back against John's hands. Recognizing this active movement (a core organizer) as the opposite of the holding pattern in Meg's body, John invites the movement to continue. Again trusting the intelligence of the body's spontaneous guidance, he perceives the movement as a key step in restoring the healthy capacity of Meg's core organizers.

John encouraged me to follow my body and let it tell me what it wanted to do. He stayed in contact with this deep tension in my groin as I first just pushed with those muscles. Then I kicked my leg, but that actually was not as satisfying as just pushing with the muscles in my groin.

Something nascent occurs through Meg's movement, and John encourages her to just trust her body's impulses, instead of imposing his agenda. Once more, he demonstrates faith in the intelligence of Meg's emerging process. He asks her to do what feels good in her body, a way of phrasing an encouraging directive for trusting her body's wisdom. She is then able to feel from the inside what is the authentic, most satisfying, expression for her body.

> John asked me to notice my experience inside when he told me that it was OK to express my anger. At first I could hardly believe it. I was afraid he would leave, or tell me I was bad. For a few moments, my leg stopped moving, which was a really familiar sensation of holding back. I felt I'd better not get angry, but I also felt resentment because it wasn't OK to get angry. A habit suddenly became clear, of how I would not express my anger, but then I would resent the other person for not letting me express it.

John is adding a verbal experiment, asking Meg to study her experience. This verbal experiment takes the form of John asking, "What happens when I say it's OK to express your anger?" Through this form, Meg's mindful attention is heightened, and she can learn how she organizes her experience in response to this statement. Her first response is disbelief in the statement's truth, and her body reverts momentarily to its old holding pattern, tightening the left groin. In terms of dissociation dynamics, the cycle of overconnected core organizers goes something like this: "I feel angry, but it's not OK to get angry, so I have to hold it in, and that leads to physical tension, and resentment, and more anger." With the verbal experiment, along with the physical, Meg can learn about the dynamic that happens among her core organizers and most likely discover what's needed to restore more healthy functioning.

> John said it *(It's OK to express your anger)* a few more times, and I finally believed that he was different from my mother, and that it really was OK with him that I got angry. I had to look him in the eyes to make sure he meant it. The muscles in my groin and my whole hip wanted to push even harder, and it felt good. I had an image of myself as a little child having a temper tantrum, which I

never really had as a child. I was really angry in the session, and it surprised me that the physical expression of the anger was just the pushing with the muscles in my leg. John also asked what words went with the movement, and it felt good to say how angry I was, but it was most satisfying to just do that movement.

A crucial, transformative moment is occurring as Meg begins to believe that her anger is OK. John patiently repeats the sentence, as both he and Meg study her reaction. John asks Meg to notice what happens if she looks at him as he says the words, providing an opportunity for Meg to literally see that he did not hold the same attitude about anger as her mother. As Meg distinguishes John from her mother, she begins to believe in another way of being, and her sensation, movement, affect, and senses align with the attitude that anger can be OK. The generalization from childhood is broken, the system begins to open, and the core organizers find a new way of responding to the inner feeling of anger. Recognizing the importance of this moment, John takes plenty of time to support the spontaneous unfolding of Meg's process.

Quite suddenly, the pushing stopped by itself. It just felt complete, and I didn't feel angry any more. John said to just notice my body. My groin and hip felt completely new. I could feel a tiny little trembling movement deep in my hip that spread down my leg. John said to keep my attention on the trembling, and I did for a long time until it stopped on its own. I felt a sense of wholeness and peace. There was energy moving freely through my body, and I felt quite open, but strong in a good way. It was a new experience for me. It was amazing to have gotten help, and then to have felt all that anger. I felt very tender toward myself, and even kind of proud. The pain in my groin was gone, and it has not reappeared in its previous, chronic form.

In this session, Meg was able to complete a long-held physical and emotional impulse (the expression of anger). Her body knew when it was finished, and at this point John released the physical contact, turning Meg's awareness toward her inner body sensation. Doing so provides an opportunity for the deep involuntary holding, often connected with the freezing response mentioned earlier, to release, as evidenced here by the trembling. Frequently, we use our cognition to truncate such spontaneous body sensations and micromovements. John verbally encouraged Meg simply to allow the trembling, not to control it in any way, but to permit her involuntary response to take over. Through his tone of voice and his words, he conveyed that it was important to track this sensation, so instead of inhibiting this movement prematurely, Meg could allow it to run its course. It took about ten minutes for the trembling to complete.

Meg had come in with a "signal" to explore: the ache in her groin, an inner body sensation. From the beginning, John had demonstrated trust in the unfolding process, soliciting Meg's guidance. Through mindful exploration, using bodywork experimentally, the dissociative patterns of her core organizers gradually became apparent. In accordance with Hakomi's information theory, as Meg gained the appropriate information from within herself, she spontaneously reorganized toward health. The ache in Meg's groin transformed in her perception from an annoying sensation to an important signal that she may be holding anger. Where Meg had been dissociated from feeling and expressing her own anger, she developed connections needed to reassociate to both her feeling and expression, and so has restored more creative options among her core organizers.

In closing, I want to offer the caveat that it is not always appropriate or desirable to study the organization of experience through hands-on bodywork. A client needs to have a sense of boundaries, ego strength, and maturity that allow her to respond constructively to this synthesis. The combination of bodywork with psychotherapy proves more powerful than either alone, having greater potential to disorganize the client if executed inappropriately, too quickly, without awareness, or with an unstable client. I noticed in the early days of experimentation that when we proceeded too quickly, clients would frequently return the following week reporting that symptoms had worsened—particularly that they felt confused, disoriented and disconnected from themselves. The trend of the times (in the 1970s) emphasized catharsis, and certainly the power of bodywork and psychotherapy combined could easily evoke a strong emotional reaction. I learned that reassociating too quickly to dissociated aspects could be antitherapeutic, often leading easily to catharsis, but also to more dissociation. The need for professional expertise, psychological and somatic assessment skills, comprehensive knowledge of both fields, practical understanding of transference, boundaries, and dissociation became apparent. In those cases where hands-on work is not appropriate, the core organizers can be studied through simple awareness using experiments other than touch. We can still work effectively with the mindbody interface through awareness of sensation, movement, and the client's self-touch. As inner awareness is built, hands-on work becomes a more viable option.

Conclusion

The more our dissociative patterns determine our experience, the less creatively we can respond to ourselves, others, and the world at large. Our habits of dissociation compromise our capacity for self-regulation, and thus our capacity to respond to life's many challenges in a way that reflects who we truly are: spiritual beings in human form (to draw from Tielhard de Chardin). To the degree we are dissociated, we have a diminished potential for choicemaking. We remain subject to unwitting compliance with patterns that perpetuate personal and collective disenchantment. While we may value kindness, connection, and cooperation, we repeatedly find ourselves and the world immersed in conflict. We desperately need to cultivate the resources and empowerment to gain our freedom from the cycles of violence, defensiveness, and reactivity currently running rampant in our world. I see the personal work being done with Hakomi Integrative Somatics and allied psychotherapeutic approaches as being part of an overall thrust toward growth and planetary healing. As we work to reassociate to dissociated parts of ourselves, we restore creative self-regulation; as our core organizers approach optimal functioning, we can being to *feel* in the larger sense. We can then hold the benefit of the whole in our hearts, and from there, become empowered to take loving, healing action in the world.

Chapter Ten

HEALING THE EMOTIONAL/SPIRITUAL BODY: THE RUBENFELD SYNERGY® METHOD

Ilana Rubenfeld

EDITOR'S NOTE: *Ilana is one of the grandes dames of the field of somatic psychology today. Throughout the thirty-five years she has been developing her method, she has impressed everyone with her energy, her kindness, and her irrepressible urge to look out for others. She came to this field through a budding career in music and conducting, and one can see its influence in her work today. Rubenfeld Synergy Method has a lyrical tone and a harmonizing effect. Ilana has had the opportunity to train with some of the original greats—Fritz Perls and Moshe Feldenkrais—and because of this she is able to look at healing from both a purely somatic as well as a psychological viewpoint. She has taught students at the university level, as well as at institutes like Omega, Esalen, and the Open Center. Though she could have chosen to be a great conductor, she chose instead to inspire greatness and integrity in this field. I suspect that she would have made a great stand-up comedian as well. I feel privileged to know her and to have shared many jokes with her.*

"*B*ody and Soul" was the cover story in the November 8, 1988 *Newsweek*. I rejoiced as I read how the scientific community finally confirmed what has been known for centuries: that our lives are lived through every inch of ourselves, body and soul and that any change must address the entire being— body, mind, emotions, and spirit.

That 1988 article was a watershed. For the twenty-five years before, I had felt like an isolated voice in the bodymind wilderness. Few people

179

understood what I was doing, and I had no colleagues to share with. Since then, interest in healing the bodymind has continued to expand, until, in 1996, "body psychotherapy" was featured at international conferences where many professionals presented and shared.

The best way for me to explain the philosophy, theory, and practice of the Rubenfeld Synergy Method is to take you with me on my life's journey of discovery—and to share with you the dramatic "Aha!"s that changed my life forever, how I discovered and researched ways to integrate gentle touch and verbal psychotherapy, and how my holistic healing system continues to evolve.

In 1957 I entered the Juilliard School of Music in New York to train to become an orchestral and choral conductor. Conducting for many hours a day—standing and moving my arms continually—was quite strenuous. In my years as a full-time musician, playing several instruments and conducting choirs, no one taught me how to use my body efficiently.

While I was preparing for a concert, my back and shoulder went into spasm, and I couldn't lift my right arm. Many doctors examined my right shoulder and arm and prescribed medications that gave only temporary relief. Desperate, I began looking for other ways of treating this debilitating condition. A musician friend suggested I go to her teacher of the F. M. Alexander Technique, a method designed to teach balanced and efficient posture. I made an appointment with Judy Leibowitz.

Judy escorted me to a room containing a padded table, a chair, and a mirror. She invited me to lie down on my back with my clothes on. Then she did something no one had ever done—she gently touched my head and asked me in a soft voice to relax and allow her to move my head. I relaxed my head—or so I thought—and was surprised when she repeated her request. Hadn't I just done that? I finally noticed that I was talking to her with clenched teeth, tight jaw, and taut neck. My head was full of tension and was immovable. I only *thought* I had relaxed. I was amazed to learn that I was not doing what I sincerely believed I was doing.

Shocked, I thought, "Do I do what I think I'm doing?" That moment was an "Aha!" experience, the first of many that changed my life and led me to create the Rubenfeld Synergy Method.

HEALING THE EMOTIONAL/SPIRITUAL BODY

Aha #1: You're not always doing what you think you're doing.

This sounds simple. It is also profound: You may think your body is following your mental instructions, when actually it's doing something else, even quite the opposite.

Judy's light touch was accompanied by her soft voice repeating words of instruction that my body and mind couldn't understand. However, my *body* understood the message in her touch, which cajoled my head and neck muscles to soften, allowing me to lengthen and find a new freedom of movement.

Aha #2: Touch is a powerful means of communication.

Her touch succeeded in communicating more clearly than her words. Her touch said that she would not hurt me and that she would teach me how to become aware of my tensions and soften them.

Judy then asked me "What do you do?"

This question startled me. None of the doctors had asked. "I am a musician and I conduct," I replied.

"Show me what you do when you conduct," she said. I stooped down with my neck sticking out and lifted my imaginary baton. "Of course you have a back and shoulder spasm!" she exclaimed. "Your neck and head are out of alignment and your ankles and knees are not supporting you."

In surprise I wondered, "Is the body connected?!"

Aha #3: The body is an interconnected system.

What happens to one part affects all other parts. In my case, an old ankle injury was manifesting as a back and shoulder problem. No health professional had observed me in action before. It seemed like a new and radical concept at that time.

Completing my first lesson, I felt taller, balanced, lighter, and more relaxed. My friend asked me excitedly, "How was it?"

"Wonderful," I replied.

"What happened?" she asked.

"I don't know," I muttered.

Aha #4: To have an experience, you don't have to know the reasons why.

You don't have to justify—or even cognitively understand—a meaningful and authentic experience. Rational understanding can come later. Interrupting an experience with explanations may weaken and stop the impact of that precious moment.

Over the next few months I continued to feel better and my back spasms dissolved. I was finally able to perform without pain. During several lessons, I began sobbing from a deep place within. These old pains had been locked deep inside of me. I realized that her way of using touch created enough safety for me to contact and express my sadness.

Aha #5: Emotions reside and are held in the body.

After several outbursts of crying, Judy explained that she was not trained as a psychotherapist and did not know how to process these waves of emotion. She strongly recommended that I see her psychoanalyst. I went, but by the time I lay down on his leather couch, the emotions released during the Alexander lesson were distant memories. We'd talk about what I had felt when Judy touched me, but the psychotherapist wouldn't use touch. Then I went to Judy, who touched me but wouldn't process or talk with me.

Aha# 6: I wanted someone to do both—talk and touch.

My yearning marked the conception of the Rubenfeld Synergy Method. I first sought to bridge somatic[1] work and psychotherapy as I struggled to integrate the physical and emotional material.[2] I came to realize that my back spasms were a link to past childhood traumas that needed attention and healing. At Judy's urging, I became an Alexander teacher while still conducting part time. Without a model for working with the body, mind, and emotions simultaneously, I began to experiment with verbal interventions when teaching Alexander lessons.

The memory of a particular student remains vivid today. Susan[3] came to me because of unremitting anxiety. By the end of a session, Susan had successfully released her bound-up shoulders and allowed them to drop down, but in the following week, she again sat in the chair with her shoulders hunched up toward her ears. During one session, she began to sob in a very high-pitched voice. Recognizing the significance of this moment, I quietly asked her how old she felt just then.

"Two years old," she replied, crying.

With my hands touching her upper back and right shoulder, I asked her to close her eyes and go back to that time. There was a sudden shudder as she squirmed in the chair and pulled her knees up to her chest so tightly that she resembled a small ball. She opened her eyes briefly to check that I was still there. A distant memory surfaced—of her hands being tied with brightly colored ribbons to the bars of her crib. Slowly her story unfolded: her mother wanted to keep baby Susan from touching her genitals. This position was frozen in her body even while the memory had been repressed for so many years.

In many successive sessions she was able to release her shoulders. Now her arms moved more freely, allowing her hands to be closer to her genitals. This new position scared her, and her shoulders often returned to their old position. After months of working through this emotional trauma and its somatic implications, she was able to express anger, resentment, and pain about her mother's behavior. Later, Susan was able to reclaim her sexual feelings in a healthy way and forgive her mother. She had integrated her re-laxed shoulders and open chest into her present life and relation-ships.

This session was a hallmark for my understanding that many physi-cal habit patterns can change and be integrated only when the associated emotional material is processed. It became clear to me that my students' bodies were physical metaphors for their lives. No longer satisfied with chang-ing their postures, I burned to know their histories and what created their dysfunctions in the first place. Listening to their physical tensions was the gateway to a larger story that began to unfold beneath my hands.

After several years, I left my analyst and joined a group led by Dr. Peter Hogan, a skilled and unorthodox Adlerian psychiatrist. I began to adapt some of his psychotherapeutic techniques when giving Alexander lessons. Intrigued by my experimental combination and its potential to effect psychophysical changes, Hogan invited me to assist at his weekend group "intensives." At first, he did most of the talking and I did all the body work. I would "listen" to people's body stories with my hands. Often, their verbal and body stories were not congruent.

Eventually he supervised me doing entire sessions myself, which made me even more curious about psychology. I then trained and apprenticed with Ruth Cohn and Dr. Elizabeth Mintz. Later I trained with Drs. Fritz and Laura Perls, the cofounders of Gestalt Therapy.

Fritz asked me to give him several Alexander lessons and consequently we developed a very special professional relationship. When Fritz invited me to sit on the other side of the client and use touch, I discovered that there was a subtle muscular response to every emotion the client expressed, as if my touch was opening gateways into the unconscious mind. As I continued to experiment with touch in this way, I added each new discovery into my integration of the Alexander Technique and psychotherapy.

A small group of somatic practitioners brought Dr. Moshe Feldenkrais to Esalen in 1970, and I was fortunate to be part of that first U.S. workshop. That summer, and for the next eight years, I trained intensely in his two-tiered method of Functional Integration and Awareness Through Movement. These creative movement exercises helped people's nervous systems to release habitual holding patterns. I used aspects of the Feldenkrais Method in my eclectic integration of bodywork and psychotherapy.

Elements of the bodymind work of F. M. Alexander and Moshe Feldenkrais along with the experimental research of Drs. Hogan and Perls[4] became the beginning harmonics in my orchestration of a powerful, new therapeutic and educational paradigm, the Rubenfeld Synergy Method.

Buckminster Fuller, the creator of the geodesic dome, suggested the word "synergy" at a conference after watching me demonstrate my work, which was still nameless at that time. He said "integration" did not accurately express what I was doing. Handing me his book *Synergetics,* he explained that a more appropriate name would be "synergy," because this work, as a whole, is greater than and different from the sum of its components. At last I had found a word that expressed the dynamics of my method. And I became a Rubenfeld Synergist.

The method's variety of tools—gentle touch, subtle movement, humor, imagination, sounds, body posture, and verbal expression—gave me the flexibility to meet clients at their point of comfort, experimenting until a way of working well together develops. That is where the excitement is for both Synergist and client—a collaboration that unfolds in the moment.

A Rubenfeld Synergy Session

Recognition and awareness of the bodymind connection exploded in the 1980s, and the demand for Rubenfeld Synergy workshops increased dramatically. I gave up my private Rubenfeld Synergy practice and devoted myself to leading workshops and training others full-time. The workshop design included bodymind exercises, lectures, "hands-on" experiences, demonstrations with volunteer participants, and humor.

For many participants, the highlight of a workshop is witnessing the demonstration session. They see how the parts fit together, vicariously experience the emotions and changes that the client undergoes, and afterwards participate in a discussion of the session.

I found that the best spatial arrangement for these demonstrations was the theater-in-the-round. This ancient Greek practice was a healing experience for everyone attending. By placing the padded table in the center and having the whole group create circles around it, we recreated this ancient healing configuration both spatially and energetically.[5]

A session can take place with a client lying on a table, sitting in a chair, or moving about. During a session, the client passes through four major phases: *awareness, experimentation, integration,* and *reentry.* These do not necessarily occur in sequence but rather overlap one another cyclically, with each repetition at a deeper level.

One of the most important moments in a session is "the first touch." It enables me to sense clients' comfort level and where they are physically and emotionally. As I get to know them, they also get a sense of me. The first touch also sends a clear message of nonviolence and gives them time to develop rapport and trust with me.

I will describe a forty-five-minute session from a recent workshop—condensed from thirty pages to three—and then I will explain the theories, philosophical underpinnings, and practices that guide Rubenfeld Synergists.

Gloria, a slight, blond woman in her late forties, comes up to the table. After a very short conversation I invite her to lie down on her back, allowing the table to support her. As I begin with the first touch, her fragile head doesn't move to either side. Her eyelids close and begin to flutter. I slide both my hands under her left shoulder blade (*awareness* of my touch). Her upper back muscles feel like tight ropes full of tangled knots. "What is happening in your back?" I ask in a gentle tone.

"It's tight, and I've got to let my son go." (Increased awareness.) Tears fill her eyes. "He's so young and helpless."

From her concerned tone, I picture a very young boy and ask, "How old is your son?" I begin to feel pulsating movements in her back.

"Oh, he's twenty-eight years old." There is a slight pause of embarrassment, and she begins to laugh. Her whole body softens. "He's leaving the nest and I'm getting older!" Clenching her fists and tightening her forearms, she crosses her arms over her chest.

"Are you willing to do an experiment?" I ask.

"Yes," she nods.

"Hold him more tightly, instead of letting him go," I suggested (*experimentation* of exaggerating what she's already doing, which is opposite to what she is saying). She squeezes until she can no longer do it. Suddenly, flinging her arms open, she lets go of her son, and her tension.

Gloria looks relieved and yet a deep furrow forms on her forehead. "I don't want to get older and lose my memory like my father. He had Alzheimer's disease and it was horrible for us!"

I ask her to roll onto her right side, which shifts her position dramatically and I place my hands on her left shoulder—moving it slowly up toward her ear and then down toward her hip. "Are you willing to do another experiment?" I ask (more experimentation).

"Yes," she whispers.

"Imagine yourself as an older woman . . . Give her a voice . . . What does she say to you?"

"I'm eighty-five years old. I love to dance, pick flowers in the field, and eat ice cream!" Her voice is full of energy now and her shoulder moves easily to and fro.

She becomes quiet and contemplative. "I never had a chance to play," she says, in a tiny little voice. "As a young child, I became old and I had to help everyone. Now that I'm eighty-five, I don't have to teach and help others in order to be loved."

I ask her to roll onto her back. Her eyelids flutter again and she winces as I slip my hands under her left shoulder. "My heart hurts. A close friend is dying of cancer."

I make an intuitive leap: "Do you have to get very sick and die not to grow old?"

"No, no, I don't want to die young and I don't want to help or teach others all the time in order to be loved," she says, shaking her head from side to side (*integration* has begun).

"Tell that to your inner child," I suggest with a playful voice.

"I love you, Little One, no matter what you do," she says, changing the sentence to suit her.

After a long pause I ask, "How old are you now, in this present moment?"

"Forty-eight years old," she says proudly and firmly.

"How wonderful! Now look into my eyes and say 'I am forty-eight years old and I can be with people without helping or teaching them,'" I say (more integration). Her left shoulder softens, releasing its tension, and energy moves swiftly through her arms and out through her fingertips.

Tears well up, yet there is no sobbing—only a deep recognition that growing older is her journey, not her father's (integration at a deeper level). She also does not have to be terminally ill to stay young (more integration). She is soft and appears peaceful as her body, mind, and emotions integrate these insights.

I invite her to sit up and, after some time, look around the room (beginning of *reentry* phase). Her face looks older, wiser, and younger as she moves her shoulders. Surprised, she smiles and announces her pain is gone. She jumps off the table, full of life and joy.

"Say your key sentence to a few people. They will be your allies,"[6] I say. We go for a walk around the room, stopping in front of several workshop participants.[7]

"I don't have to help everyone so that they will love me. I can just be with people the way I am right now," she tells them (continued integration during reentry). There is a sacred silence.

Some people's faces are damp with tears, while others are laughing and applauding. Her story has touched many as they recognize her themes in their lives: aging, children leaving home, taking care of an ill parent, being loved only if you are a helper, the death of beloved friends.

Gloria's story is full of universal themes that participants recognize as they witness, identify, empathize, project—often sharing their own anger, laughter, and grief.

When the many components of Rubenfeld Synergy flow seamlessly and elegantly from one to another, the Method appears to be simple and effortless. I am reminded of a Zen story:

Once again, as so many times before, the Roshi took the brush and seemingly without effort made a perfect circle.

The student could contain himself no longer. "Master, how do you make such perfect circles, time after time? It looks so simple when you do it."

"Yes," replied the Roshi, the barest hint of a smile on his lips, "fifty years of simple."

This parable is a reminder that simplicity develops with time and practice. The outward appearance of "simple" may fool us because it masks what's underneath—the years of learning, researching, practicing, refining, questioning, starting over again, and appreciating the mysterious process of creation.

PRINCIPLES, PHILOSOPHY, AND THEORETICAL FOUNDATIONS
OF THE RUBENFELD SYNERGY METHOD[8]

The following principles, philosophies, and theoretical foundations guide Rubenfeld Synergy sessions:

1. Each individual is unique.

The Rubenfeld Synergy Method respects the uniqueness of each individual. Some systems rely on characterological maps or templates, which purport to correlate emotional behavior to various areas of the body—for example, back pain means anger, chest constriction means sadness, and so on. That may be the case sometimes, but not necessarily. I have supervised many young therapists who miss the obvious because they rely on a specific map that the client does not fit.

Working without a preset agenda allows the session to develop spontaneously. Rubenfeld Synergists tailor each session to the needs of the individual client.

2. The body, mind, emotions, and spirit are part of a dynamically interrelated system.

New discoveries from the last part of the twentieth century point toward interconnections between many fields of science and the arts. Research in each separate field demonstrates interrelationships that acknowledge that people must be treated through an integrative (not specialized) approach as whole human beings.

Ludwig von Bertalanffy's general systems theory suggests that the parts of a system affect each other through their interactions, constantly changing the equilibrium of the entire system.

Each time you introduce change at one level, you change every other level and affect the whole person. This is not a linear process but rather a cyclical one that involves all aspects of the nervous system—emotions, perceptions, beliefs, cognition, and learning capacities.

The way we move our bodies and the way we hold our postures reflect our emotions, attitudes, and thinking patterns—and vice versa. Clients are invited to experiment with movements and postures so that they can recognize the underlying cause of their problems and become aware of alternative ways to use their bodies.

3. Awareness is the first key to change.

As I refined my work, I noticed that it wasn't enough for *me* to listen and notice what was going on with my clients. *They*, too, had to become aware. By the end of a session a client often looks different, with major changes in posture, complexion, or expression. Sometimes, even though the changes are obvious to me and to any observers, the client does not see or experience them. For example:

> David arrived complaining of a terrible neck pain. It was obvious to me that his right shoulder was much higher than his left. By the end of the session both shoulders were even. I asked him what he was experiencing. With his eyes closed, he reported that now his left shoulder felt much higher. I asked him to open his eyes and look into the mirror. He shook his head in disbelief when he saw that they were even. Reality and his old habit of perception were still at odds. We had to practice these distinctions quite a few times before he could integrate them.

By increasing his self-awareness and self-observation, David developed a clearer sense of the differences between his inner and outer worlds. Only with this awareness could he then begin to bring them into agreement.

Change cannot happen without this awareness. Physical and emotional habit patterns are learned unconsciously and, as long as they remain in the background, the client cannot choose to do otherwise. The Synergist's use of a creative experiment—involving touch, verbal intervention, and movement—heightens the client's awareness so that these habit patterns come to the foreground. When clients recognize these patterns, they have the opportunity to explore alternative choices and develop possibilities for psychophysical change.

Rubenfeld Synergists' gentle touch creates safety and support for clients' focusing inward and becoming more aware. I believe this inward focus, called "mindfulness" in Eastern disciplines, is basic to every mind-body approach.

4. Change occurs in the present moment.

Clients may experience their memories of the past and fantasize about the future, but change itself occurs in the present. With the use of active imagination and visualization, clients relive the experience in real time and review the past. For instance, survivors of trauma need to voice their unspoken stories, but too many repetitions would only embed the trauma more deeply in their nervous system. With enough time, clients can rescript these remembered events and look at them from another vantage point. They can resolve unfinished business and integrate new insights in the present, embedding the somatic and emotional changes in the nervous system.

5. The ultimate responsibility for change rests with the client.

Awareness is necessary for change, but it's not sufficient. There is a wonderful joke: "How many psychotherapists does it take to change a light bulb?" (pause) "One, and only if the light bulb wants to change."

The ultimate responsibility for change rests with clients. There is no way a therapist can force an individual to change. Sometimes, the very resistance to change is what keeps the client together, even though it may be dysfunctional. The Synergist can help clients recognize the dysfunction—emotionally and physically—and slowly guide them to try a new behavior. Eventually this newly-learned behavior can replace the old habits of the past.

When Synergists touch a tight holding area, they may palpate it gently and slowly while verbally exploring various themes. If that area does not change, soften, or release, that's a clue pointing to the possibility of resistance. Synergists, respecting this resistance, do not force an entry but return there at another time.[9] When change does occur, it is initiated by the client (from the inside out), not forced or pushed by the practitioner (from the outside in). The Synergist's touch and verbal processing may serve as a catalyst for the client's change.

6. People have a natural capacity for self-healing and self-regulation.

The work of Candace Pert, Bernie Siegel, Norman Cousins, and Andrew Weil documents the existence and power of self-healing. The client's innate healing ability already exists, waiting to be actualized. The Synergist doesn't "correct" it but facilitates its development.

A basic axiom in Gestalt psychology is that every organism has the capacity to attain an optimum healing balance within itself and in its environment. Studies from Harvard show us that the simple act of remembering how it feels to care for someone, or to be cared for by a loved one, can drive up—and sustain for one hour!—the body's level of the antibody immuno-globulin A.

Other studies show a link between loneliness and lowered cellular immunity. Candace Pert, in her exploration of neuropeptides (hormones that govern communication between the brain and body cells) found that the limbic system—the part of the brain responsible for mood and emotions—has forty times more neuropeptide receptors than other parts of the brain. Work that is both somatic and emotional fosters self-healing by giving clients access to the limbic system.

7. The body's life force and energy field can be sensed.

There are many ancient energy systems, in use for millennia, that have been become known in the West in the twentieth century.[10] In the process of working with thousands of people, I discovered I could read someone's energy pattern by moving my hands about an inch above the body. For example, "stuck" energy has a dense and stationary quality. When clients work through feelings and memories connected to a part of their body, the quality of energy changes markedly. Previously blocked areas begin to pulsate; muscles soften and relax.

Slowing our pace and consciously practicing with "listening hands" opens the door to experiencing this energy field and the life force that resides in every body. This free-flowing movement of energy is strongly associated with spiritual experiences.

8. Touch is a viable, accurate system of communication.

Touch is a very sophisticated language that is communicated through our hands, both receiving and giving information. It bypasses words and rational concepts housed in the neocortical brain. In early infancy, the baby receives and understands the nonverbal language of touch long before it comprehends words. Touching supports the growth of the nervous system, including the development of the five senses and the abilities of orienting in space, moving, and thinking.

The message and quality of touch depends on the *intention* of the toucher. What Synergists think and feel is communicated through their hands to the client. Therefore, the intention, attitude, and quality of touch are considered with as much care as are the choice of words and timing used in verbal therapy.

Touch that evokes trust and safety develops new gateways to emotional awareness and can create dialogues with the unconscious mind. It offers a direct channel with the neuromuscular system and provides immediate feedback about the client's state of being.

9. The body is a metaphor.

Seeing and dialoguing with parts of the body can lead to life issues. And the Synergist's "listening hands" can hear the body's story.

> As Burt lay on the table, I observed his legs. They looked very different from each other—one was pointing to the ceiling and the other was rotated to the right.

> Touching and gently moving his feet verified this difference dramatically. It was as if one leg *wanted* to stay on a straight path and the other *wanted* to go off to the side. When I checked this idea out with him,[11] he laughed, saying "How did you know I'm struggling with being pulled in two directions in my life right now!?"

> It was clear to me that his ankles, knees, and hip joints had been in this state since childhood. This was not a new behavior pattern; it was a metaphor for a life issue that had begun years before. This is an interesting phenomenon—to see, feel, and sense the visceral translation of a body state to a life situation.

10. The body tells the truth.

Our words and our bodies often tell incongruent stories, as these two sessions illustrate:

> Lucille, a short, lively woman about seventy-five years old, fairly

flew out of her chair and onto the table when I asked for a volunteer. She began to sob and complain about how, after forty years, her husband had left her to find his own "space." Slipping my hands under her back, I discovered that it was relaxed, soft, pulsing with energy—"juicy." I asked her what was going on in her life right now. She looked at me sheepishly and said "I have two boyfriends." We both started to laugh. Gasping for air, she exclaimed that her sex life is wonderful and both men shower her with affection and attention. Lucille thought she should be miserable; after all, her husband had left her. Yet her body told a different story, one that didn't agree with what she was saying.

John, a depressed and sad young man, lay motionless on the table. I tried to gently move his head. It was stuck. When I slipped my hands under his back it felt like a sheet of steel. He explained that his fiancée had left him suddenly and he was confused. I asked him to imagine his fiancée and speak to her.

In a soft, placating voice he said, "Joan, I forgive you. . . " As he spoke, his back tightened even more, as if it were saying "You must be kidding! I'm furious!" His back clearly contradicted what he was saying.

"If your back had a voice, what would it say?" I asked.

He began to pound the table, yelling, "I'm so angry at what you've done!" Even though he thought he should forgive her, his body was expressing his inner emotions.

After several sessions, he was able to contact and express his grief and sadness. Then, looking and feeling more relieved, he was genuinely ready to forgive her. His body, mind, and emotions were now congruent.

In both sessions my "listening hands" were able to detect the discrepancy and use it as a guide for my questions and verbal interventions.

11. The body is the sanctuary of the soul.

The ancient Jewish mystic tradition of the Kabbalah is studied as a guide to understanding the unity of body and spirit. All beings embody spirit—from the smallest creature to the most complex systems of the universe. This concept also appears in yoga and other Eastern traditions, which value acceptance of everything that is happening in the moment.

The natural progression and deepening work of integrating body, mind, and emotions may invite transpersonal and spiritual growth. Rubenfeld Synergy sessions may progress toward a spiritual dimension when clients deal with their "soul" issues by questioning their life values in relationships, families, communities, and the world.

In the last decade, I've noticed that people yearn to find aspects of themselves that are more than just their material life. I believe that when people work with a method that addresses the emotional and energetic blocks in their body, their spiritual dimension can unfold.

12. Pleasure needs to be supported to balance pain.

Grief, anger, pain, joy, and laughter are all housed in the body. Many people have gotten into the habit of repeating their most painful stories and thereby ignoring opportunities to create or contact joy and pleasure in the present. Many adults discover that they have "lost" their playful child within and have forgotten how to have fun and how to enjoy pleasure.

Harry A. Klopf, author of *The Hedonistic Neuron: A Theory of Memory, Learning and Intelligence*, claims that the nervous system learns from pleasure, not pain. According to his theory, each time we make sense of new information, the brain rewards us by releasing large quantities of endorphins and other pleasure-producing neurochemicals.

Clients need to contact their joyful resources and learn to use them in order to have a well-balanced life. They can benefit from making contact with their joyous playfulness, lost since childhood.

13. Humor can heal and lighten.

Humor has certainly lightened painful situations in the life of my clients, students, and colleagues as well as in my own life. It was a powerful, positive, and healing tool for my transformative journey.

Clients can get stuck somatically and emotionally in a painful and repetitive loop. Using appropriate humor, not sarcasm, interrupts this habitual pattern and allows the pain to lighten, creating a possibility for clients to delve more deeply and see their stories from another perspective.

Laughter can dissolve fear, create pathways to creativity, insights, and healing, and make it possible for clients to deal with past emotional wounding that is otherwise too painful to bear. Using humor is most successful when clients respond spontaneously—creating a more relaxed atmosphere.

Laughter, provoked or stimulated by appropriate use of humor, can free tight holding patterns, invite deeper breathing, and enhance creativity. Consider this session, from a workshop in which a psychotherapist asked me if I could demonstrate how I use humor:

Margery, a short, fragile, pale, blond woman volunteered and sat down in the empty chair next to me. With slumped shoulders, rounded spine, and a white, ashen complexion, she rolled her tearful eyes towards me. Touching her back and shoulders lightly, I felt waves of grief, pain, and sadness roaring through her body. She was very tense, as if she was frozen in a posture of loss.

"What's been happening to you lately?" I asked.

"I'm a choreographer and in the last four years, half of my troupe has died of AIDS." The group became suddenly very quiet. Some eyes were downcast; others shed tears.

"Last month, Arthur, a 6-foot, 3-inch black dancer, died. His passing was like a death knell to my creativity. I feel like I can't choreograph and create dances anymore. I'm so depressed!" she said softly and began to wail. My hands helped her emotional energy to pass on through and out of her body.

"When did you see Arthur last?" I whispered softly.
"In his hospital room during the last hours. He used to be so muscular, buoyant, and full of energy. Now he was skin and bones, with hollow, big eyes."

"What was going on in the hospital room and who was there?" I continued.

"Well. . . his father was singing gospel songs very loudly and his mother was holding a small ugly dog." The hint of a smile crept over her face. "She kept shoving this drooling dog into his face." Now some group members started to laugh. "Finally Arthur begged his Mom to stop doing that. 'Is this the last vision you want me to have before I check out—of this dog I hate so much?' he moaned."

Margery started from a rolling laugh to boisterous upheavals. The group joined in, creating quite a raucous sound. Her body softened and currents of healing energy began to flow through. A dam of grief had just broken and allowed her creative self to reenter.

"Are you willing to do an experiment?" I asked.

"Yes," she replied with curiosity.

"Choreograph a dance for Arthur right now!"

She stood up, pulled her shoulders back, threw her chest forward, and looked up at the ceiling. We shifted all the chairs to the side to create space for her to move. Transformed, she channeled all her emotions into this dance—Arthur's dance. The room bristled with excitement. Before our eyes she became a magnificent goddess, moving with beauty, strength, and grace. Concluding, she melted to the floor and held her arms up towards the heavens.

No one moved; tears flowed down faces, including mine.

The humor and laughter had lightened that last scene and finally softened her frozen creativity into exquisite expressiveness. I turned to the psychotherapist who had originally asked the question and said, "Well, do you understand now how I use humor?"

"Yes," she replied, sobbing. "I do!"

Postscript: Margery announced that she would dedicate the following year to creating a dance for all those who died of AIDS and a special trilogy for Arthur. Indeed, she did—to rave reviews. I know because I attended every performance.

14. Reflecting clients' verbal expressions validates their experience.

Margaret Mead said she smacked her lips "to taste the words." Initially, I repeated the client's words to myself, experiencing them on another level. Sometimes I would change a word, the emphasis, or my vocal tone while reflecting it back to the client.

Feedback from clients indicated how important it was for them to know that I heard them accurately and that the repetition validated their experience. Continuing to develop this as a technique, I experimented with many variations of their words.

15. Confusion facilitates change.

Intrigued as I am by the construction of words, I see much meaning in the word "confusion." "Fusion" means "union." But "con" can mean either "with" or "opposed to." Thus the word "confusion" implies pulling apart and joining, both of which are important in the process of change. As Nobel Laureate physicist Ilya Prigogine has stated, "Falling apart is only a phase of falling together."

Clients are encouraged to allow their feelings of confusion without negative judgment. One has to be willing to be disorganized (con-fused) in order to get reorganized (re-fused or fused again).

Spasms, tension blocks, lack of energy, and the repetition of the same behavior indicate the existence of habitual holding patterns. People generally seek help to change these dysfunctions only after the resulting discomfort has reached an unacceptable level. Even then, they remain unaware of the holding patterns that underlie the discomfort.

Confusion interrupts dysfunctional habit patterns. During this "window of opportunity," the Synergist invites clients to experiment with a new, nonhabitual behavior. After some time, the new behavior can be integrated into their lives.

16. Altered states of consciousness can enhance healing.

Altered states of consciousness—particularly trance states—are natural phenomena and are more common than most people believe. During a trance state, the client's attention may focus acutely on certain sensory modalities and internal states of being. There are many indications that a client is in a trance. These include time distortions, fluttering eyes, changes in breathing patterns, skin color, eye movement, and tone of voice.

I have noticed that clients tend to go into a trance quite readily when I touch them lightly at the beginning of a session. Trance states can also be induced by confusion and by the simultaneous use of touch and verbal processing. Some clients are "triggered" into a trance by specific odors, sights, sounds, or words.

Altered states can facilitate the client's ability to contact old physical and emotional memories that are still present in the body and can expand the practitioner's ability to dialogue with the unconscious bodymind.

17. Integration is necessary for lasting results.

Unless clients incorporate their new insights and behaviors in their daily lives, they are likely to revert to old, habitual patterns. Integration within a session can take place on many levels. Slowly, the client integrates movements and sensations, memories and emotions, images and insights. Gloria's "reentry" phase (see page 186) included several stages of integration: from lying to sitting, from sitting to standing, and from standing to walking. At each stage, she was integrating her insights from a somatically young age to

HEALING THE EMOTIONAL/SPIRITUAL BODY

adulthood.

18. Self-care is the first step to client care.

Richard, a very compassionate psychotherapist, complained to me that he was feeling very drained and tired after seeing clients. When I tried to move his neck and head, they were frozen—stuck together without any mobility. I asked him to show me how he sat when he talked and listened to his clients. He assumed an attitude of attentive listening—with his neck stuck out, back stooped, and chin jutting forward. He spent hours every day in this postural "trance," believing that it conveyed contact, concern, and total focus.

In reality, this posture did the opposite, by giving him terrible pain and making it harder for him to remain present with his clients. As he let go slowly during our session, relaxing and leaning less, he grew very anxious and sad. His habitual way of listening to his clients was literally "sticking his neck out" for them. As we explored his childhood, he remembered going into this posture every time he took care of his younger brothers and sisters and had to listen to their cries and pain. In that moment, he forgot about himself and lost his boundaries in order to empathize with them. Now, in his adult life, he still listened to others in the same way.

Over the next few months he was able to work through his need to be the "superempathizer" and gradually changed this dysfunctional habitual posture and sustained a new way of being with his clients, physically and emotionally.

Burn-out has become a catch-all phrase for the dangerous effects borne by those helpers and healers who give too much—professionally, personally, and spiritually. How do we maintain compassion, concern, and empathy without losing our boundaries? This is a pivotal question for Synergists, clients, and anyone who is in relationship with others—couples, families, and community members.

Ilana Rubenfeld

Practitioners and clients alike need to learn to heed the warning signals of burn-out before fatigue and illness set in. Synergists face additional challenges in self-care: When using touch we need to guard against transmitting our problems and tensions to the client through our hands. And we need to avoid taking on the somatic aches and pains of the client.

Rubenfeld Synergists learn to practice self-care during a session by paying attention to posture, breathing, centering, the physical environment, and maintaining personal boundaries—being able to identify with the client and have compassion for the client without merging with the client. An important element of self-care for the Synergist is continued professional supervision.

The Training of Rubenfeld Synergists

Having this philosophical and theoretical foundation prepared me to teach my work to others. In 1975, professionals from both spheres—bodywork and psychotherapy—approached me to train them in the Rubenfeld Synergy Method.

In those days, there were no schools or training programs to use as a model. How would I teach students the individual elements—somatic/touch skills, psychotherapeutic interventions, self-care, respect, and compassion for clients—while also showing them how to integrate all of these elements into an organic whole? This was the challenging puzzle I had to solve.

My training as a music conductor rescued me. Keeping track of twenty or more simultaneous activities while retaining the entire *gestalt* of a composition is part of every conductor's education and daily practice. Whether I was conducting Bach's long *St. Matthew's Passion* or Mozart's brief *Ave Verum*, the need—to know the parts while holding the whole—was the same. That was it!

Aha #7: To become practitioners of the Rubenfeld Synergy Method, trainees would learn the skills of a conductor!

After this major "aha!," the training design fell into place. I accepted the first group of trainees in 1977. I designed the program to be highly experiential, with an abundance of "hands-on" practice, theoretical discussions, bodymind exercises, lectures, creative group exercises, and practical application of the material. We consciously created a community that supported an atmosphere of safety for risk-taking and experimentation.

In those first several trainings I was a one-woman show—playing the roles of Synergist, organizer, trainer, supervisor, and administrator. Now, after more than a dozen trainings, I have a large faculty and staff to assist me as the teaching materials and methods are continually refined. Having one supervisor to every four-to-six trainees guarantees that everyone gets highly individualized attention.

True integration is not achieved by simply putting a smattering of methods together; mastery comes from commitment to in-depth learning and training. The Rubenfeld Synergy® Training Program, leading to professional certification, meets for three intensive seven-day modules and three weekends per year for four years. The total of sixteen-hundred hours includes contact hours, supervised practice with clients (during and outside of the training modules), personal Rubenfeld Synergy sessions, and independent research.

Being a musician, I created a way of "scoring" a Rubenfeld Synergy session.[12] Every moment of the session can be seen in detail or as a whole. Trainees learn how to recreate a session by analyzing and "scoring" it.[13]

An example of a Rubenfeld Score is shown on the following pages.

SAMPLE RUBENFELD SCORE

RUBENFELD'S SOMATIC INTERVENTION	RUBENFELD'S OBSERVATIONS AND REFLECTIONS	RUBENFELD'S VERBAL INTERVENTION	CLIENT'S VERBAL AND PHYSICAL RESPONSE
Slides both hands under right shoulder blade and upper back, keeping fingers flat.	Client's back feels like a sheet of steel. No energy is passing through her chest. Her breathing is very shallow. She is in a holding pattern that may be a defense against feeling her emotions. Gentleness is crucial at this juncture in order to establish trust and heighten her awareness to this area.	"I sense a lot under my fingers." Voice soft, matching the touch, a long pause.	Her eyes are closed. She opens and closes her mouth a few times without any sound.
Hands are still under right shoulder blade and upper back.	There is a slight movement in her back.	"What is happening in your back?" Another long pause.	She moves left hand toward her mouth.
Fingertips slightly curve upward, moving into this area at a different angle.	Back and chest begin to soften, more energy is passing through.	"How do you feel about the area that I'm touching?"	"Should I tell you?" A few tears gather around her eyes.
Fingers flatten out again.	Right shoulder releases tensions in several waves. She decides to trust and let go. Rubenfeld watching her face and listening to her voice while hands listen to her body.		"I'm separating from my husband, John." Voice mildly choked.
Hands follow her movement until last wave of energy is complete. Hands slowly move away from her body.	The movement away from client is in the soft rhythm that has been set. Rubenfeld returns to herself for a few moments of centering and self-care.		Mouth continues to open and close without words and tears begin to run down her face.
Synergist walks around to the other side and slips hands under left shoulder blade and upper back.	The left shoulder is tight and feels out of balance compared to the right one that just released.	"How do you feel about separating from him?"	"I think it's the right thing to do." Hands move with mouth as she speaks.

RUBENFELD'S SOMATIC INTERVENTION	RUBENFELD'S OBSERVATIONS AND REFLECTIONS	RUBENFELD'S VERBAL INTERVENTION	CLIENT'S VERBAL AND PHYSICAL RESPONSE
Fingers curve up and gently palpate the muscles.	Exploring the theme of "unfinished" business held in her body and psyche.	"Is there anything you would like to tell John about how you are feeling?"	She begins to cry softly, then deeper sobs emerge.
Fingers flatten out. One hand remains under shoulder, while other hand moves from underneath and is placed gently on the stomach (solar plexus).	Intense feelings are quickly moving. Client needs contact in the emotional center and support in moving it through her body.	"Your feelings are okay. [pause] Imagine John here in front of you. [pause] What would you like to say to him?"	She continues to cry more loudly.
Both hands are under left shoulder and upper back.	There is great heat pouring from her back and chest. Shoulder begins to release in several large waves.		"I'm not who you thought I was!"
Hands follow the movement of the release until it is complete.	Shoulder and back dramatically soften as tension begins to melt.		
Still facing client's left side, left hand returns to stomach, while right hand gently passes up to head and is placed on top of head.	Left hand is touching the emotional center and sensing the breathing patterns. Right hand is on the crown of the head which symbolizes unconditional compassion in the ancient Eastern energy systems. These two areas are connected and heightened through touch and strong intentionality.	"Tell John who you are." Giving client plenty of time.	She swallows a few times. Her left hand continues to move around as she speaks haltingly. "I'm very disorganized . . . very unstuctured. I'm not able to handle things." Takes a deep breath. "I'm needy." Her voice is choking up again. "You think I'm strong . . . I'm not as strong as I appear. . . "
Right hand moves from crown of head to under her neck. Left hand continues softly rocking her lower ribs.	Remembering the myth of Wonder Woman with bulletproof steel bracelets around her wrists. The metaphor of strength on the outside covering any weakness or neediness. (cont. p.206)	Smiling . . . "Oh! You're a member of the Wonder Woman club? I resigned several times but I keep getting another membership card in the mail."	She laughs from a deep place and nods her head.

Rubenfeld's Somatic Intervention	Rubenfeld's Observations and Reflections	Rubenfeld's Verbal Intervention	Client's Verbal and Physical Response
	Introducing humor lightens and eases her shoulder and neck areas.		
Hands are still in the same places.	Many women have presented themselves as so strong that they are afraid to admit that they need support.	"You want John to think you are strong?" "Can you resign from that club?"	"Yes." "Not yet." A big grin spreads across her face.
Right hand begins to move away from top of head and touch her forehead.	In the ancient Eastern energy system, the forehead is the home of the third eye, which symbolizes wisdom.	"What happens when you're not strong . . when you feel needy?"	"I cry!" She says this amidst her laughter.
Right hand still on forehead and left fingertips on upper chest.	Her forehead is cool and much more relaxed. There is a steady stream of energy moving from her stomach through her chest and out the top of her head. Her heartbeat is steady.	"Instead of *I need,* start with *I want.* What do you *want?*"	"I want to feel peaceful inside."

WHO BENEFITS FROM RUBENFELD SYNERGY?

Many people ask me about the benefits of having Rubenfeld Synergy sessions. Any ordinary individual can benefit, as illustrated in Gloria's session, which dealt with many life issues common to us all. Others who can benefit include:

◆ People in high-stress occupations, such as performing arts, business, government, and education;

◆ People suffering from acute anxiety, panic disorders, and Post-Traumatic Stress Syndrome, such as survivors of war, displacement, sudden loss, or violence;

◆ Those with addictive behaviors and eating disorders

◆ People dealing with debilitating health problems, e.g., chronic pain, cancer, neurological diseases such as muscular dystrophy, autoimmune diseases such as multiple sclerosis and rheumatoid arthritis, chronic fatigue syndrome, fibromyalgia, AIDS

◆ Couples and families suffering from dysfunctional patterns

◆ Caregivers—individuals caring for their family members as well as health care professionals

There are no known contraindications for the Rubenfeld Synergy Method. Synergists are trained to recognize situations for which they need to refer clients to other professionals.

BACK TO THE FUTURE

Interdisciplinary influences have always excited me. When I met Virginia Satir in the 1960s, I was struck by her concept that it is vitally important to look at clients in the context of the family, which is a system of interacting individuals. In the 1980s, I began to meet regularly with some of her senior trainers, experimenting with using the Rubenfeld Synergy Method with couples and families.

An unusual and outstanding event brought hundreds of people together for a weekend of mind-body integration in the early 1970s. At the New School of Social Research in New York City, Margaret Mead, Joseph Campbell, Jean Houston, and I rotated teaching sections of the audience, each with our own style of leading. I was inspired by the synergistic effect of our presentations.

In New York in the early 1990s there were several small conferences on somatic education and movement. However, it was at conferences in 1995 and 1996[14] that I recognized that the ancient paradigm of body-centered psychotherapy had reemerged and was being accepted by a much larger professional population. I was filled with joy and excitement as we met and demonstrated and discussed ideas and theories with each other. Inspiration had come from the past and was being reignited in the present. We then took steps to assure that this open dialogue will continue in the future.

As part of a fast-growing field, we in somatic psychology and body-centered psychotherapy need to be willing to go further in our practice than we have ever gone before. I would like to see us go "out on a limbic." The more integrated and integrative we are as healers, the more powerfully we can serve as the allies of positive change, bringing a balance of forces back into this fragmented world.

I am honored to be part of this project and to share the space with a group of esteemed colleagues.

REFERENCES

Claire, T. (1995) "Rubenfeld Synergy Method: Touch Therapy Meets Talk Therapy," *Bodywork*. New York: William Morrow and Company, 151-65.

Junglas, D. (1994) *The Experience of Becoming an Integrated Self Through Rubenfeld Synergy* , Cincinnati: The Union Institute.

Lerklin, J. M. (June, 1995) "Sing the Body Electric," *Changes*, 30–35. Includes instructions for a Rubenfeld Body-Mind Exercise.*

Markowitz, L. (Sept.–Oct. 1996) "Minding the Body, Embodying the Mind: Therapists Explore Mind-Body Alternatives," *Family Therapy Networker*, 20–33. A comprehensive overview of the field, including the Rubenfeld Synergy Method.*

Rubenfeld, I. (1995) *Growing Old Means Forgetting to Retire.* A Time for Spirit Video Series from the Third Annual Conference on Conscious Aging, sponsored by the Omega Institute, *New Age Journal* and *MetaMedia Arts.**

Mishlove, J. and Rubenfeld, I. (1992) *Mind-Body Integration.* An InnerWork™ videotape. Berkeley, Cal.: Thinking Allowed Productions.*

Rubenfeld, I. (Spring/Summer 1988) "Beginners Hands: Twenty-five Years of Simple, Rubenfeld Synergy—the Birth of a Therapy," *Somatics.**

——. (Autumn/Winter, 1990–91) "Ushering in a Century of Integration." *Somatics Journal*, 59–63.*

——. (1992) "Gestalt Therapy and the Bodymind: An Overview of the Rubenfeld Synergy Method," *Gestalt Therapy: Perspectives and Applications*,

HEALING THE EMOTIONAL/SPIRITUAL BODY

ed. Edwin C. Nevis. New York: Gardner Press, 147-77.

———. (1973) *Rubenfeld on the Road.* An album of four audiotapes (eight exercises) that foster flexibility, awareness, breathing, and strength.*

* Asterisks indicate the availability of reprints from the Rubenfeld Synergy Center.

1. The words *soma* and *somatic* refer to the bodymind as a system, rather than to the physical body alone.

2. I hadn't heard of Wilhelm Reich, the psychoanalyst who demonstrated that manipulating muscles could bring into consciousness past memories of experiences held unconsciously in the "body armor."

3. All of the clients in these examples have given me permission to use their sessions. I have changed the names to protect their privacy. Any similarity to other individuals is purely coincidental.

4. Summers during the 1960s, I learned a great deal from Ida Rolf, Charlotte Selver, and Virginia Satir, who were teachers at the Esalen Institute in Big Sur, California. Being with these giants and innovators reminded me of my excitement when I studied music with Pablo Casals and assisted conductor Leopold Stokowski.

5. Many Synergy sessions are private, with only the client and Synergist present.

6. In private sessions, the Synergist and client may create allies by substituting an imagined group of people—relatives, friends, and coworkers—who normally populate the client's life.

7. The psychophysical sequence of lying, sitting, standing, and walking—while integrating the material from the session—recapitulates important stages of early childhood development.

8. The following eighteen principles, © 1997 Ilana Rubenfeld, are reprinted here with her permission.

9. This is an important difference between our approach and that of other kinds of body work, which locate stuck, tight areas and loosen them by massage techniques and manipulation.

10. The body's energy has many names. *Chakra* is a Sanskrit word that describes swirling circles of energy at various locations in and around the body, from the base of the spine to the top of the head. The Japanese *ki* and Chinese *chi* refer to the life force that circulates along meridians in the body. *Orgone* was Wilhelm Reich's term for the life force.

11. Note: I checked this out with him; I didn't use a characterological map.

12. Musical scores show the different vocal or instrumental parts on separate horizontal lines.

13. Reprinted from *Gestalt Therapy: Perspectives and Applications*, 1992, with permission of Ilana Rubenfeld and Ed Nevis, ed.

14 . International Somatic Conference, San Francisco, California, October, 1995, and *First U.S. National Conference on Body Oriented Psychotherapy: Building Bridges and Celebrating Diversity*, Beverly, Massachusetts, June, 1996.

Chapter Eleven

THE BRADDOCK BODY PROCESS®

Carolyn Braddock, MA, PC

EDITOR'S NOTE: *Carolyn Braddock represents one of our newer voices. She enters this august body as a dynamo of networking, creative collaborations, and passionate advocacy. She is highly attuned to women's issues in this field, as well as to body-centered addictions recovery. Her ability to communicate her vision, with the interests of diverse agencies in mind, has gained her entrance into many previously inaccessible institutions, who all end up being converted to a body-centered perspective.*

What struck me as I got to know Carolyn was how attended to I felt in her presence. By this I mean she literally turned her attention fully on me in a way that felt nourishing and at the same time stimulating. I suspect that it is partly this quality that has made her work into one of the upcoming forms of this decade. Carolyn has large vision. She wants to see embodiment come into the lives of recovering women and men as well as large institutions. Her tender heart and body demeanor enable her to work well with survivors. Her love for this work, alongside her high energy, makes her one of our most effective voices.

*M*y journey to realizing the moving connection of body, mind, and spirit began early, coming out of a sports background. As a "superjock," I was acutely aware of the need for attaining balance and support on both feet while remaining flexible in my body. Full, connected breaths, feet solidly on the ground, and loud grunts helped my tennis serves become fast and into the hard-to-reach corners. My work continues to be influenced by what was learned in those early days. Even now, as a result of balance, flexibility, and breath, along with voicing a few grunts and groans, my golf game plays a part in my work. I am reminded to center, balance, and breathe as I hit the ball.

My mentor in the sports world reminded me (and I hear her voice even now) to stop struggling and get out of the "victim position," a position of weakness and rigidity or collapse. As someone who wanted to do everything quickly and forcefully, I learned to be softer and more gentle with myself while remaining strong. Injured knees ended my sports career, and my life shifted to my later career choice, the study of families, adolescents, and those who have been traumatized sexually, emotionally, physically, and spiritually. In those days (late 1960s) literature was sparse, and few people knew much about the field of trauma. In fact, although trauma directly affects the body, little training was offered about the body and trauma.

In the beginning, I emphasized sexual trauma in my work, but it gradually expanded to include other forms of trauma. My definition of trauma includes body trauma (sexual, emotional, physical, and spiritual), surgeries, loss of body limbs or body function, trauma from natural disasters, life-threatening illnesses, family or relationship trauma, and more. My interest in the field increased as I became aware of many friends and others who had experienced trauma but had few choices available to them for healing.

A minister in college influenced my work by encouraging me to develop my voice by singing and playing guitar in a coffeehouse and by working outdoors with adolescents in body, mind, and spirit-oriented activities. My music was my form of Tai Ji. I began to sing my feelings—using different tones, pitches, loudnesses, and various ways of opening and closing my jaw. Spiritually, my work might have been labeled then as that of a "wounded healer."

Influenced by several theologians, I became interested in the many schools of spiritual direction, in Eastern and Western thought, and in the use of breath, sound, and movement by spiritual teachers. I became increasingly aware of the commonalities in the bodies of trauma survivors and noticed some significant patterns. I observed the prevailing types as the rigid body, the collapsed body, and the inanimate body, each with its respective breath, sound, and movement patterns. Observing a body and hearing the words were like watching a movie—they had stories to tell.

I was fascinated with balance which is important in sports and life in general. I watched people walking and observed how my clients walked and moved. I noticed how they wore down their shoes. Trauma survivors walked differently, and many seemed off-balance. People's feet should support them like a tree with roots solid, spreading out, reaching down into the ground, strong and planted, while their ankles should be like hinges, allowing their upper bodies to move freely, flexibly, and easily. I noticed that frequently in trauma survivors one side moved more than the other, or the survivor would lean more to one side or the other. I would ask the survivor what each side of his or her body was experiencing. Each side had a voice and a story. I might ask a trauma survivor what it was like to reach out and to have clarity about what he or she wanted in life. I might observe one foot moving forward while the other seemed glued to the floor without movement. Both feet had things to say. Dialoguing with each foot gave voice to the movement. From there, an individual could notice the movement, be encouraged to say what his or her body was experiencing, and choose an action.

Commonly, trauma clients reach out and then immediately back up as they say what they want. I was intrigued by this, since the movement of the body was incongruent with what was being said. It means they believe they can't have what they want, they don't deserve it, and if they get it it will be taken away.

The trauma survivor may be hypervigilant, waiting for the good feelings to disappear, since trust and safety are critical issues. The therapist needs to pay particular attention to being *with* the client. Working with trauma takes the development of special skills. This work is based on paying attention to what clients are saying and how they are saying it—that is, how the trauma is manifested in their bodies. Particular attention is paid to breath—where their breath stops or is held, how they use their voices, and how they walk, which reflects how they walk through everyday life.

My studies led me into Gestalt, Bioenergetics, systems theory, and many forms of bodywork, including spiritual healing, the laying-on of hands, trauma release, Esalen massage, and other energy systems, largely from Brazilian healers. From these, I learned about intentionality, safety, and trust, all of which are now focal points in my work.

One of my most significant teachers was Carl Whitaker, often called "the father of family therapy." I learned about waiting from Carl—waiting for the process to happen, having patience, and opening doors of responsible options for the client. For me, this work was also similar to playing team sports—involving a team (the family or parts of a family) and having to be aware of where the ball was at all times. I also learned about trusting the process—listening with all my senses and exploring all angles. This led to observing the body from all dimensions. Carl's direct style helped me to be more specific about how my work would develop in years to come. The evolution of the Braddock Body Process continued. Teachers like Brother David Steindl-Rast encouraged me to be more conscious of how, when we as therapists "touch" another human being, whether verbally or nonverbally, a spiritual relationship is begun. That "touch" can help release many years of stored trauma.

I learned from other bodyworkers and from their commitment to integrity and excellence. Aston Patterners Linda and Walter Krier, Ann Brode, Christian A. Hendricks, and bodyworkers Char Pias and C. Jay Bradbury offer alternatives to traditional ways of working. All this has helped my work evolve so that the client is actively involved in the healing journey.

The Braddock Body Process was developed in response to my observation that many survivors have no voice to express the kind of anger, sadness, frustration, or pain they experience. With trauma, the body was the scene of the crime. This memory is expressed directly through "body voices" in the way a person breathes, moves, and makes sound. Listening to these "body voices" facilitates a survivor's next stage of growth by integrating body, mind, and spirit.

The central focus of the process is using breath, sound, and movement intervention strategies as a path of healing. The body is honored as sacred. The client recognizes his or her own pace. This form of healing is gentle and effective. The Braddock Body Process helps clients to access their *own power* more deeply. The process involves the *entire* body. Empowerment for the client increases through making new choices and developing a set of tools with which to practice a new, strong voice. Awakening from trauma so the body becomes movable and is breathing is the key to my work. Clients recognize for themselves where they are holding trauma, and then they can make a choice about their healing (many have not had a choice before).

Joann[1], for example, realized she was dragging her right foot. (I could hear her foot shuffling as she walked.)

"Joann, I'm noticing your right foot is dragging behind your left foot," I told her. "I'm curious about what your foot might want to say."

She stopped and took a breath into her feet. After she took a breath into her feet, she held her breath and began going into a flashback (memory) of her trauma. Her left arm became stiff and swung against her body and her chin dropped against her chest. I encouraged her to keep breathing and keep moving her body so she would move into and through her trauma, a technique that is also taught in martial arts. As she moved, her body loosened; there was more movement in her pelvis (her place of power), and she began breathing steadily in and out. Her body lengthened; she appeared taller. In her past, her experiences of flashbacks would leave her immobile for days. With this method, she was able to move through her memory.

In subsequent sessions, Joann learned to take full, deep breaths. As she exhaled, her jaw loosened, allowing more sound. She also learned some martial arts theory and practiced movement exercises that created a new way to walk—one that was more centered and balanced. Her walk kept changing as she trusted that her feet would support her and keep her from falling. She could shift her weight from one side to the other in her stride, almost as in ice skating. She learned that each side can have a chance to rest briefly on every other step. On her exhale, she would imagine her breath falling downward through her body and feet.

With further research, I found some common cognitive characteristics of father/daughter incest survivors that related to how they were carrying those messages in their bodies. Again, those messages could be found in the three embodiments: rigid body, collapsed body, and inanimate body. I co-founded the Institute on Child Abuse and Neglect (ICAN), which was designed as a center to train other professionals how to work with trauma. Experts from across the country assisted, and ICAN evolved into what is currently the Braddock Body Process.

I continued to observe the three embodiments in my clients. As I explain in my book *Body Voices: Using the Power of Breath, Sound, and Movement to Heal and Create New Boundaries* (PageMill Press, 1995):

> The rigid client is physically locked and stiff, hoarding energy within so that no one can get close and, thus, holding on to the trauma. The collapsed body signals in every way an attitude of

surrender and a system of belief predicated on the acceptance of total defeat. In this pattern, the body takes on an expression of complete hopelessness and despair. The inanimate pattern is characterized by paralysis and lack of free movement, but with the purpose of dissociating from surrounding life and remaining numb to the pain and fear.

The rigid body can be heard walking down the hall, heels hitting heavily on the floor. The collapsed body may wear shoes out on the sides or along their toes, a signal of an "I give up" belief system. The inanimate body barely touches down to the floor and when it does, it's generally lightly on the toes or balls of the feet.

I developed eight topics for sessions to guide the client through the healing journey: Building a Relationship of Safety and Trust; Breathwork; Regaining Voice through Sound; Body Movement; Somatic Symptoms; Expressing Feelings; Memories, Dreams, and Flashbacks; and Cognitive Belief Systems. These topics addressed the common complaints and issues of trauma clients.

The Braddock Body Process and *Body Voices* also emphasize the emotional body (dissociative states, victim belief, shame and guilt, accepting the good, getting what we want); the physical body; body image and touch; the sexual body (sexuality); the spiritual body (spiritual journey, addictions, cultural issues); and the relational body (support systems and the struggle for intimacy).

Consistently I have found that clients enter body-centered psychotherapy, workshops, or consulting after numerous years (often twelve to fifteen years) of long-term cognitive therapy as their primary experience, and may feel dependent on the therapist. They may still feel tension and pain, and they may experience a list of somatic symptoms. Many kinds of somatic symptoms are manifested from repressed feelings resulting from trauma. Common ones are headaches, stomach aches, chest pains, gynecological problems, and foot, back, or neck problems. These individuals are searching for ways to express what their bodies are saying. When I ask them the reason for coming to work with me, they point to the work as body-oriented and feeling stuck in their bodies with the emphasis on resolving trauma. The manifestations of their trauma experiences affect relationships and the ability to be intimate emotionally, sexually, and occupationally. They want something more than going to weekly therapy sessions to talk—they are seeking some form of forward movement. One of the mechanisms in my work is the use of what we would call "intensives." I have found that even clients who live in the area might come in more than the average fifty-minute sessions because more time allows us to go much deeper. We can discover where trauma is held in their bodies and help them to release and feel more centered. Another way of working is to schedule several days, usually six hours per day.

I avoid trying to "fix" a client. My work is really about *being with* clients and their healing processes and *helping* them to release tightly-held trauma in their bodies, minds, and spirits. Clients reclaim their cores—who they are beneath the trauma. They find their spirits. Many of my clients are psychiatrists, psychologists, clergy, medical doctors, and others in the medical and alternative medicine fields. Many feel locked into their own work and into their own professional role and are having difficulty dealing with clients or patients on a daily basis. Burnout and stress are clear signals to practitioners that they are stuck in their helping roles. It is interesting to note that once some of the traumas are cleared from their own bodies, they find it much easier to spot and then help their patients, in an easy and friendly way, to release the trauma in their own bodies. The Braddock Body Process is particularly well-suited for people who feel stuck in therapy and who have been telling their stories over and over again. The inclusion of the body in the healing process provides a focus for moving into a deeper healing.

Then there are the people who have never been in therapy and feel traumatized. These people can also be helped with this process. Starting the body process after a trauma, or when someone realizes that he or she is having difficulties in life as a result of trauma, is effective because it involves the body *immediately* and gives the client some ways to feel stronger and more empowered, even in the first session. When a breathing technique or help in breathing is offered, the client can feel stronger, standing on his or her feet, more grounded, and more centered. This gives clients the beginning of what I might call a "toolbox" to use when they do feel stuck.

An important message in my work is that healing from trauma can be gentle, without struggle (or force), sensitive, and friendly. It can also be effective, and it can be whole-body healing in which clients feel empowered, balanced, and good about themselves. The process allows clients to work through and move through the trauma more effectively and more quickly than they can with many other modalities. A real key to my work is about moving forward, *with* and *through* the trauma, so that the trauma does not become something that is looming over the client like a black cloud, causing the client to feel stuck and labeled "victim." In essence, I keep reminding clients that if they feel stuck, they should get up and move. That way, the trauma is constantly moving through their body.

Martial arts theory and practice play an important role in my work. The goal is to help a client achieve balance through selected martial arts exercises, to notice where a client struggles in his or her body, and to listen carefully to the body's wisdom. This way I will know where to intervene to help the client. In groups (workshops and trainings), each individual can access his or her unique places of holding trauma.

Laurie came into a session with relationship problems. As she discussed her problems, I noticed she kept closing her pelvis with her right leg, her breathing was shallow, and her back leaned backwards with the back of the chair. Her body suddenly froze and her eyes were glazed and dissociated.

"Where are you?" I asked three times (I ask three times so my voice can move through the dissociation). I waited, staying present with my own breath. Her breathing shifted quickly and her breath became a panic breath— what we call fight-or-flight breathing from her upper chest. Trying to breathe wasn't working, so I told her to take a big breath into her belly and then hold it as she tightened her entire body. Then I encouraged her to release her breath with sound. "Haaaaaaa. . . works well." She repeated this process three times, then she became conscious, had direct eye contact, and was breathing easily.

In later sessions, her pelvis began to have a voice, speaking about her fears of becoming intimate with her partner, relating to her sexual trauma as a child. The pelvis is a trouble spot for many trauma survivors. Laurie felt cramping and pain in her pelvis. These feelings could be called a "body voice." Using these somatic symptoms, her body was saying, "Hear me, I want to speak with you."

Pain may be the only way a client can hear or pay attention to her pelvis. Sometimes I will tell a client to imagine she has a camera and a microphone and that she is interviewing parts of her body. I told Laurie she could interview her pelvis and ask it what it might want to say. Then she would take a deep breath and listen to what came out—that is, listen to how it felt. Giving her pelvis a voice, a chance to say what it is feeling or what it wants, can be helpful with intervention strategies. She may hear her pelvis say, "I'm feeling tight . . . your jeans are too tight . . . you're not giving me enough air . . . you're angry with me . . . you don't appreciate me," and more. She also may hear, "I want to dialogue with you. I want you to say some affirming words to me. I want you to let your breath fall down into me."

Clients learn to listen to various parts of their bodies. In Laurie's case, her body had carried a memory of sexual abuse for 38 years. Now, using this process, she can heal the memory.

Pain in a traumatized part of the body is a typical posttraumatic stress reaction. This reaction also occurs when trauma survivors become intimate with partners. Using the Braddock Body Process, they learn how to recognize when this response is about to emerge, and then make a choice to breathe and move their bodies through this trauma.

Although the participant already may have had years of therapy, the trauma may still linger in the body in the leg-hip connection, shoulder, trunk connection, stomach, abdomen, chest and, of course, the *feet!* This work helps the body to expand and create more space so more healing can take place. I pay attention to verbal and nonverbal clues from clients. Those signals include repetitive motions, eye contact, holding patterns, weak spots in the body, words that are incongruent, a "victim stance," and victim statements. This is an active process, in which the participant and the therapist participate together in healing. Clients develop specific tools to facilitate freer breath, and to feel better and stronger emotionally and physically. These are tools they can use when they get stuck or off-balance. Much of the work is helping clients to be more balanced physically, which creates more balance mentally. When clients are more balanced and feel better in their bodies, they can release more readily the trauma stored there. All of this directly affects their belief systems and how they see themselves.

Clients learn to breathe full breaths, and to connect their "in" breath with their "out" breath, helping them to access and express feelings. Increasing breathing skills can actually help the participant move through flashbacks and difficult, intense feelings. I use gentle martial arts theory and exercises in which *anyone* can participate. These exercises also are designed so participants can recognize where and how they struggle, mentally and physically. Clients learn how to listen to their bodies and how to get out of the way. Many of these exercises were designed in collaboration with Christian Hendricks, a JuJutsu instructor and Aston Patterner.

Participants report that they feel taller and have more space, which means that they are not holding tension in their bodies. Boundaries and limits are set more easily. Their bodies actually set limits through movement. They have a sense of more internal control and feel more empowered. From there, healthy choices are made more easily and frequently. I focus on body image, sexuality, and relationship issues and then on ways to improve social and occupational functioning. Clients are more motivated and feel better and clearer about what they want because they have a stronger voice and can move through their trauma and continue to grow. This process creates a balance between intensity and lightness.

Art therapy and music therapy are also used. These often help clients go deeper into their healing and see more choices in their lives. They learn they can be heard and also have a voice to express themselves and that their body voices can be expressed through these modalities.

My work is also about the client taking charge of his or her own healing. I help my clients as I would if I were the coach of a baseball team. I help them to open their eyes, to see choices, to listen, to know that, even though they may *not* have had a choice back when the trauma was occurring, they do *now*. One choice involves getting up and moving and/or breathing *into* and *through* those feelings which sometimes can cause immobility. "Walk, get into your feet, move your body," I say.

Another important part of the Braddock Body Process is the spiritual aspect, which concerns the questions of "Why me?" "Why did this happen to me?" "Why do I still need to live with the pain?" "Am I to blame?" "I feel shame about myself and my body as a result of what has happened to me." "Where is God? I feel so alone." Trauma affects a person's views about God, about a higher power. I inquire and listen to clients as they tell me about their beliefs.

When clients work through their traumas, I notice that the rigidity within their bodies begins to soften. They become more flexible, which invites more choices and more ways of letting go of struggle when they begin to get agitated. They are then better able to move out of uncomfortable situations and avoid getting into a victim position. They learn to trust their bodies, tuning into exactly *when* their body says to move.

I help clients identify the signals in their bodies that tell them when to get out of the way. In my own body, my moving signal is in my upper chest. The moment I notice a tight and tingling sensation in my chest, I know that an uncomfortable conflict, person, or situation is coming close to me. When I feel this sensation in my chest, I know it is time to move out of the way. One client listens to his left thigh, which actually twitches when he needs to move. A client learns to pay attention to these signals and then move immediately at the signal.

An exercise we do in working with couples and groups is to have one person (let's say it's a woman) close her eyes as her partner moves closer. The woman needs to listen to her body to determine when to move. Rather than watching the other person, the client learns to honor the wisdom inside her own body. Couples who do this work are able to be aware of when they are having trouble and to choose whether or not to engage. They learn to listen to their body voices.

Unlocking the frozenness and numbness in their bodies helps clients to be more conscious. It increases flexibility, which is its own strength. I am helping the client to acknowledge what is external—the way they connect with the world with their hands, feet, and head—both cognitively and in relationships. I'm also helping each client find what actually is at his or her center, at the core, without the trauma. When the knowledge "I am a trauma survivor; I am a victim" becomes a dominant part of a person's identity, then there is no movement. When someone says "I am a trauma survivor," a collapsed position often follows, which signifies, "I give up."

In the Braddock Body Process, I find a balance between listening to the client's words or story and observing *how* the words are expressed in the client's body movements, breath, and sound. I may observe a block in the throat, manifested by clearing of the throat, lack of eye contact, shortening of the body, clenching of the fist, collapse of the chest, or other areas of collapse, rigidity, or numbness.

I always look at how a client is being supported. Does the client have a body split, in which the upper part of her body is moving and the lower part holds still? Or does she have a left/right split, one side moving and expressing while the other is holds still, remaining in trauma. Or is there another split?

I'm particularly interested in observing a client's feet and patterns of walking. My clients may walk or move through much of the session. In fact, some people will say I have a "foot fetish" because of my emphasis on feet. But to me it is important to help clients stand on their own feet. For some, it may be the first time they feel strong, as if they're rooted into the ground. This means that they can step forward instead of having to step back or not step at all.

Centering, moving downward into the earth, feeling the ground, and touching the ground with the entire foot is essentially a way of saying, "Yes, I am ready to be here, to be present with myself." I remind my clients to push down on the ground with their feet, get longer, stretch out their joints, even the ankle joints, stretch out the connection between their legs and hip joints, and rest two fingers on their upper sternum as a reminder to let that part also stretch. That doesn't mean reaching upwards with the chin and it doesn't mean lifting up with the shoulders. It means simply *feeling* taller, *being* longer, *taking up more space and allowing more space in the body for more air.* More air means more space, more freedom, more breath, more life, and more spirit.

Another important part of my work involves the client "being heard." The therapy session may be the first time the client has told his or her secret. As the client progresses at her own pace, the reaction of the therapist is critical, because the client must know the therapist is truly with her. My belief is that hearing a client's story is important, but hearing the story and noticing what is happening in her body is even more important, because then I can help the client to recognize how the story is affecting how she is in the world, in her body. I frequently ask questions like, "What is it you want me to hear?" or "What's important for you to tell me right now?" Then the client has an opportunity to focus in on what it is that is important to her. This is especially important for clients who have not been heard before, or not been believed. In the process of telling stories, or in the process of breathing or using sound or movement, I also invite *process.* Although some clients can be addicted to a familiar, repetitive way of processing, I invite them to notice what's underneath, what else is trying to emerge as a voice from their bodies. For instance, a client may be used to expressing anger by hitting pillows, or otherwise expressing herself externally. I inquire about what else could be expressed, what other feeling is there, and then help the client to embrace that deeper feeling.

Many trauma survivors fear sound, loud noises, or yelling, because these were a part of their traumas. Many know chaos well. Even a small sigh can be important in my work, as that shows a client he or she has a voice. A client may inhale through his nose, let go of the air through his mouth, and on the exhale, allow his breath to release his jaw. This allows breath to move the jaw naturally rather than forcing it. In this way, on the exhale, the client can experiment with a sigh, and even a little more sound, and gradually move towards using sound as an avenue for healing. When these new sounds occur, clients in my work can learn new ways to move through the fear and experience a voice from the center of their bodies, their core. If the client has trouble expressing with words, gibberish (nonsense words that you can just make up) is a wonderful way of allowing at least some sound to come through.

When Jim feels fear, his entire body pulls inward—joints, feet, legs, hips, pelvis, neck, shoulders, chest, and even his eyes. He has learned to take a deep breath as he lies on the floor, and, on the exhale, to let out his breath and gently, with a sigh, stretch his legs out, leading with his heel and feeling more space between his leg/hip connection. This helps him move through his fear.

This process is like a dance, a two-step dance, with exercises to increase flexibility, balance, and strength. In this way clients can quickly release trauma from their bodies and be supported by their feet and breath.

When I ask someone a yes-or-no question, I listen for a full-body response. A client may say "yes," yet her head may move side to side, indicating "no." I may ask several times. This allows for a dialogue between the body and parts of the body that are speaking loudly through the voice of pain and somatic symptoms.

Samantha was in bed with severe back pain until she dialogued with her back. She did this by asking her back questions, which she did in several ways. For example, she used her dominant hand to write questions like, "What is it you want to tell me? I'm ready to listen. I feel your pain. What is the pain about?" Then the non-dominant hand would answer, writing and speaking for her back.

A second way for her to dialogue was to talk aloud to her back and then change her voice slightly as she became her back, talking and responding. She would talk and then listen, keeping this process going until she felt complete and had nothing else to say.

As she listened, her back responded, "I'm tired. I'm not wanting any more weight of anyone else's problems." She listened further. Her back felt numb and needed touch. Yet, as a trauma survivor, she wanted only safe touch. She kept dialoguing and listening. As she did, her back began to improve. She began to set clearer boundaries in her life, to protect herself from the weight of others' problems.

I want to see the body from all dimensions—to see what is actually happening, and what the relationship is between one part and another, especially the part that has been affected by trauma and how that part relates to others. Each body is unique and requires my full attention as a therapist. To me, each session is an adventure. I empower the client to have his or her *own* experience with questions or observations such as: "I'm noticing that . . . I'm curious about . . . Tell me about your left hip, what you're experiencing." "Whose arm is that?" I'm interested in their story *and* what attracts my nonjudgmental attention as they speak and move. My role is to encourage clients to embrace their bodies, to be aware of their bodies, and to have curiosity and openness. The body is sacred, and my process honors the sacredness of each individual body.

Awakening from trauma is sometimes fearful. A client may wonder, "What will it be like to be without my pain?" or "Will I be believed?" or "How can I trust again?" or "Is it OK to be OK?" So, I keep inquiring, getting to know those parts of the client that have experienced trauma as well as those that have not and integrating both. *My work is about life, vital life, with movement, breath, and sound increasing as the trauma is released from the body.* Clients learn to move so their spirits can be alive again.

My process honors where the client is. The answers are already inside. Age doesn't matter. When clients have experienced trauma, their body image or sexuality may be unbalanced. Awakening, affirming, and listening carefully to the Body Voices while rewiring the circuits helps release trauma. My direction to clients is always, "Move, stretch, get longer, take up more space!"

Video analysis can help clients to see places of holding. This develops body awareness and can help clients develop new patterns. For example, my client Judy was shocked when she viewed herself and where she was carrying her trauma. She noticed that as she talked about her feelings, she backed up, curled her toes, and collapsed inward. The visual picture helped her to notice this, then make a new choice to stretch, get longer and create more space. Each day we videotaped, she could see more openness.

Tammy learned "conscious dissociation"—a way to notice when she would numb out and move away from her pain with glassy eyes and shallow breath. She began to notice when she was beginning to "go away," and could then make a choice—either to move away or to breathe and be present, even with uncomfortable feelings.

Breathing techniques can teach the client to breathe through memories and fears, which allows more openness and vulnerability, more space in the body.

As Lorie's breath fell downward into her pelvis and into her feet, she felt fear as she began to experience a tingling in her body. She was afraid of losing control (a fear common for sexual trauma survivors). The more she breathed and used her voice to say out loud what was happening, the more she moved through her fear. She began to feel sensations for the first time since her childhood trauma. Her pelvis began to have feelings and she let go of the fear of feeling sensations, even pleasant ones.

Learning about the self and solitude is another aspect of working with trauma. I remember participating in a workshop where we each spent a full day alone. Many of us were afraid to be only with ourselves, afraid that uncomfortable, painful emotions would surface. Yet, this is an important step in listening inside and getting stronger, reclaiming the emotional, sexual, physical, and spiritual body. As Brother David Steindl-Rast says, "In order to listen, you have to be silent inside the body."

Breath, sound, and movement are the three key elements that help clients work safely, effectively, and solidly with and through trauma. Clients learn that they can feel balanced and can *do* something to help feel better immediately. This process is action-oriented. With martial arts theory and practice helping the client to feel more empowered, the client learns where the trauma is stored in the body, ways of releasing trauma, and ways to move out of the way of struggle. This allows space for more breath and movement in the body and more life. The client realizes more choices and moves through life and relationships in a more balanced way.

---

1. All clients' names have been changed.

Chapter Twelve

ETHICS AND TECHNIQUES FOR TOUCH IN SOMATIC PSYCHOTHERAPY

Christine Caldwell, Ph.D.

Touching others and being touched by them is a powerful and healing tool. When used with clear intention and focused attention, it can accelerate self-awareness, deeper experiencing, self-acceptance, and effective action, both within a therapy session and in our daily lives. Touch is underused in most therapeutic encounters, primarily because due to its power, touch can cause harm. As a society we fear this power/harm combination. We have feared it so deeply, and in many cases so correctly, that we create laws, cultural mores, taboos, and conventions to control it. The ability to do harm with touch always will exist as long as there is a power differential between individuals, sexes, classes, and races. Yet we also are beginning to realize as a society that touch is so necessary to human existence that there are times in our lives that we would die without it.

Psychotherapy is often seen as a remedial return to the unmet needs of our formative years. As newborns and infants if we do not receive regular touching and holding we literally can fail to thrive and even die. Both lack of touch and inappropriate touch can permanently warp our being. We also know that our need for touch never goes away—it simply becomes more self-directed.

Another primary need is for safety, particularly physical safety. Only recently has the world culture begun to question the age-old practice of physical punishment of children. In many clinical practices, between sixty and ninety percent of a therapist's clients come from physically and/or sexually abusive households. As we look at the rampant misuse of touch as a tool for coercion, domination, and control in our culture, we can understand why we are fearful of retraumatizing ourselves through touch.

How then do we use touch as an effective and nourishing tool in psychotherapy, particularly in forms of psychotherapy that value and address the body as a crucial factor in healing? What is called for is a thorough method of training in touch for helping professionals that addresses the clients' needs for both safety and physical nourishment.

The first component of touch training is ethics. Most states do not have specific laws about touch. In the broadest sense, we can generalize that in order to violate civil or criminal law, touch must be unwarranted, unwelcome, and have the potential to cause physical or psychological harm. In the fields of psychotherapy and counseling there are more specific guidelines, though they primarily focus on sexual touch. In psychotherapy, any sexual touch is rightly considered unwarranted and is strictly censured, even if it is invited by the client. But this is where guidelines fall short. Beyond these important strictures, therapists have little ethical guidance about how to touch their clients in only healing ways.

The glaring omission in our laws with respect to the physical punishment of children is, I believe, the prime cause of the ambiguity and upset regarding touch that we encounter as adults. Even though as adults we are protected by law from any physical violence done to us, this same basic right is not extended to children, who are more vulnerable and in need of protection. Parents have the right to inflict physical pain on their children at any time that is deemed appropriate by the parent. Granted, we have become more alert to the most heinous excesses of the abuse of children and the law will remove children from such situations in extreme cases, but we still guarantee, protect, and even value the hitting of children in our society. It would be unthinkable as adults for us to allow a person to hit us, even if we had done something to bring it on. We would sue and expect restitution.

Indeed, our culture has historically (and bizarrely) sanctioned physical violence against any person in a low-power position. Thus, we see institutional violence perpetrated against women, political protesters, racial minorities, inmates, old people, and children. The implicit message, that we can get away with hurting someone who is subordinate to us, is a fundamental sickness in our society and is the root of all the furor around the ethics of touch.

Given that many of us who walk into a therapist's office are likely to have been touch-deprived *and* touched inappropriately in the past, how do we help to remedy this? Ethically, here are a few guidelines everyone can start with:

1. Choose a therapist who has touch training.

A therapist who has studied touch has a framework for reading the body in terms of energy and tension patterns, defensive blocks, tissue structure, and touch technique. This framework gives the theerapist clinical information that can inform the decision whether to touch, where to touch, and how to touch. It also in many states empowers therapists to touch legally, from the framework of having legitimate background and skill. Many bodywork systems provide this type of training. The time and energy output to become certified in a bodywork method can be formidable, though it is highly recommended. However, a good old-fashioned massage license will provide this training also.

2. Give your touch history to your therapist.

Tell your therapist about your experiences of touch growing up in your family, from the standpoints of affection, control, punishment, and sexuality. Report both touch you received, and touch you gave, as well as touch you witnessed. Tell the therapist if you have ever been touched inappropriately as an adult, and whether or not touch has been nourishing for you. Be straightforward if you have any concerns about touch in your current life or in the context of therapy.

3. Pre-contract with the therapist for touch as a possibility in the sessions.

Ask the therapist to explain her or his philosophy of touch. Have the therapist give examples of when touch would be inappropriate, and when it might be called for. Find out if touch is required for your work together, and whether you can ask at any time that touch be stopped and whether it immediately will be stopped. If you have any inkling that you might not have good touch boundaries (inability to sense or express your NO; overriding your NO in order to feel loved, safe, or in control; using touch as a bartering tool), touch is not appropriate for you until this issue is thoroughly worked with as a therapeutic issue.

4. When in doubt, don't touch or get touched.

When in doubt, bring up the doubt as a clinical issue. An example of this would be when you have an urge/intuition to be held, but you also are feeling a sense of trepidation about it. Don't do the action, but trust that the urge and the trepidation arose for a good reason. You may want to say at that moment what is true for you, such as: "I was never held or comforted when I felt this feeling as a child," or "I had an urge to be held just now, along with a worry about doing that. Does this feel relevant to this experience?"

5. Understand your motivations for touch.

Do you clearly see the therapist for who he or she is at that moment, and do you have a precise vision about the touch? Or are you feeling an urge to be held or touched in a way that is controlling? The deciding factor can come from knowing where your attention is located. Is it on the therapist and his or her actions, or is it arising from your own feelings? If you don't have a clear feeling, pause a minute, and be curious about the feelings that touching may stimulate in you. Rather than touching, ask yourself about the relevance of your urge to be touched. One of the most frequent inappropriate therapeutic touches is one that rescues the client from whatever uncomfortable state he or she is feeling. Running a close second is touch that rescues the therapist from uncomfortable feelings. If we examine these urges, we can get an interesting look into how the client or the therapist may be enrolling the other into his or her historical life scripts. We also can make conscious our own needs to be appreciated, liked, or touched.

6. In touch, timing is crucial.

If done too soon, it will sedate our important experience, and potentially give us the message that it's not OK to feel intense feelings, or that we need to be protected from intense feelings. If done too late, it can reinforce old imprints of control or deprivation. Paying attention in this area can be very beneficial in fine-tuning one's sense of timing.

7. Never let a therapist touch you in a sexual area or an area that you consider private.

This is obvious, but needs to be stated. Therapists must pay particular attention to cultural differences. For example, many Asian cultures consider the head a private area. Cultures can have different mores about touch between men and women.

8. Trust your intuition.

Our intuition is very accurate in shaping our primal need for touch. Intuition is a simple "yes" or "no." Relying on cognitive analysis to shape touch will rob it of its most vital energies.

9. Use touch boldly and sparingly.

Once we value and trust our intuition, we can become exquisite bearers of nourishment in our lives and in the lives of our loved ones. For this same reason, we want to make sure we are challenging ourselves to proactively and appropriately find sources other than therapy for this nourishment. The therapeutic relationship cannot for long be the only place where we are touched. Otherwise, we foster a deep dependency that would be counterproductive.

Touch Techniques

When therapists are willing to use the tremendous power to heal that touch represents, they also commit to providing the best and most accurate form of touch for themselves and others. In this light, we can look at our various conscious and unconscious touch intentions, some specific forms that touch comes in, and some general tips for therapists on how to use touch.

TOUCH INTENTIONS

There are five conscious intentions involved in touching and five unconscious ones. I will speak of these intentions in a clinical way, but these ideas apply in our daily lives as well. Looking at our intentions reflects whether we are acting in service to our healing, or acting to enroll others in our old personality strategies. The conscious intentions are to support, to nurture, to challenge, to reflect, and to provide space. The unconscious intentions are their mirror opposites, and are respectively: sedation, codependency, aggression, mindlessness, and abandonment.

Support

A supportive touch can literally provide physical backing for our experience. My support intention as a therapist might be to contribute a stabilizing influence. A supportive touch intention allows the client to practice a new movement sequence (expressing a feeling through the body) with the therapist's initial help. It can also provide physical encouragement. It mirrors a developmental stage when we needed our parents' direct intervention in order to progress, such as holding onto dad's hand as we learned to walk, and supplies us with a sense of a basically benevolent and caring world. When done well and at the appropriate point in our healing, supportive touch actually supports our emergent progress.

Sedation

When we are confused about or unaware of our own unresolved support issues, we have a tendency to touch or be touched in a sedating way. This often occurs when we unconsciously take responsibility for someone else's experience, and in therapy it looks like a taking over of the client's responsibility for movement. It may involve touching too soon, so that an emerging experience is not allowed to develop on its own (for instance, a client begins to cry and the therapist holds and pats the client in a patronizing way). The result is that any charge or energy that we have to move through a feeling is lost, either through distraction or disempowerment. It can give us the message that we can't do it ourselves, or that we don't have to do anything to get through life, somebody will make it better for us.

Nurture

Just as we were (one hopes) held and greeted and loved when we were born, so a nurturing intention conveys a sense of love and acceptance. It is being held after we have completely and deeply expressed. It comforts and shelters. It literally nurtures our breakthrough into physical truth-telling and accurate expression. It signals us that our essence is welcome here, when it may not have been so originally. It often takes the shape of hugging and holding.

Codependency

When I need to touch you to reassure myself that I am all right, I am being codependent. We often touch codependently in the disguise of nourishing others. This type of touch often has a look to it of the frightened parent nervously squeezing the child while saying, "There, there, you'll be all right." This move actually smothers the emergent essence of the client, and should alert us to our unconscious need to seek approval outside ourselves, at the expense of our essence.

Challenge

Touch also can challenge, much as the birthing process challenges a fetus. This touch intention arises from our need to have something to push against, something to hold up under our weight. Oftentimes, we need some boundary in order to feel met by life. An intention to challenge involves helping to intensify our experience so that we can fully participate with it. Perhaps we just need to push against a therapist's hands and feel the returning push in order to feel reassured that people in our lives won't cave on us. At times, a challenging touch may help us fight an addiction. Metaphorically, a challenging touch would be like staying the hand that is trying to take one more drink.

Aggression

When we have not completed our issues around being challenged, primarily because we have challenge confused with control, we will unconsciously aggress with touch. Here we will use touch for purposes of domination, power, or authority, and will unwittingly retraumatize ourselves and others. This is rarely obvious, however, and we need to look for subtle ways in which we can be using touch to control rather than facilitate our own and others' experiences.

Reflection

The intention to reflect manifests through our interest in seeing ourselves accurately, and is often called mirroring. We want to be reflected back to ourselves; we want know that the world sees us. It is a statement of "I see you, I see this shape of you, this size of you, this energy in your body." It can look like simply resting our hands on another's arm. Reflection allows us to form safe and healthy relationships with the outside world.

Mindlessness

We engage in mindlessness when we have not been adequately reflected. If we do not have a history of being seen, deeply seen, we are not able to stay present to ourselves. We literally cannot see ourselves. When we cannot observe our own process, we fall asleep to others. We touch without thought or reason. We touch out of a lack of anything else to do. We lay our hands on people when it is not necessary and not appropriate.

Providing Space

Sometimes the best intention is simply to bear witness. In this case, the touch intention comprises a conscious act of not touching. Paradoxically, this can be very "touching." By not touching, we can foster a sense of separateness, of autonomy, of distinctness that can be exquisite. It is important to see that both touching and not touching are active interventions, and can be used consciously to further our own and others' rich experience of the world.

Abandonment

An unconscious intention to abandon is a reenactment of our own issues in this area. If, just when touch is needed, we don't touch, we can be acting out our own loneliness in the world. We unknowingly abandon someone's fledgling feeling, and send a message that the other person must do it alone, always alone. Sometimes we do this thinking that we are providing space, but sometimes space can be an absence rather than a permission.

TYPES OF TOUCH

There are four types of touch, which are generally used therapeutically as a session progresses through four organic stages of development. In the initial stages of a session, awareness touch is usually the touch of choice. In the second stage of a session, when a client is struggling with owning his or her physical and behavioral patterns and taking responsibility for them, an intensifying touch is often appropriate. As the client enters the third stage, when he or she has completely felt and expressed what is inside, the possibility for true experience then arises and a nurturing touch is often called for. And lastly, when a client is working to integrate his or her new sense of authenticity into daily life, a teaching touch can be used.

Awareness

In the first stage of a session, a client is typically opening up to him or herself. The client is exploring sensation, feeling, and energy in an attempt to access the fuel for their transformational journey. At this point awareness touch can be used. Awareness touch is a light resting of the hand on or above some part of the client's body. The purpose is to focus or magnify the attention the client gives to this spot. It is important to allow the hand to be soft and to relax it into the shape of the area beneath it. This touch does not "do" anything, but is more about being a witnessing presence that assists the client.

Working

This type of touch is highly specialized in bodywork and can be transferred to body-centered psychotherapy. It is a touch that uses directed pressure to change the tissue in order to free blockages, promote energy flow, or exaggerate a holding pattern. I often call it an intensifying touch in that it provides the client's energy system with more input and more direction. It frequently involves either doing more of what a client is already doing (like squeezing a gripped hand) or providing a physical boundary or limit that the client can push against or along. Either way, this touch can deepen the client's experience. It is not recommended that any therapist engage in this touch form unless he or she has had specific touch or bodywork training.

Nurturing

When a client has moved completely through a feeling and has fully committed to and engaged in a complete movement/expression sequence, nurturing touches may be in order. These are perhaps our most familiar forms of touch. They involve holding and stroking and allowing the client to rest all or part of his or her body in a nourishing field. Because this often is the form of touch clients have not received in their lives when they needed it, it also can be the most misunderstood. In a sexual abuse survivor, this is the touch form that will tend to be the most confusing. For this reason, I sometimes will stroke a client's hair or hand very gently, in lieu of holding him or her more fully. And I let the client decide if and when he or she is ready for a full hug or complete holding.

Teaching

As a client completes a session and seeks to integrate the work that has been done into daily life, a teaching touch is often called for. This touch helps clients practice new movement behaviors and apply them to their everyday bodies. It can mean placing my hands on the front and back of a client's ribcage and asking her to breathe into the pressure of my hands, thus promoting increased breath capacity. Here again, bodywork training can prove valuable, as it can give the clinician a framework for how to proceed.

GENERAL TOUCH GUIDELINES FOR ALL OF US

Do not touch until intention is clear. This is not to say that we have to have an intentional analysis completed and filed away before we reach out to someone. Touch is highly intuitive and often spontaneous, and as long as we consciously check in and feel clear, our intentions also are clear.

Always stop touching when the intention is complete, or if your attention goes elsewhere. It actually is clinically toxic if I leave my hand resting on someone's body for no reason, especially when my attention has gone elsewhere.

Touch obeys laws of synchrony. If I am touching mindlessly, it likely has its roots both in my history and in the history of the person I am touching. By being alert and committed to my own healing around touch, I can see more clearly others' scripts for touch and avoid getting enrolled in them. I also can glean information from the moments when I was unconsciousness in relation to another person. These moments can reveal clues as to who that other person's abusers or neglecters might have been. If I find myself unwittingly playing a knight in shining armor, I can become aware of issues of rescuing in which both the client and myself might be engaged.

Touch works best when we combine training with trust, especially if we have been touched inappropriately in the past. Training secures our abilities. The more I trust that my ability to touch effectively will arise, the more my abilities are supported and cultivated. Trust actually fosters conscious creativity, and the more I trust myself, the more trustworthy I am to others.

If I make a touch mistake, I acknowledge it and reveal everything that I am aware of. I have seen this one move be more healing than any other intervention I have made with a client. By becoming totally visible, I transform my unconsciousness into conscious relationship. I once realized in a session that I had touched a client in a controlling manner. I revealed this and described to her my embarrassment, and when and how I had felt the urge to touch her that way. She began to cry and told me that it was exactly at these moments that her mother used to grab her and shake her when she was growing up. We both marveled at how compellingly we had both reenacted that moment, and she was then able to see how she would set herself up to get that familiar result, by allowing herself to lose control and expecting others to provide it. After the session, I was able to unravel an uncon-

CHRISTINE CALDWELL

scious intention in myself to aggress as a way to validate my sense of authority in the face of out-of-control situations.

Touch intentions and techniques are profound and lasting elements in the therapeutic relationship and in our daily lives. We can take part in a great social healing around the issue of touch by training ourselves thoroughly and consciously to use this primal act as a means of transformation.

Appendix One

AUTHOR RESOURCES

THE MOVING CYCLE INSTITUTE
(formerly The Moving Center)
P.O. Box 19892
Boulder, Colo., U.S.A. 80308
(303) 415-3774
FAX (303) 413-9003
Founded and directed by Christine Caldwell, Ph.D., LPC, ADTR.

THE HENDRICKS INSTITUTE
1187 Coast Village Road, Suite 109
Santa Barbara, Calif., U.S.A. 93108-2794
(805) 565-1870 or
(800) 688-0772
Founded and directed by Kathlyn and Gay Hendricks.

THE HAKOMI INSTITUTE
P.O. Box 1873
Boulder, Colo., U.S.A. 80306
(303) 443-6209

ARNY AND AMY MINDELL
2305 NW Kearney #320
Portland, Ore., U.S.A. 97210
(503) 796-0779

THE ROSENBERG-RAND INSTITUTE, INC.
1551 Ocean Avenue, Suite 230
Santa Monica, Calif., U.S.A. 90401
(310) 394-0147

THE RANCHO STROZZI INSTITUTE
4101 Middle Two Rock Road
Petaluma, Calif., U.S.A. 94952
(707) 778-6505
FAX (707) 778-0306
Founded and directed by Richard Strozzi Heckler.

THE PESSO-BOYDEN INSTITUTE
Lake Shore Drive
Franklin, N.H., U.S.A.
(603) 934-5548
Founded and directed by Al and Diane Pesso.

HAKOMI INTEGRATED SOMATICS
P.O. Box 19438
Boulder, Colo., U.S.A. 80308
(303) 447-3290
Founded and directed by Pat Ogden.

THE RUBENFELD CENTER
115 Waverly Place
New York, N.Y., U.S.A. 10011
(212) 254-5100
e-mail: rubenfeld@aol.com
Founded and directed by Ilana Rubenfeld.

For information about the Synergist's Code of Ethics, and for referrals to
certified Rubenfeld Synergists, contact:
NATIONAL ASSOCIATION OF RUBENFELD SYNERGISTS
1000 River Road, Suite 8H
Belmar, N.J., U.S.A. 07719

AUTHOR RESOURCES

THE BRADDOCK BODY PROCESS
P.O. Box 260123
Lakewood, Colo., U.S.A. 80226-0123
(303) 985-7310
FAX (303) 989-9813
Founded and directed by Carolyn Braddock

THE NAROPA INSTITUTE
SOMATIC PSYCHOLOGY DEPARTMENT
2130 Arapahoe Ave.
Boulder, Colo., U.S.A. 80302
(303) 444-0202 or
(303) 546-5284
Founded by Christine Caldwell.

CALIFORNIA INSTITUTE FOR INTEGRAL STUDIES
SOMATIC PSYCHOLOGY DEPARTMENT
Box CB
765 Ashbury Street
San Francisco, Calif., U.S.A. 94117
Founded by Don Johnson.

HOW TO CHOOSE A SOMATIC PSYCHOLOGIST

Christine Caldwell, Ph.D., LPC, ADTR

Entering this field of work reminds me of what it is like to enter a jewelry store. There are so many sparking gems! In order to choose among them, I can take a look at what I want, my budget, and the characteristics of the jewels. First let's take a look at the characteristics.

Because this field has been operating without a unifying professional organization until just recently (the United States Association for Somatic Psychotherapy was formed in June of 1996), little has been done to articulate to the public the language and names under which we operate. The first issue for a consumer is the type of work a practitioner does.

Some somatic disciplines focus exclusively on bodywork, movement education, and stress reduction. I will call these professionals "somatic practitioners." They include methods such as massage, Rolfing, Hellerwork, Aston-Patterning, Alexander, Feldenkrais, Traeger, and many others. These systems almost always use touch and body coaching, mostly to effect change in body tissues so that they function in harmony with the whole bodymind. Somatic practitioners do not necessarily have any psychotherapeutic training and are typically not empowered to work with the psychological component of illness. They have typically studied anatomy, physiology, kinesiology, and the specific discipline for which they trained, and often practice under massage licenses. These therapies work alone or hand-in-hand with traditional verbal therapies or alongside somatic psychologists.

In choosing a somatic practitioner, it is a good idea to investigate the extent of an individual's training. For instance, some states allow massage licenses to be conferred with as little as one hundred hours of training, while others require two thousand hours. Do not expect too much from a system that can certify people after a few weekends of study. Because most somatic practitioners use touch, you should find out how this is employed. Some systems use simple touches on the upright, clothed body to educate a client about how to move more efficiently. Other forms require a nude body on a massage table, and involve touch everywhere except private areas. The more extensively touch is used, the more you should feel sure of the training and professionalism of your practitioner.

In some cases these disciplines are covered by health insurance policies, usually in the general category of physical rehabilitation. They typically require a physician's prescription.

Somatic psychologists are the type of practitioners represented in this book. Usually, they have had extensive training and/or licensed in psychotherapy, as well as specific training with one or more of the leaders in the field. These professionals are on par with clinical psychologists, psychiatrists, social workers, and counselors. Often somatic psychologists have had as much training in verbal therapy as they have had in body disciplines. This is the type of practitioner to go to if you want to do serious psychotherapy that includes and values your body.

A somatic psychologist is able to work with what are typically thought of as psychological problems, both neurotic and psychotic. However, if you are looking at severe disturbance (psychosis, suicidal ideations), I would not recommend going to a somatic psychologist who is not also trained and/or licensed in more traditional clinical settings, one in which the psychologist has had extensive exposure to and experience with severe populations. Historically, the pioneers in somatic therapy could not arrange for their apprentices to work and get experience in these settings.

Many of the trainings set up by the somatic psychology pioneers are extensive enough to expose trainees to the intricacies of working with all kinds of human problems. Several trainings require years of intensive study before people are certified as practitioners. If trainings are less extensive, the system either accepts only already-licensed therapists, or they do not claim to be doing psychotherapy and/or do not work with involved problems. Beware of any form of somatic psychology that does not fall into those categories.

An exciting trend is occurring now in the field: training programs in body psychology that are housed in accredited universities. Currently, there is one, founded by Don Johnson, at the California Institute for Integral Studies in San Francisco and one, founded by myself, at The Naropa Institute in Boulder, Colorado. These institutions can provide students with the "in the trenches" training that is required for working with severely disturbed populations. I see this as a growing trend in the field, and one which may promote state licensing as somatic psychologists.

A branch of somatic psychology that quickly responded to this trend is dance/movement therapy and many of the creative arts therapies in general. Creative arts therapists have historically benefited from being trained in college and graduate-level settings, complete with extensive internships and supervision. They have had organized professional associations for decades, confer internal licenses, and have high standards of training. A dance/movement therapist will specialize in blending one's psychology with one's creativity, through the use of expressive movement.

In choosing a form of somatic psychology, think about the format and setting you want. Do you want daily individual therapy, or weekly? Do you want group intensives? Are you looking simply to understand your body better, or do you need to deal with a life that is falling apart? Some systems blend in Eastern disciplines such as martial arts or meditation, while others help you integrate your body with your spirituality or your career in corporate America.

In regards to finances, some systems lend themselves to more cost-effective one-time-only group formats, while others operate best as individual weekly sessions held over a period of time. Somatic psychologists that have state licenses or work under a licensed therapist can often be covered by one's health insurance. Some require a therapist's referral, others do not.

Here are some general tips for choosing a somatic (or any) therapist:

Be a good consumer: shop around, ask questions.

Ask friends and associates whom they go to or can recommend. This is often the way to find the best therapist.

If going into private therapy, interview several therapists. Most therapists will offer a free "meet and greet" session that discusses the type of work and its parameters.

Trust a practitioner who shares his or her credentials freely and who has clear, written policies and works in a professional setting.

Be aware that promises that sound too good to be true usually are.

Any system that claims it is the one true system is usually organized around dogma, right and wrong, and unquestioning adherence. In such a case, you are signing up more for a fundamentalist religion than you are a for a form of therapy.

Trust your gut. In choosing a somatic therapy, after assessing an acceptable level of professionalism and training, your instincts are your best guide. Studies upon studies have shown that the best therapy is done when the client likes, trusts and feels comfortable with the therapist, regardless of the therapist's theoretical or technical orientation. The therapist/client fit is extremely important, and your best way of assessing that is with your heart and your belly and the intuition that resides there.

RECOMMENDED BOOKS IN
SOMATIC PSYCHOLOGY

Baginski, Bodo, and Shalila Sharamon. *Reiki: Universal Life Energy.* Mendocine, Calif.: LifeRhythm, 1988.

Berry, Carmen R. *Your Body Never Lies.* Berkeley, Calif.: Page Mill Press, 1993.

Bertherat, Therese, and Carol Bernstein. *The Body Has Its Reasons.* Rochester, Vt.: Healing Arts Press, 1989.

Boadella, David. *Lifestreams, and Introduction to Biosynthesis.* London: Routledge and Kegan Paul, 1987.

Braddock, Carolyn. *Body Voices: Using the Power of Breath, Sound and Movement to Heal and Create New Boundaries.* Berkeley, Calif.: Page Mill Press, 1995.

Brown, Malcolm. *The Healing Touch.* Mendocino, Calif.: LifeRhythm, 1990.

Caldwell, Christine. *Getting Our Bodies Back.* Boston: Shambhala, 1996.

Campbell, David. *Touching Dialogue: A Somatic Psychotherapy for Self-Realization.* New York: In Hand Books, 1989.

Conger, John. *The Body in Recovery: Somatic Psychotherapy and the Self.* Berkeley, Calif. : Frog, Ltd., 1994.

Cousins, Norman. *Anatomy of an Illness.* New York: Bantam, 1979.

Dychtwald, Ken. *Bodymind.* New York: Pantheon Books, 1977.

Ford, Clyde. *Where Healing Waters Meet.* Barrytown, N.Y.: Station Hill Press, 1989.

Goodbread, Joseph. *The Dreambody Toolkit.* New York: Routledge and Kegan Paul, 1987.

Hanna, Thomas. *Bodies in Revolt: A Primer in Somatic Thinking.* Novato, Calif.: Freeperson Press, 1970.

___. *Somatics: Reawakening the Mind's Control of Movement, Flexibility, and Health.* New York: Addison-Wesley, 1988.

___. *The Body of Life.* New York: Knopf, 1987.

Heckler, Richard S. *The Anatomy of Change.* Boston: Shambhala, 1984.

Heller, Joseph, and William Henkin. *Bodywise.* Berkeley, Calif.: Wingbow Press, 1991.

Hendricks, Gay. *At the Speed of Life: A New Approach to Personal Change Through Body-Centered Therapy.* New York: Bantam, 1993.

___. *Conscious Breathing.* New York: Bantam, 1995.

Hendricks, Gay, and Kathlyn Hendricks. *Radiance! Breathwork, Movement and Body-Centered Psychotherapy.* Berkeley, Calif.: Wingbow Press, 1991.

Hutchinson, Marcia Germaine. *Transforming Body Image.* Trumansburg, N.Y.: Crossing Press, 1985.

Johanson, Greg, and Ron Kurtz. *Grace Unfolding: Psychotherapy in the Spirit of the Tao-te Ching.* New York: Bell Tower, 1991.

Johnson, Don. *Body.* Boston: Beacon Press, 1983.

___. *The Protean Body.* New York: Harper and Row, 1977.

Johnson, Don, ed. *Bone, Breath, and Gesture.* 1996.

Keleman, Stanley. *Embodying Experience: Forming a Personal Life.* Berkeley, Calif.: Center Press, 1987.

___. *Emotional Anatomy.* Berkeley, Calif.: Center Press, 1985.

___. *Living Your Dying.* New York: Random House, 1974.

___. *Somatic Reality.* Berkeley, Calif.: Center Press, 1979.

___. *The Human Ground: Sexuality, Self and Survival.* Palo Alto, Calif.: Science and Behavior Books, 1975.

___. *Your Body Speaks Its Mind.* New York: Simon and Schuster, 1975.

Kepner, James. *Body Process.* New York: Gestalt Institute of Cleveland, 1987.

Kurtz, Ron. *Body-Centered Psychotherapy: The Hakomi Method.* Mendocino, Calif.: LifeRhythm, 1990.

Kurtz, Ron, and Hector Prestera. *The Body Reveals.* New York: Harper and Row, 1976.

Lessac, A. *Body Wisdom.* New York: Noble Offset, 1978.

Levine, Peter. *Walking the Tiger: Healing Trauma Through the Body.* Unpublished (obtained through the Ergos Institute, telephone: 303-651-0500).

Levy, Fran. *Dance and Other Expressive Art Therapies: When Words are not Enough.* 1996.

Lowen, Alexander. *The Betrayal of the Body.* New York: Macmillan, 1967.

___. *Love and Orgasm: A Revolutionary Guide to Sexual Fulfillment.* New York: Signet, 1965.

___. *Pleasure: A Creative Approach to Life.* New York: Penguin, 1970.

Luce, Gay. *Body Time.* New York: Bantam, 1971.

Mindell, Arnold. *Dreambody: The Body's Role in Revealing the Self.* Boston: Routledge and Kegan Paul, 1983.

___. *Working with a Dreaming Body.* Boston: Routledge and Kegan Paul, 1985.

Montague, Ashley. *Touching.* New York: Harper and Row, 1971.

Murphy, Michael. *The Future of the Body.* Los Angeles: Jeremy Tarcher, 1992.

Pesso, Albert. *Movement in Psychotherapy.* New York: New York University Press, 1969.

Pierrakos, John. *Core Energetics.* Mendocino, Calif.: LifeRhythm, 1987.

Rosenberg, Jack L., et. al. *Body, Self and Soul: Sustaining Integration.* Atlanta: Humanics Ltd., 1985.

Sheets-Johnstone, Maxine, ed. *Giving the Body Its Due.* New York: SUNY, 1992.

Smith, Edward. The Body in Psychotherapy. Jefferson, N.C.: McFarland and Co., 1985.

Todd, Mabel Elsworth. *The Thinking Body.* New York: Dance Horizons, 1937.

INDEX

INDEX

INDEX

QUEST BOOKS
are published by
The Theosophical Society in America
Wheaton, Illinois 60189-0270
a branch of a world organization
dedicated to the promotion of the unity of
humanity and the encouragement of the study of
religion, philosophy, and science, to the end that
we may better understand ourselves and our place in
the universe. The Society stands for complete
freedom of individual search and belief.
For further information about its activities,
write, call 1-800-669-1571, or consult its Web page:
http://www. theosophical.org.

The Theosophical Publishing House
is aided by the generous support of
the Kern Foundation,
a trust established by Herbert A. Kern
and dedicated to Theosophical education.

Praise for
Getting in Touch

"The body-centered therapies so beautifully articulated in *Getting in Touch* help people respect the exquisite intelligence their bodies possess. From such teachings, people grow to experience their bodies as allies and teachers, blessed with marvelous healing capacities and perennial wisdom."

—John Robbins, author of
Diet for a New America and
Reclaiming Our Health

"Our body is often the last place we look to find healing. This book is a valuable key to unlocking the majesty and mystery of the nearest healing potential we have: our own body."

—Larry Dossey, M.D., author of
Prayer is Good Medicine and *Healing Words*

"This book is a much needed help in a field that sorely needs literature to describe the many fine works that are going on everywhere. It assembles an outstanding group of representatives to articulate the major strands in the promising and fertile field of body-oriented therapies."

—Don Hanlon Johnson, Ph.D.,
Professor of Somatics,
California Institute of Integral Studies